D0212500

TRADERS PRESS, INC.
P.O. BOX 6206
GREENVILLE, SOUTH CAROLINA 29606

BOOKS AND GIFTS FOR
INVESTORS AND TRADERS

800-927-8222

Climate

The Key to Understanding Business Cycles

The Raymond H. Wheeler Papers

Climate

The Key to Understanding Business Cycles

With a Forecast of Trends into the 21st Century

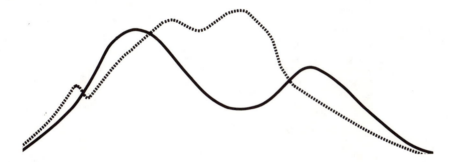

edited by

Michael Zahorchak

TIDE PRESS
POST OFFICE BOX 477
LINDEN, NEW JERSEY 07036

Associate Editor: Ralph D. Cato

Composition: Tide Press

Art and Cover: Gail Arnott

Book Design and Mechanical: Ralph D. Cato

FIRST EDITION

LIBRARY OF CONGRESS CATALOG CARD NUMBER: 83-70136

STANDARD BOOK NUMBER: ISBN   0-912931-00-0

To
S. Howard Bartley

who preserved the Wheeler manuscripts for their eventual dissemination to the scientific and business communities.

Some forthcoming books in this series

The Principle of Unity
A Guide to Understanding the Process of Change

Raymond H. Wheeler's World Weather Maps — 600 B.C.-1930 A.D.
A pictorial summary, with explanatory text, showing the relation of culture, military, and population movements to world climatic cycles.

Wheeler on Cycles
The major rainfall cycles and their relation to business cycles.

Wheeler and Kondratieff
The Kondratieff Wave analyzed back to 600 B.C. in correlation with the primary Wheeler climate cycle.

Also by Michael Zahorchak

The Art of Low Risk Investing
A simple yet precise system that links stock market activity to investor psychology.

Favorable Executions
The Wall Street Specialist and the Auction Market

Contents

Preface

This volume deals with the long climatic cycles of history and how each phase of these cycles generates a different sequence of economic conditions. It is the result of a painstaking analysis of well over 3,000 reference sources by a team of several hundred researchers over a span of more than 20 years. The conclusions to be drawn are of vital importance to every businessman, political leader, economist, analyst, investor, historian, social scientist, meteorologist, philosopher, medical researcher, astronomer, geographer, agriculturalist, conservationist, planner, and futurist interested in improving the accuracy of forecasts and projections, in understanding current events more clearly, and in comprehending past events more holistically. This book is an important reference source to everyone interested not only in economics and the changing level of business activity, but also in stock and commodity prices, the weather, politics, cycles, and human health and vitality.

The data base from which this volume is derived covers not merely the past few years, decades, or centuries but encompasses the full spectrum of human activity and achievement since 600 B.C. Throughout this book, the case for a correlation between climate and business conditions is clearly, simply, and forcefully made. And for those too busy to read the full details of certain aspects of this case, each chapter contains a summary highlighting the principal points covered in the chapter.

Wheeler begins by observing that, within any climatic belt, people exhibit changing levels of physical strength, moods, and mental alertness according to changes in the weather and in the seasons. This suggests that prevailing temperature and humidity levels have much to do in determining human energy and efficiency. Moving on, a survey of world climate demonstrates that in those areas where climates are extreme, populations are both sparse and primitive. Further, it is concluded that advanced civilizations are, and have always been, exclusively associated with climates that do not drain the energies of the population and that permit the growth of adequate food supplies.

Geographically, if the number, distribution, and industrial character of the world's largest cities is an indication of the level of civilization, then the highest civilizations have occurred, now and in the past, in areas with similar temperature, rainfall, and storm characteristics.

The relation of climate and human behavior has been the subject of investigation throughout history. Wheeler summarizes the thinking in this area ranging from Hippocrates and Aristotle through Thomas Aquinas and Montesquieu to modern investigators including Edgar Lawrence Smith and Ellsworth Huntington. Although most people refuse to accept the fact that humans are subject to the forces of nature because they believe that this admission subjects them to slavery or makes them victims of these forces, Wheeler shows that freedom comes from learning what these forces are and turning them to one's own account.

Experimental and statistical studies show that the reason warm-climate people remain primitive and backward is related to their energy levels. Contrary to popular opinion, high temperatures retard physical growth and delay the process of maturing. Experiments with animals also demonstrate that high temperatures cause serious mental and physical deterioration.

The evidence from throughout the world points to the fact that climate is not stable but is always in the process of moving either toward or away from temperature and rainfall extremes. This evidence further points to a succession of weather phases that regularly repeat themselves. Throughout history, certain transitions of phases have been attended by cultural revivals and eras of prosperity, while others have accompanied economic depressions and the declines of civilizations.

After determining that tree-ring growth is related to long-term climatic fluctuations, tree-ring patterns were analyzed back to 600 B.C. This was examined along with over 20,000 items of miscellaneous evidence to determine what the climate was at different times in history. This analysis concluded that miscellaneous weather reports, when accumulated in large numbers, accurately point to the successive phases of the climatic cycle. Further, a significant relationship between the sunspot cycle and prevailing climatic conditions was discovered, including an explanation for the varying length of the sunspot cycle.

An analysis of world weather records shows that climatic fluctuations, whether long or short, follow the same pattern, which is a repeated succession of phases where temperature and rainfall always occupy the same positions with respect to one another. With this information it was possible to deduce the probable location, within the climatic pattern, of any decade in history.

The history of climate has been characterized by cycles of varying length, the most important of which range from 1,000 years down to those of less than 7 years in a pattern of rhythms within rhythms. Although the pattern of a climatic fluctuation is always the same, making it possible to predict a trend well in advance, no two rhythms are exactly alike. Nothing of any consequence in business or economics escapes the influence of the two most important cycles in this series. The current position of these two cycles, with their probable significance for future events, is discussed.

At least since the Greek city-states, definite human behavior patterns were found to repeat themselves through the centuries on tides of climatic change, including likely periods of war and peace; of Civil and international wars; of class struggle between rich and poor, liberals and conservatives; of emancipations and slavery; of strong leaders or inept ones; of prosperity or depression; of industrial revolution or stagnation; of the expansion or contraction of trade, commerce, and travel; and of the revival or decline of learning. All this and more has occurred regularly at the same times in the primary climatic cycle.

Wheeler found a close correlation between the climatic cycle and economic activity in the United States from 1794 to 1930. When examined by decades, the correspondance is almost 100%, while on a year-to-year basis it ranged between 56% and 85%, depending on the phase of the climatic cycle, with an overall correspondance of 74%. Without exception, every boom period since 1794 occurred at a time the climatic theory called for a boom period. With only one minor exception, every depression era also occurred at a time the theory suggested a depression era. In each case Wheeler shows that economic facts and principles, like specific forms of government, specific styles in art, and specific concepts in science are all subordinate to the prevailing cultural pattern of the time. Changes from boom to depression and back are not isolated events but are a part of the overall cultural field within which the event occurs. For this reason a satisfactory economic theory of the business cycle can never arise simply by examining economic phenomena because something more basic is involved.

This more basic factor is the weather, which is the only factor common to all booms and depressions and to all peoples at all times in history. It is the only factor relating economic cycles to corresponding cycles in numerous other areas of human behavior in the manner that existing synchronicities demand, and it is the only possible means of interpreting the correspondance between weather and business.

Wheeler's forecast of business conditions through the end of the century has so far been remarkably accurate. He forecast that the prosperity of the 1950s would be followed by a long depression period during which the depression years would far outnumber the years of prosperity. This is exactly what happened from the mid-1960s through the early 1980s. The rest of this forecast, along with his forecast of climate through the middle of the twenty-first century and his projections relating to other historical, economic, and political matters, are contained in a comprehensive Postscript to the manuscript, which also updates, from the Editor's perspective, matter covered in Wheeler's text.

Acknowledgements

On behalf of everyone who will read or hear of this book, I am deeply indebted to the late Professor Raymond H. Wheeler for perceiving what no one before him, or since, has observed: that, over long periods of time, climatic changes evolve in an orderly progression of temperature - rainfall relationships similar to those prevailing in the annual progression of seasons, and further, that important changes in cultural, political, and economic patterns accompany, and can be anticipated by, these long-term climatic changes.

A word of thanks is also in order to the hundreds of associates who worked under Dr. Wheeler's direction over the years as research assistants, secretaries, readers, analysts, statisticians, filers, compilers, indexers, and artists. These are the people who read, analyzed, and assembled into Dr. Wheeler's data base significant information from more than 3,000 encyclopedias, books, diaries, maps, articles, papers, and reports.

Equally as important to the publication of this and forthcoming volumes in this series is Dr. S. Howard Bartley, a former student and later friend and associate of Dr. Wheeler. Without him the Wheeler papers may have been lost forever. On Wheeler's death, his manuscripts, most of which were still unpublished, were entrusted by Mrs. Wheeler to Dr. Bartley, who promised her not only that the papers would someday, somehow be published, but that the research effort so nobly started in the 1930s would be reinstated. Were it not for this pledge, so faithfully kept over the years, these papers may well have been lost and Wheeler's lifetime of work may have been for naught. As my pledge to Dr. Bartley, in return for permission to publish this, and forthcoming volumes, royalties from these books will be utilized to fund a research effort to update, clarify, and expand on what Wheeler and his associates have already accomplished.

My thanks to Steve Dendrinos who, aware of my interest in cycles, directed me to Dr. Bartley; to Gertrude Shirk for stressing to me the importance of Dr. Wheeler's contribution to science and mankind; to Gail Arnott for taking the faded charts and figures in the original manuscript and redrawing them into the sharp, clear illustrations that add so much to this text, and for designing the cover; and to Ralph Cato, without whose assistance this volume could never have been published. As associate editor, Ralph has become my alter ego, engaging in all phases of the book's editing, design, and production.

Finally, I extend my appreciation to the buyer of this book for providing the werewithal and the confidence to publish the remaining Wheeler papers and to continue his research efforts. If you are interested in keeping apprised of our work, or can add to our knowledge of Wheeler in any way, please write to me care of Tide Press, P.O. Box 477, Linden, N.J. 07036. I don't promise to answer all your letters personally because this would take time away from the project, but I do promise to keep you apprised of important events in this area as they occur.

Michael Zahorchak

Introduction

The present book is an edited version of one of the notebooks of Raymond H. Wheeler, a pioneer in the study of the relationships between climate and human affairs. We all know that weather has something to do with what we do or even feel like doing at any given moment. Since childhood, many of us have been taught that climate affects the plants and animals around us; certain behaviors of wild animals, for example, are traditionally understood to foretell something about what kind of season to expect.

This kind of thinking had never been applied, at least in any extensive way, to long-term human motivational patterns — particularly in the realm of economics. But Wheeler, assuming that humans are a part of nature, set about examining the matter. The magnitude of his endeavor was such as to eclipse any hasty conclusions. He began his research in the 1930s while teaching at the University of Kansas. He enlisted the help of over 200 individuals, including 95 historical researchers. His studies cover a period from 600 B.C. to 1950 A.D. and survey 18 different areas of human activity in relation to climatic fluctuations.

A number of notebooks grew out of the findings, each notebook on a separate general topic. The topic of the present book pertains to weather trends and cycles as they affect business. The 12 chapters constitute a cluster of related considerations all bearing on the fact that climatic change is a cyclical, not a random process.

From the very start, climate had to be something concrete and measurable. Two variations were chosen, namely, temperature and rainfall. Of course seasons of the year and belts of the earth from equator to pole were taken into account. The temperature-rainfall factor provided for four combinations: warm-wet, warm-dry, cold-wet, and cold-dry climatic phases. The significant climatic descriptions concerned these combinations. Hypothetically, one might have expected that these patterns would follow each other in no set order, and for no set length of time. Wheeler's findings did not turn out that way. The results disclosed distinct cycles, the longest of which was approximately 1000-years, with 500-year, 100-year, and lesser cycles as components. While these conclusions might seem too simplistic to be believable, the data undeniably substantiate them. Even more amazing and significant was that each of these climatic phases gave rise to its own distinctive type of human activity, with particular influence on the type of government that tended to hold sway during each period.

Naturally, one of the things business is interested in is predicting the future. In this pursuit, however, even expert opinions often conflict distressingly. To find a basic orderliness underlying certain major factors in the business cycle would be invaluable. The import of the Wheeler study is that there is an orderliness underlying climatic flux as well as the kinds of human behavior tied to it. This is something that all those engaged in business ought to be aware of, yet the curious fact is that business in general has been conducted for centuries in ignorance of it.

I knew Dr. Wheeler, for he was one of my university teachers and mentor for my advanced degrees. He was so devoted to this long study, and particularly to the basic philosophy of scientific reasoning, that he seemed too serious at the time. But the value of his insights and his endeavors are not surpassed by anyone my education has made me aware of.

In this book there is nothing that any intelligent person cannot understand and benefit from. It simply brings more of the significant features of climate and human activity together than have heretofore appeared in a single volume. Thus it should be a most worthwhile book for the business community.

S. Howard Bartley, Ph.D.
Distinguished Research Professor
July, 1983

Climate

The Key to Understanding Business Cycles

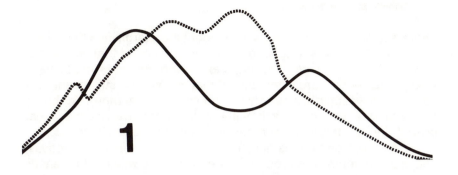

1

Climatic Belts of the World

Who, on a hot, muggy midsummer day has not felt the debilitating and suffocating effect of the oppressive heat and fatigue that follows even the slightest exertion? In contrast, who, on a cool but not too humid day in spring or fall, has not felt distinctly euphoric? Who is not worn out at the end of a long, hot summer or a long cold winter? We can all attest to the profound effects of climatic changes on our individual moods and even our physical well-being.

In the Temperate Zones of our planet the atmosphere is more active during spring and fall, and quieter during midsummer and midwinter. As the seasons are changing, it is stormier, windier and wetter; temperatures are more variable and changes in humidity are greater and more frequent. Everyone has experienced lethargy and depression before a thunderstorm, when the barometer is rapidly falling, and has enjoyed the relief and stimulating effect of the cooler temperatures and rising barometer that follow the rain. Everyone living in a temperate zone has experienced the exhiliration, happiness, optimism and activity that comes with spring:

> Now is the high-tide of the year,
> And whatever of life hath ebbed away
> Comes flooding back with ripply cheer,
> Into every bare inlet, and creek and bay;
>
> Everything is upward striving;
> 'Tis as easy now for the heart to be true
> As for grass to be green or skies to be blue,
> 'Tis the natural way of living.
>
> James Russell Lowell

1

There was no doubt in Lowell's mind about the energizing effect of the shift from winter to spring, and of the overflowing of that energy not only into joy but *strength* — strength to put sorrows aside and to make wise judgements. Here is the insight that warmer but still reasonably cool spring weather brings activity and a high moral tone, in contrast to the fatigue, instability, irritability and comparative weakness that prevail during the dreary weather of middle and late winter.

All these conditions have to do with human feelings, motives, and states of mind. These commonly experienced weather influences are very quick in their effects and can change one's moods in only a few hours. Just as each day's weather affects people's health, ambitions, moods, and judgements, so do *different combinations of temperature and rainfall that prevail over long periods of time* in the different phases of long climatic cycles affect how people feel, how they react, how they think, what they do, what they want, and what they will or will not tolerate.

Multiply these influences by millions of people and you can visualize the influence of weather trends and climatic changes on the activities and achievements of peoples and nations throughout history. It is well-recognized that commerce tends to decline in winter and revive in spring; to decline in midsummer and pick up again in the fall. Wars have a habit of breaking out in spring, not only because physical conditions make it more difficult to wage war during cold, snowy weather, but because human aggressiveness and morale are highest in spring. There is frequently a lull in war during the heat of summer, when man's energy level is obviously low, but warlike activity revives again in the fall. We know the human conception rate is highest in spring, next highest in fall, lower in winter, and lowest in the intense heat of midsummer. Commerce, war, and even human procreation are all closely tied *to seasonal weather change.*

Changes in seasons are not only changes in weather, they are changes in climate. *Weather becomes climate when repeated or extended over months and years.* In the United States, we are living in a climate mostly cold and dry in midwinter, warm and wet in spring and early summer, warm and dry during middle or late summer, and cold and wet in the fall.

There are longer changes in climatic conditions than the seasonal shifts during the year. These longer changes are designated *cycles,* and the combinations of temperature and rainfall likely to appear during the 12 months of a year occur in like sequence in a complex patterning of long climatic fluctuations. *The long cycles in weather follow the same pattern as the seasonal shifts: from cold-dry (winter) to warm-wet (spring) to warm-dry (summer) to cold-wet (fall) and back again to cold-dry.*

The Old-Fashioned Winters

Many older people remember how much colder it was during the 1880s and early 1890s, when there were longer and more severe winters than in the 1920s and 1930s. It was not uncommon for ice from 18 to 22 inches thick to form on midwestern rivers, yet there has been no such thickness in recent years. In fact, during many of the years between 1920 and 1940 the ice on these rivers has not been thick enough for safe skating.

From time to time, observers say the earth is becoming "warmer." It is not generally realized that we are actually passing through the warm phase of a recurring climatic cycle, averaging close to 100 years in passing through the four phases of cold-dry, warm-wet, warm-dry, and cold-wet. The heat and dryness reached a warm-phase climax in the 1930s over much of the earth. The Dust Bowl in the midwestern United States is a striking example of this phenomenon. But why was it, one may ask, that one of history's worst economic depressions also occurred at the same time? Because *catastrophic depressions often occur historically during cyclical periods of hot drought.*

The Influence of Weather Environment

Most of us readily concede that plants and animals are creatures of their environment. Therefore, why should we be surprised that man is also? Should one expect human life to be exempt from the natural laws and conditions to which plant and animal life are subject? True, the problem regarding plants is the most obvious of the three. Who has ever worked on a farm, raised a garden, or nurtured plants in the home without discovering that environment is all-important? Not only must the soil be just right, but each variety of plant requires its own set of temperature, sunshine, and moisture conditions. Depart from these even slightly and the plant develops defects or fails altogether.

On a larger scale, the dependence of plant life on environment can be seen in the vast differences in plant life found in different climatic zones. Each climate produces a different flora. Witness the palms and broad-leafed evergreens that grow in the tropics, the banana and coconut trees, the rubber trees, the exotic orchids and profusely flowering creepers that fill the air with the scent of jasmine and almond. Yet the luxuriant plants of the tropics, while beautiful and imposing, are seldom hardy or vigorous. How different they are from the trees and plants of the temperate zones that shed their leaves with the seasons or are reduced to dormancy by frosts, only to revive and flourish again the following spring. How different still the scrubby pines and firs of high mountain altitudes, and the mosses and lichens of the cold polar regions.

While differences traceable to climate are not as striking in the animal kingdom, nevertheless they are unmistakable. One does not find monkeys, baboons, apes, or gorillas living natively in the cool parts of the temperate zones, nor temperate-zone animals living natively in the tropics. Even animals belonging to the same family are quite different when native to different climatic zones. There are reindeer and caribou in cold regions along with musk ox and yak; bison, moose, elk, and white tailed deer thrive in the temperate zone; and eland, kudu, okapi, gnu, water buffalo, and giraffe fluorish in the tropics.

A further glimpse of the effect of climate on plant and animal life is obtained from the study of paleontology, the science of fossils. Time after time during geologic history, most of the earth was much warmer than it is now. Tropical plants and animals lived in what is presently the United States and Canada, and even in the polar regions. Times like these followed very cold periods and, in turn, gave way to more cold times.

On several of these remarkable temperature recoveries, which sooner or later were accompanied by corresponding recoveries in rainfall, there burst forth great empires of life both in the seas and on land. At one time, vast areas blossomed with huge reptiles, the dinosaurs, whose bones can be seen in many natural history museums today. This happened from approximately 100 to 200 million years ago. But the boom period for dinosaurs ultimately came to an end. The rains ceased, vegitation declined, food became scarce, and dinosaurs, the ruling class of animals at the time, died out. If any were left, they succumbed to falling temperatures as the next cold period set in.

This springing up and dying out of large plant and animal populations has happened again and again in the history of the earth on recurring climatic changes. In recent times, from 2 million to about 30,000 years ago, these climatic changes occurred more rapidly as warm periods were interspersed with ice ages. There were mammals on earth in great variety, including the half-ape, half-human ancestral cousins of man himself. Time after time, plant, animal, and prehuman life had to change or die. Animals were forced to migrate long distances in their struggle with the elements. In those cold climates there existed elephantlike creatures with long tusks and shaggy coats, and woolly rhinoceroses that have since evolved into bare-skinned, warm-climate animals. An undetermined number of subhuman "races" emerged, only to become diseased, to die of hunger and cold or, falling behind the evolution of other and smarter races, to be exterminated by them. And so it has been all through the history of the earth: The main promoter or destroyer of plant and animal life has been environment — in the form of *weather* and its long-term manifestation, *climate.*

Weather, Human Vitality, and Aggressiveness

Just as in early geologic time, when great empires of animal life blossomed as climate changed from excessively cold-dry periods to times that were warm and wet, so from the dawn of recorded civilization to the present, similar shifts in climate on a smaller scale have repeatedly generated great human empires sparked by revivals of human vitality. Then, quite as regularly, when it turned cold again these empires fell. *The process is still going on.* This fact is of the utmost importance to the businessman, no less than to the historian, not only because political and economic success are interdependent but because in its own right the business world, and the structures that constitute it, prospers, declines, and undergoes drastic change on these same tides of weather and climatic fluctuation.

The most advanced human races today live in those regions of the earth where the climate has certain characteristics not generally found elsewhere. Among these characteristics are: a certain degree of coolness and a certain range of average annual temperatures; a certain kind of rainfall and storminess; a marked variability in the weather throughout the year; a moderate-to-wide daily range and a moderate-to-wide annual range in temperatures.

In order to better understand the significance of these conditions, it will be necessary to take a brief excursion into the climates of the world and into some of the more elementary facts of geography.

Climatic Belts Unfavorable to Civilization

Generally speaking, average annual temperatures are highest in the tropical zone, a wide belt extending around the center of the earth on both sides of the equator. This belt has no temperature seasons; it is warm the year around. The average annual temperature is near 80° or above, with very little difference between day and night temperatures.

Here the sun's rays penetrate the earth's atmosphere vertically twice a year, on approximately the 21st of March and 21st of

September, and at noon each day the sun is always high. In the center of this zone the sun heats the air to a maximum throughout the year, especially in the spring and fall. Heated air expands and rises. Therefore, at the equator there is always a column of rising air. This means the air pressure against the earth is always comparatively low. As the air rises and expands, it cools and its capacity to hold moisture decreases; hence it rains. So in this belt it rains almost every day, generally in the afternoon; the average rainfall is considerably more than 80 inches a year. (In comparison, New York averages 42 inches; St. Louis, 39; Chicago, 33; Denver, 14; and San Francisco, 22.) This is the region of rain forests, with jungles so dense that very little sunlight reaches the ground. This zone lies, for the most part, within about 7° latitude north and south of the equator. Regions of this type are found in the upper Amazon, central Africa, and many of the East Indes.

On both sides of this zone are other regions well within the tropics and extending to about 15° north and south latitude. Here it is always hot and rainfall averages from 40 to 80 inches a year. However, there is always a short dry season in winter when the sun is lowest. The rainy season follows the sun back and forth across the equator. When the sun is highest in the southern hemisphere, it is raining there and is dry in the corresponding belt of the northern hemisphere. In these regions the jungles are also thick but sunlight can reach the ground. As a result the ground is matted with a dense growth of shrubs and vines, making the forests impenetrable. Here the shade temperature is 80° soon after sunrise. The calm air becomes hotter and moving about is unpleasant by 9 a.m. The air is laden with moisture and is very oppressive. By midafternoon, it may be 85° or 90° and depressingly humid. Then it may begin to rain. Travelers describe *the resulting weakness and prostration as almost unbearable. Both physical and mental work are difficult.* At night the temperature is still high. It is stuffy and almost impossible to sleep. When it rains at night some relief comes from a slight drop in temperature, but not much. The discomfort may be compared to the mugginess preceding a summer thunderstorm in the American Midwest but the tropics are at least ten times more intense. This belt includes parts of Central America, northern South America, southern Brazil, Abyssinia, Madagascar, southern India, Indo-China, the East Indes, some of the West Indes, and parts of Northern Australia. *Nowhere in the rain forest and jungle belts is there an advanced native civilization.*

Overlapping this second belt and extending farther north and south, from 10° to 20° latitude but still within the tropical zone, is a third belt of tropical shrub. Here it is always hot but there is a long dry season. On account of the intense heat, these areas are semideserts except along the rivers. *Here the population is moderate to sparse and still primitive.* Examples are areas in Central America (especially in northern Yucatan), parts of southern Mexico, parts of central and south Africa (especially the west), a large plateau in south-central India, and a belt in northern Australia. *These regions are too hot and too dry to support a thriving and vigorous population.*

Next in order, reaching as far as 25° from the equator and overlapping the third belt, is a fourth called the tropical savanna. This belt is always hot or very warm with a wet and dry season. The dry season lasts too long for tropical jungles to exist, and results in much of the land being covered with a tall grass, hence its name. The pampas of northern Argentina and a large area of Brazil belong to this belt, as do the higher plateau regions of central Africa and India, and a belt immediately south of the Sahara desert, stretching across the Sudan. The northern Philippines lie in this belt, along with the northern horns of Australia and the region around Mexico City. There are only moderately dense native populations in these areas and they are still primitive.

Next comes an interesting belt extending in many places to 35° latitude according to local conditions. This is the desert belt taking in parts of northern Mexico, the coast of Peru and northern Chile, the west coast of South Africa, the Sahara, Arabia, Iran and parts of northwest India. It also includes southern California, Arizona, New Mexico and parts of southwestern Texas, southcentral Asia, parts of Argentina, and a large part of Australia. In these regions it is always dry, winters are warm, and summers are very hot. There is some relief in winter from the oppressing monotony of high temperature and there is more chance for coolness at night. In many of these regions winter nights are actually cold, perhaps freezing or below. The hottest spots on earth are in this belt though they are some distance from the equator. The native population of the desert belt is sparse but of a higher mentality than in the tropics.

Why should so much of the earth on both sides of the equator be mostly desert? The trade winds of these regions consist of warm air descending from high-pressure belts along the inside edges of the temperate zones near the tropics. This air is dry and, as it descends, its capacity to hold moisture is increased. Before this moisture can be dropped it has to be cooled, but this doesn't happen unless a mountain range is in the way. Consequently these winds keep the land areas dry over which they flow.

Now let us consider the climatic belts starting at the poles. From the poles to about 75° latitude *it is always winter.* This is the polar desert belt *and contains no native inhabitants.* A large continent, visited only by a few expeditions, surrounds the South Pole. Northern Greenland and the islands north of the mainland of Canada are in this belt.

Between 65° and 75° latitude lies the tundra belt with very long, cold, snowy winters and short, cool, rainy summers. No trees grow here and crops cannot be raised. *The native population is very sparse and primitive and of the Mongoloid type.* The northern coasts of Canada and Alaska are in this belt.

Climatic Belts Favorable to Civilization

The previous discussion leaves us with scarcely more than 30° of latitude, approximately one-third the distance between the equator and the poles, within which to find civilization. The temperate zones extend from 23.5° to 66° latitude so it is obvious at once that *civilization is definately a temperate-zone phenomenon.*

Beginning at 30° and extending to about 40° is a subtropical dry forest belt, covering parts of southern California, parts of Spain, the south coast of Asia Minor, a part of central Chile, a small section of the southwest coast of Africa, and a smaller portion of southwest Australia. These regions have what is known as Mediterranean climate — cool, rainy winters and warm, dry summers. Elsewhere along these same latitudes exists a subtropical humid climate, as is found along the northern shore of the Gulf of Mexico and in the southeastern United States.

The largest areas in the temperate zone with approximately the same climate are the prairie or steppe regions running generally from 35° to 45° latitude in both hemispheres. Their main characteristics are cool, dry winters and hot, rainy summers, although these conditions vary considerably from place to place. Perhaps the best examples are Iowa, Illinois, Indiana, Missouri, eastern Kansas, Hungary, parts of Argentina, the Ukraine, parts of eastern China, Rhodesia, and an inland belt in eastern Australia. In all these regions the prairies are bordered, generally as one travels inland, by semiarid regions that merge into desert.

Middle latitude deserts are found in eastern Argentina, northern Chile, several western states in the United States, and central Asia from the eastern edge of the Caspian Sea eastward and northward to include Russia, Chinese Turkestan, Tibet, parts of western China, and Mongolia. These inland deserts cover wide areas. Sometimes they are

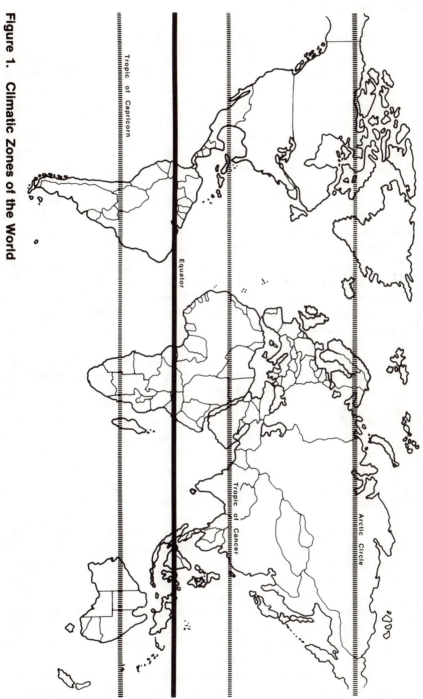

Figure 1. Climatic Zones of the World

Tropic of Capricorn

Equator

Tropic of Cancer

Arctic Circle

extensions of the trade-wind deserts of 25° to 35° latitude.

In the prairie regions that generally lie along the eastern or southern borders of the deserts, the population is dense. These are the granaries and corn raising belts of the world, with grazing lands for cattle in some sections. Spring and summer rainfall and warm to hot days provide a good growing season for agricultural crops

Some of these regions, such as Indiana and Illinois, would also be classified as having a moderately warm, humid continental climate. In the United States this climate extends from northeastern Texas, eastern Kansas, Nebraska, and Oklahoma to North Carolina, Virginia, Pennsylvania, and New York, and takes in the northern half of the cotton belt. In Europe it includes Austria, Hungary, the southern Ukraine, and the Balkans. In Asia it includes the eastern edges of the northern half of China, Korea, and parts of Japan.

From central California along the coast north through Oregon and Washington, the climate is still Mediterranean, but gradually the temperature becomes more like that of the southern and middle prairie belt. The north Pacific coast is warmer than inland regions of the same latitude because the prevailing westerly winds have been warmed by the Japanese current.

North of this region in the northern hemisphere is an extension of the same climate, except that the winters are longer and colder and more of the annual rainfall comes as snow. This belt extends roughly from 42° to 55°, and overlaps the prairie belt. This belt has a good rainfall and is characterized by deciduous forests rather than large open tracts. Parts of this belt have a marine rather than continental climate but, like the latter, are humid. This is generally the most stormy region. In the United States it begins roughly with Minnesota and extends eastward to New England. New England and eastern Canada are affected by their proximity to the Atlantic Ocean and therefore do not have winters as cold as those further inland. A somewhat similar but less favorable situation (more like Idaho and Montana) is found in Poland, the Baltic States, and eastward across Russia to the Ural Mountains. Parts of Manchukuo have a fair to good climate of like character. The winters are cold and snowy, the summers warm to hot and rainy. *In this belt the population is generally dense.*

The best example of the marine variety of this climate is Great Britain and western Europe, including southern Norway and Sweden. New Zealand has much the same climate. *It is in this belt that populations are the most dense and the most industrialized.*

Westward from Minnesota through the Dakotas the northern prairie belt merges into the middle latitude desert. In the northern

Rocky Mountain states, however, the altitude is high, with enough moisture to resemble the climate of the coniferous forest belt.

North of this, from 55° to 65°, lies the belt of coniferous forests. Here the winters are very long, cold, and snowy, and the summers short, warm, and rainy. *The population is of moderate density,* as in northern Sweden, inland southern Canada, parts of north-central Russia, and western Siberia. One cannot go far northward in this belt without observing that *civilization begins to thin out. Native populations are likely to be more primitive.* The growing season becomes shorter until it vanishes.

Summary

It is common for people to feel different in different kinds of weather. Physical strength and mental alertness decrease on hot, muggy days. It is often too warm for maximum vitality and comfort even when it is dry. Depression and lassitude increase as the barometer falls. Warm, humid weather produces irritability.

It is also common for people to feel better and have more energy during certain seasons than others. Vitality and aggressiveness decrease during the winter and revive in spring. They decrease again in summer and revive in the fall. These facts suggest that prevailing temperatures and humidity have much to do in determining human energy and efficiency.

A survey of world climates demonstrates that *native populations are primitive over large areas of the earth where it is very warm or very cold.* In these same areas it is generally excessively wet or dry and in most instances the population is sparse as well as primitive.

Only relatively small areas on earth have a climate favorable for human life. These lie in the temperate zone. Only limited areas within these zones receive a type of rainfall suitable for agriculture and grazing. Wherever the latter exists there also exist moderate to cool average temperatures. *Advanced civilizations are exclusively associated with climates that do not drain the energies of the population and that permit the growth of adequate food supplies.*

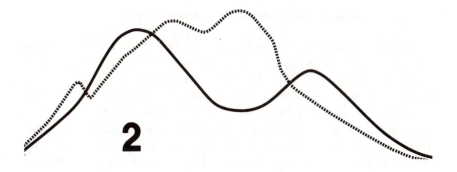

2

Climatic Influences and the Industrial Centers of the World

Geographic Location of Population Centers

On those parts of the earth with the densest populations are found some 750 cities with populations of 100,000 or more. Figure 2 illustrates the distribution of these cities according to latitude (north and south latitudes are combined). Remember that the temperate zones end at 66.5° latitude north or south in one direction and at 23.5° latitude in the other direction. Thus each zone is about 43° or 3,000 miles wide.

Nome, Alaska and Archangel, Russia, lie practically at the same latitude of about 65° almost in the arctic zone. Several large European cities are situated as far north as 60° latitude. Because warm westerly winds blow inland from relatively warm Atlantic Ocean currents, these cities are considerably warmer than corresponding cities in North America. The mean annual temperature of Leningrad at 59° north latitude (opposite the northern tip of Labrador and the southern edge of the main body of Alaska) is 39° F, about the same as that of Duluth Minnesota, at latitude 46° north — a 13° difference (Duluth is roughly 900 miles farther south than Leningrad). Moscow is 2° farther north than Dutch Harbor, Alaska, but mean annual temperatures are nearly the same for these two cities, in the neighborhood of 40° F.

Most large European manufacturing centers are in latitudes 50° to 53°, but Montreal is only 45.5°. The mean annual temperatures of all these cities range from 47° to 50° F. Most American industrial centers,

900 to over 1,000 miles farther south are only slightly warmer. Boston and Chicago average 50° and New York averages 52°. The latitude of London is about 51.5° north but Boston is around 42.3°. New York is nearly opposite Barcelona but Barcelona averages 7° warmer temperatures. Mukden, in Manchukuo, Chicago, Rome, and Tiflis in the Caucasus are all about 42° north latitude. Mukden, however, averages only 44° F whereas Rome averages 60° and Tiflis, 54°. The reason Mukden is so cold is that cold, dry, inland winds prevail during winter. The coldest spot on earth is not very far away, in Eastern Siberia, where the average annual temperature is only 3° above zero and where it can get as cold as -94° F in winter. Rome is warmer because of warm westerly winds and because the mountain ranges to its north help to hold back the cold north winds of winter. Quebec and Odessa are located at about the same latitude, between 46° and 47° north, but their temperatures are 38.5° and 50° F, respectively. Most of France is north of Minneapolis, but Bordeaux, close to the same latitude, is 10° warmer. Conversely, Philadelphia and Madrid are roughly at the same latitude and the temperatures are nearly the same, 54° and 57° F. The latitude of about 40° that marks the northern boundary of Kansas also runs close to Peiping, yet Peiping's temperature is about 52°, much the same as that of New York and Belgrade.

Washington, D.C., Cincinnati, and Naples lie practically at the same latitude, 39° north. The temperature of the American cities is 55° F, but that of Naples is 60°. Palermo, on the island of Sicily, Athens, and San Francisco are all close to 38° north latitude, yet the mean annual temperature of San Francisco is 55° F while that of the Mediterranean cities is 63°.

Familiar localities of the same latitude of Tokyo, 35°, are Gibraltar and Memphis, Tennessee. Tokyo is the coolest of the three with a temperature of 57° F, while Gibraltar is 63° and Memphis 61°. Memphis is nearly the same distance north as Buenos Aires and Adelaide, Australia, are on the south. Their temperatures are all about the same. The mean annual temperatures of southwest Australia, the tip of South Africa, and the Mediterranean are about the same.

Travelling south, we come to San Diego at 32° north latitude, the same as Fort Worth, Texas, and Nagasaki, Japan. We are now far south of Europe and nearly opposite Alexandria, Egypt, and the northern edge of India. New Orleans and Cairo are opposite one another at 30° north latitude, and average almost the same temperature, 68° F. Havana is opposite Calcutta and Hong Kong and about the same distance from the equator as Rio de Janeiro.

Temperatures are much higher; Rio de Janeiro averages 73° F, Havana, 77°, and Calcutta, 78°.

Mexico City is only a little farther north than Rangoon, but because it lies over 7,400 feet above sea level, it is relatively cool (60°) compared with 81° for Rangoon. Localities at 17° latitude or less from the equator generally have annual temperatures of about 80° if they are near sea level. But just as the coldest spot on earth is some distance from the North Pole, so the hottest places are some distance from the equator, namely, in Death Valley, California, and the Arabian Desert, where temperatures well over 130° F have been recorded.

Mean Annual Temperatures

These comparisons are interesting in themselves, but they also afford a beginning of the understanding we are seeking. If we take these 750 cities and "plot" them against their mean annual temperatures, we obtain the picture shown in Figure 3. The bottom numbers represent mean annual temperatures. Note that these temperatures run from 30° to 84° F. The cities at the cold end of the range are all in Siberia; those around 40° are in Canada and northern Russia, with northern Norway and Sweden in between. The coldest city of any size in the United States is Duluth, with a mean annual temperature of 39°, about the same as Moscow and Trondheim, Norway. Other cities in the neighborhood of 40° are Calgary, Leningrad, Oslo, Vladivostok, and Bismark, North Dakota.

Note the tremendous peak of cities from 47° to 50°, inclusive. Of these cities, 33 have a temperature of 47°, 82 a temperature of 48°, 78 a temperature of 49°, and 40 a temperature of 50°. *Obviously this is the temperature range within which civilizations, as measured by the growth of industrial cities, are overwhelmingly concentrated.* This is the range within which lie the cities of Britain, western Europe, southern Canada, and the northern United States.

There is a small peak of cities between 55° and 57° F, including 25 cities with temperatures of 57°. This group includes San Francisco, Kansas City, St. Louis, Washington, Wichita, and Baltimore in the United States; Tiflis, Milan, Madrid, Istanbul, Marseilles, Tokyo, and Baku.

Another peak occurs at 60° where there are 43 cities including Raleigh, Oklahoma City, Nashville, Shanghai, Nagasaki, Bahia Blanca, Rome, Naples, and Genoa. Near this temperature are Valparaiso, Melbourne, Auckland, Barcelona, San Diego, Buenos Aires, Teheran, Mexico City, Cape Town, Addis Ababa, Hankow, and Little Rock.

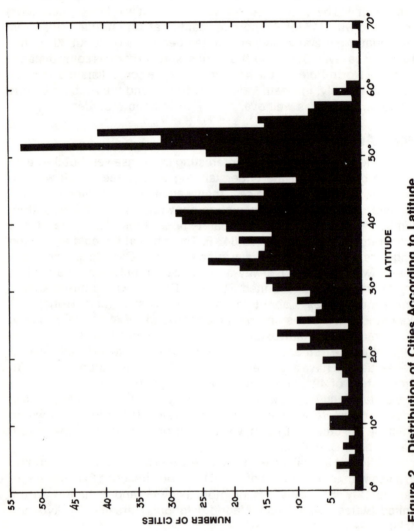

Figure 2. Distribution of Cities According to Latitude

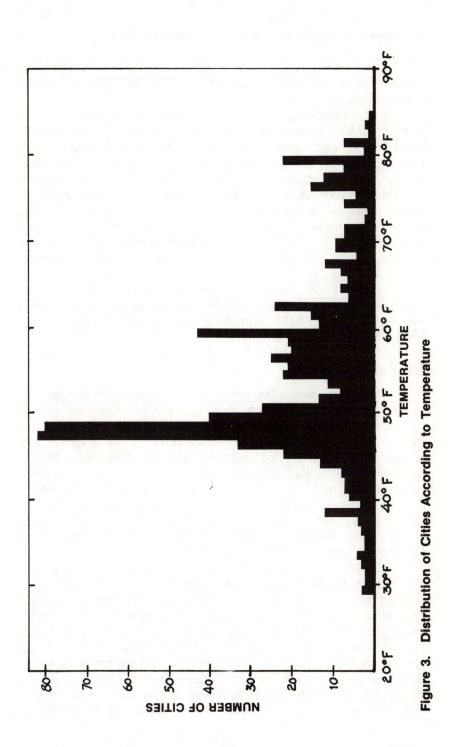

Figure 3. Distribution of Cities According to Temperature

Some of the cities around 70° are San Antonio, Brisbane, Peshawa, New Orleans, Jacksonville, Phoenix, Houston, Monterrey, and Hong Kong.

A final peak comprises cities with mean temperatures ranging from 78° to 80°. Among them are most of the cities of India, such as New Delhi, Calcutta, Nagpur, Bombay, and Madras. This group also includes Manila, Singapore, Batavia, Georgetown, Freetown, Pernambuco, Mandalay, and Panama. One of the hottest tropical settlements is Berbera along the Red Sea in British Somaliland, with an annual mean temperature of 85°. *None of these latter cities has as dynamic a population as those that lie just above or below the mean annual temperature of 50°, and most have been modernized by European or American capital and by European and American immigrants, especially the British.*

Therefore the temperature range containing the greatest industrial advancement and those qualities we regard as "highly civilized" is from 47° to 52°, with the broader range from 38° to 70° not presenting too much of a handicap.

Population Density

Along the same lines, consider the regions with the densest populations per square mile of territory. Here, of course, we run into many complications. In countries like India and China, extensive areas are only thinly populated but congestion is terrific in other areas, due in part to geography, to traditional settlement patterns, and to economics. In mountainous countries the valleys support most of the people. In dry countries the population centers around available water supplies, where the land is arable, or where soil can be irrigated. Naturally, dense populations concentrate where commerce is possible. Nevertheless, the most congested areas of the world, taking countries as wholes, do not include China or India.

There is another complicating factor. When congestion reaches a certain limit, depending on the standards of medicine, sanitation, and living, the congestion itself works against further increases in population. This factor has undoubtedly been at work for centuries in the tightly packed cities and valleys of Japan, India, China, and Java.

The area next to Britain and western Europe in order of population density is Japan with around 400 people per square mile. Germany, by contrast, has only 380. Italy is next with 350. The number then drops off sharply: India has only about 180, but this is relatively high in relation to the land area involved; China has about 100; the

United States only about 45; and Russia about 25. The statistics for other countries are as follows:

Puerto Rico	500	Turkey	50
Denmark	250	Egypt	45
Switzerland	250	Sweden	45
Austria	250	Norway	35
Hungary	250	Canada	30
Haiti	250	Fiji Islands	25
France	220	Mexico	25
Roumania	200	Iran	20
Poland	200	South America	15
Portugal	175	New Zealand	15
Bulgaria	150	Africa	13
Yugoslavia	150	Brazil	11
Europe (average)	140	Argentina	11
Greece	130	Borneo	10
Spain	130	Chile	9
Cuba	100	Bolivia	6
European Russia	70	Australia	2
Asia (average)	50		

The point of these figures is that, of all the areas where populations have had a chance to grow, *the greatest population per square mile is found, all other things being equal, within exactly the same temperature range in which are located the most dynamic civilizations — 47° to 52° F.*

Of course, the argument might be advanced that these are the most favored areas geographically, in terms of land, harbors, and distances, for the development of commerce and, therefore, for prosperity. This, however, is not true. There are many excellent harbors around the Mediterranean and distances between them are short, but the area has neither the right soil nor the right climate to support large populations. Why, then, were ancient civilations clustered around the Mediterranean when western Europe and Britain were still in a state of savagery? The answer is quite simple: In ancient times the simple inventions had not been discovered by means of which people could, with comfort, withstand the rigors of a very cool climate. Houses had no chimneys and could not be heated in winter. But as soon as man had achieved sufficient control of fire for heating — chimneys with fireplaces — *civilization moved north.* Civilized man actually prefers cool to warm climates. It is interesting to note in the history of India how centers of political control and culture moved north and south on tides of climatic change. In the absence of heating systems, these centers moved south when it got cooler and north when it got warmer. *In either case they followed the moderately cooler temperatures.* In the warm countries the more advanced of the primitive civilizations have, almost without exception, been located at higher altitudes where it is cooler, not in the hot, stuffy valleys. *Geographical conditions other than climate which favor commerce will not of themselves produce a dense and advanced population.*

Mean Seasonal Temperatures

If we examine the climates of the most densely populated areas — Great Britain, western Europe, the northern United States, and southern Canada — other interesting facts come to light. Anyone who has lived in the tropics knows how monotonous and devitalizing the climate is. There is practically no temperature difference between summer and winter; January temperatures are only one or two degrees different from July temperatures. The coldest month of the year is practically as warm as the warmest month. At Colon on the Isthmus of Panama, for example, the range of mean monthly temperature is only 2°. Similar conditions prevail in the Dutch East Indies. At Andagoya, Columbia, the yearly range is only 1°, and at Singapore it is only 3°.

The other extreme is eastern Siberia. At Verkhoyansk, the difference between the average temperatures of the coldest and warmest months is 117°, and the absolute range of temperature *between the coldest and hottest temperatures is 188°* (from 94° F above to -94° below zero). Compare this with the absolute range in the *tropics where differences from 20° to 30° are rare.* Thus, the warmer it is the year round, the less is the annual temperature range; the colder it is, the greater the range. *Few people live where the summer-winter temperature range is extremely wide or extremely narrow.*

Now if we compare the cities of the world regarding their respective seasonal differences, the greatest concentration of cities is to be found where the seasonal differences in temperature fall between 35° and 55° F. These are the same cities that produce the tall peak in Figure 3. There is another concentration of cities having a summer-winter range of 20° to 40°. These cities are warmer the year round than those of the first group. Several important European cities, namely, Copenhagen, Amsterdam, Hamburg, and Brussels, have a seasonal range of only 25° to 30°, but they are cooler the year round, and also have a marine climate, the seasonal ranges of which are not as large as those of continental climates. Iowa and Nebraska, for example, have a seasonal range of 51° to 55°, while Portland, Oregon's range is only 26° to 30°. The temperature range of San Francisco is smaller yet, only 6° to 10°, but San Francisco is cool the year round. Cities in the tropics but at high altitudes, such as Quito, Equador, and Bogota, Columbia, have practically the same temperature the year round, and their inhabitants frequently go to the hot valleys below to find relief from the monotony of temperatures that are too constant. (Even a change to higher temperatures is for the moment refreshing!) All this adds up to the fact that *part of the climatic picture favorable to human vitality is a certain range of difference in the seasons.*

Absolute Temperature Ranges

If we consider absolute temperatures, we find that the differences between the hottest and coldest days of the year give us similar results. *Again there is an optimum range for dynamic civilization.* The most advanced civilizations are in regions where absolute range is not less than 60° nor more than 160°. Again, continental temperature ranges are wider than those in coastal or island regions. Here are a few illustrations:

Location	Absolute Temperature Range *		
Verkhoyansk, Siberia	188°	Seattle	100
Ft. Vermillion	174	Houston	115
Winnipeg	149	Paris	115
Boston	140	London	85
Leningrad	140	Rome	85
Denver	135	Buenos Aires	80
New York	110	Santiago	70
Omaha	140	San Francisco	65
St. Louis	120	Batavia	30
Vienna	115	Ceylon	20
Amsterdam	105		

* The range between the hottest and the coldest temperatures.

Daily Temperature Ranges

There is still another feature of climate important to human dynamism: the difference between day and night temperatures. Peculiarly enough, these differences are likely to be highest in hot and dry desert regions such as the Sahara and the southwestern United States. The daily range is also high in the mountains where the difference between temperature in the shade and the sun is significant. Daily temperature ranges for various parts of the earth are as follows:

Area	Degrees Farenheit
Southwestern United States	30 and above
Iraq	30
African Sudan	30
Spanish Interior	30
Argentine desert	30
African high plateaus	25-30
China	20-30
Central United States	25 (average)
Buenos Aires	25
Western Europe	15 (average)
United States Gulf Coast	10-15
English coast	8
English inland	15
Southwestern Australia	15-20
Northern Brazilian coast	10-12
Northern Brazilian interior	20
Argentina	20-25
United States cotton belt	15-25
Russia	25-30

Other things being equal, *civilization is found in areas having a daily temperature range of from 10° to 30°.* If this range is as low as 10°, coolness must prevail. Unless it is generally cool when the day-night range is low (excluding areas that are always too cold), the nights are too warm as compared with the days. Southwestern Australia, for example, is relatively warm the year round, but it has a moderately large day-night range of 15° or better. San Francisco, which has a low daily range, is cool. Buenos Aires, which has a low annual range, has a wide daily range of 25°. Whenever the daily range rises above 30° or 35°, the region is almost invariably a desert or is too far north for civilization.

Rainfall Characteristics

In addition to temperature considerations, regions supporting the most advanced civilizations also have certain characteristics in regard to rainfall. The extreme humidity of the tropics and the aridity of desert regions, both of which encourage small populations, low-level civilizations, or both, have already been mentioned. *The most civilized areas on earth enjoy a specific type of rainfall — the cyclonic storm.* Storms move from higher to lower pressure areas with the prevailing winds. These meteorological conditions combine to produce tracks over which the storms travel. Storms of the "cyclone" pattern bring with them, as a rule, wind, moderate to strong changes in temperature, and moderate to strong changes in barometric pressure. The general direction of the tracks is from west to east. The storms are frequently attended, especially in summer, by thunder and lightning, and precipitation is irregular but with a distribution that is more or less general through the 12 months of the year. Most of the United States, Canada, Great Britain, and Europe east to the Caspian Sea and Ural Mountains have this type of rainfall, although depending on the location, it may rain more in one season than in others.

Other than rainfall in a Mediterranean type of climate (mentioned in Chapter 1), where precipitation is largely confined to winter and spring and is followed by a long summer drought, there is one other basic form of rainfall — the monsoon. Practically the only rainfall that Asia receives is of this type, which occurs in summer. It is caused by the fact that in summer there is a large low-pressure area over the continent and a high-pressure area over the ocean to the south, causing warm, moisture laden winds to flow to the continent. India, China, southern Japan, and some of the East Indies have this type of rainfall, and practically nothing else. Hence, they have long winter droughts that frequently extend into spring. In winter the high- and low-pressure areas change places, producing cold, dry winds from the continent out toward the ocean. The monsoon season is very humid, especially in the many places where it rains almost continuously. The winters in the higher latitudes are characterized by strong, dusty, cold-dry winds. *No country not supplied with cyclonic storms has developed a high level of industrial civilization.*

Summary

The parts of the earth with the most advanced civilizations enjoy a climate with certain characteristics. They are located in a temperate, cool, humid climate with a mean annual range of temperatures of 45° to 55° F. Beyond this range, either way, the vitality and level of advancement of the population begins to decline, although the total feasible range extends from about 37° to 70° F.

The same parts of the earth that have the preferred *mean annual temperatures* also are favored with a *preferred range of mean monthly or seasonal temperatures*. This range extends from 15° to 55°, with the most advanced populations living where this range extends between 20° and 50°. Even with a difference as slight as 10°, it is possible to have an advanced civilization.

These same areas, for the most part have an absolute range of daily temperatures, summer to winter, of 60° to 160°, with the highest civilizations located mostly between 85° and 130°. Only low or retarded civilizations exist in regions having an absolute range either below 60° or over 140°.

Again, these very same parts of the earth have a daily temperature range from night to day running from 10° to 30° F depending on their location. Smaller ranges exist where there is a cool marine climate, as in San Francisco, but in general the range is close to 20° at the lower end and not over 30° at the upper end.

The rainfall of these "preferred" parts of the earth is invariably based on the cyclonic storm pattern. Cyclonic storms not only provide optimum moisture for agriculture in terms of an annual rainfall from 20 to 60 inches per year, with 20 to 40 prevailing, but also in terms of an adequate distribution throughout the 12 months of the year. Regions of cyclonic storms do not ordinarily have marked wet or dry seasons.

Parts of the earth receiving their rain in winter, as in the case of the Mediterranean, are generally above the preferred temperature range and must often rely on irrigation during the growing season. Certain regions like the United States Northwest are cool enough to be in the preferred temperature belt. Here the winter rainy season is much longer. With few exceptions, precipitation over 60 inches occurs where it is too warm. High rainfall in the warmer half of the temperate zones, such as in the United States Southeast and along the coast of China, is associated with a debilitatingly high humidity. Although some parts of the earth are well within the preferred rainfall range, rain comes only in summer in the form of monsoons. Here annual temperatures are too high and the summer-winter difference is too small.

Preferred rainfall and temperature conditions are related. The cyclonic storms that prevail where civilization is highest provide still another kind of variability in temperature, namely, fluctuations either during the day or night. In summer, for example, when it is hot and sultry a storm comes up and the temperature drops by 10° to 20° F, or, as in the case of the United States Midwest, temperatures may drop as much as 40° or 50° F in a very short time. On the other hand, during the fall, winter, and early spring, especially when the seasons are changing, sudden warm or cold waves are common. The inland portions of western and central Europe are subject to these changes, especially in winter, although they are not likely to be accompanied by much moisture. New England "northeasters" are common in winter.

bringing snow, and in the northern half of the United States, winter cyclonic storms frequently reach blizzard proportions. Sometimes these blizzards reach into the southern states, especially in the central west.

If the number, distribution, and industrial character of cities are an indication of the degree to which civilization has advanced, then the highest civilizations are located in areas with a cool, humid, continental or marine climate of definite characteristics, including moderate to cool annual temperatures, westerly winds, and cyclonic storms, generating considerable but not extreme variability in seasonal and absolute temperatures, and temperature contrast between day and night. These are the conditions under which man has prospered most through the centuries. These are the regions where he has settled to build his cities and his commerce; where he has progressed the most in the arts and sciences; where his intelligence is the highest; and where, from his achievements, it is obvious that he is most vigorous. Neither these qualities nor the climatic factors associated with them are found elsewhere in the world, even in regions that might otherwise be geographically suitable.

This conclusion is not new. Its observation dates beyond Ancient Greece and has been repeated many times by scientific minds through the centuries. Yet this conclusion has been denied equally as often. An inquiry into the nature of this longstanding historical debate is the subject of Chapter 3.

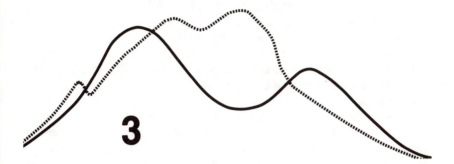

3

History of Investigations on Climate and Human Behavior

The Ancient Observers

Several centuries before Christ, Greek historians, geographers, and travellers noted that people living in the cooler, northern countries were lighter colored, larger, and stronger than those living in warmer, southern climates. The northern people, they observed, were more vigorous, braver, more aggressive, and ferocious in battle, were less prone to sensuous indulgence, and were more modest and trustworthy. Their societies were more democratic and they had an aversion to slavery. They were, however, not as interested in reflective pursuits. On the other hand, people in the warmer countries were less rugged, darker skinned, more passionate and prone to sexual indulgence, more sensitive, irritable, and hot tempered, more inclined to slavery, more prone to tyrannical government, more given to political assassinations and intrigues, and generally more cruel. Yet, according to the Greeks, people of the warmer countries were more intelligent. (It has already been noted in Chapter 1, however, that the more civilized regions on earth in ancient times were all located in warmer belts because heating systems did not exist.)

The essential features of these two patterns have been found again and again. The Greek physician, Hippocrates believed that environmental conditions supplied the necessary stimulus for foresight, ambition, alertness, and bravery. The historian Herodotus noticed that "soft" countries produced "soft" people; "delightful fruits" and "warlike spirit" did not compliment one another.

Aristotle wrote that the north European had more spirit and vigor than the native of the warmer Asiatic countries, who was content to remain in subjection and slavery. He believed that an intermediate climate between the cold of Europe and the warmth of Asia produced superior people.

Two centuries before Christ, the Greek historian Polybius, in his *History of Rome,* was very specific in his comments on the relation of climate to human achievement. "We mortals," he said, "have an irresistible tendency to yield to climatic influences. To this cause and no other may be traced the great distinctions which prevail among us in character, physical formation and complexion, as well as in most of our habits, varying in nationality or wide local separation."

Strabo, the greatest geographer of antiquity, noted that a too fertile country made people peaceful and prosperous but bred a desire for luxury, caused a loss of ruggedness, and fostered a decline in moral fiber.

Vitruvius, Roman scientist, architect, and contemporary of Strabo, concluded that people from the colder, northern countries were larger, more vigorous, braver in battle, and had heavier voices than the people of the south, who were more timid, smaller, darker, and had higher pitched voices. He also believed, however, that the greater intelligence of the southern races was due in part to the fact that warmth was conductive to greater reflection.

Other ancients voicing similar views were the Roman naturalist Pliny, the Greek physician Galen, who echoed the beliefs of Hippocrates, the Roman military writer Vegetius, and Paul the Deacon, who at a later date was perhaps the first to observe that inhabitants of northern lands were generally more healthy and enjoyed a *higher birth rate* than those of southern lands.

Medieval and Renaissance Contributions

Ibn Indrisi and Ibn Khaldun, twelfth century Arabian geographers, agreed that warm-climate people were more passionate and given to physical pleasures, while people of the north were emotionally stolid and slower to become excited. Like many of their predecessors, these investigators believed that intermediate climate produced superior races, but unlike their predecessors, they also noted that the temperament and behavior patterns of races that had migrated from one climate to another *changed until they resembled the characteristics that prevailed in the new climate.*

Thomas Aquinas, widely conceded to be the greatest mind of the Middle Ages recapitulated the beliefs of Aristotle. He concurred that a "middle" climate, neither extremely warm nor cold, produced people of general superiority.

In the sixteenth century, Jean Bodin, founder of political science and the first to define the sovereignty of the state in his *Commonwealth,* discussed the subject in considerable detail. He decided northerners were more faithful to government, were indifferent to sexual indulgence, prized their liberty highly, and were not so fixed in their ideas. They found it easier to abandon one religious faith for another and had more cheerful dispositions. Southerners, on the other hand, were more melancholic, grave, "internally cold", effeminate, malicious, foxy, and cruel. They were also more licentious and prone to practice polygamy. While wiser and more courteous than people of the north, they were more deceptive and less well adapted for stable political activity. Thus, according to Bodin, problems of government varied with the climate; the north was more democratic and valued individual life more than the south, where intrigue and tyranny were more likely to prevail.

Studies from the Age of Reason

In 1733, John Arbuthnot wrote *An Essay Concerning the Effect of Air on Human Bodies.* Northern individuals, he said, were hardier and more suited for difficult physical work, whereas southern people were indolent and favored a slave economy. "Governments," he wrote, "are powerless to change the genius and temper of a race against the forces of air and climate." The French naturalist Georges de Buffon, who wrote *Natural History of Animals, Vegetables and Minerals* in 1743, essentially agreed with Arbuthnot's views.

The most complete analysis of the problem to date was made by E. L. Montesquieu, the famous French lawyer and political philosopher, whose ideas on government (contained in his *Spirit of the Laws,* 1748) greatly influenced the authors of our own Constitution; he believed that different branches of government should be set up as checks against each other. Montesquieu is perhaps less well known for his intensive study of the phychological characteristics of different races in relation to their governments. He found that warm climate races were weak, timid, apathetic to physical exertion, avaricious, sensitive to pleasure and pain, sexually indulgent, and exhibited little "mental ambition." They were also more religious, their manners and laws were less flexible — often immutable — and they were stubborn and willful; their codes of law were stricter and their governments more tyrannical. Because there was often a considerable excess of women in their population, polygamy was practiced. On the other hand, the inhabitants of the north were physically stronger, braver, had more endurance, and were generally the conquerers in war. They were also more democratic, more apt to be honest, franker and less suspicious, emotionally more stable, and less prone to expending their energies in sensuous pleasures.

Adam Ferguson, a Scottish philosopher, repeated these observations in his *History of Civil Society* in 1768. Northern individuals, he believed, were on the whole sounder in their judgement, but less imaginative than the southernors. Man thrives against obstacles, reasoned Ferguson, and nearly everywhere possesses a surprisingly wide range of adaptability, yet northern peoples were more successful in adapting themselves than southerners. Climate gives people definite traits, he wrote, the explanation for which is eventually to be sought in the effect of climate on human physiology.

Nineteenth Century Determinism

L. F. Maury, French historian and archeologist of the College of France, claimed in his *Earth and Man* (1857) that climate affects people and types of government. Because warm-climate people are lazy and indolent, and lack enough energy to desire freedom, *tyranny in government is almost essential for their well being!* On the other hand, because cool-climate people are energetic, more stable and ruly, and easier to reason with, for them a more democratic form of government is desireable.

John W. Draper, an eminent American scientist, wrote *History of Intellectual Development of Europe* (1863). According to Draper, physical circumstances go far in controlling the characteristics of the human race. He wrote, "Where there are many climates there will be many forms of men. For every climate and indeed for every geographical locality there is an answering type of humanity." This phenomenon, however, did not commit man to slavery by the elements, for man had learned to turn night into day and cold into warmth. Nevertheless, the superior nature of European and American civilization was to be accounted for in terms of the human energy generated by the right form of climate.

In Germany, geographers Karl Ritter and Friedrich Ratzel made such a good case for the influence of geography and climate on man's behavior that they initiated an entire school of thought that stressed geographical factors in explaining history. An American pupil of Ratzel, Ellen Churchill Semple, was active in spreading these ideas in the United States.

Recent Research in the Age of Analysis

In the United States, Edwin Grant Dexter made a pioneer study of weather in relation to human health and behavior entitled *Weather Influences, An Empirical Study of Mental and Physiological Effects of Definite Meteorological Conditions* (1904). Two of his findings were particularly interesting. First, crimes against persons, as opposed to crimes against property, are more frequent in the warmer months. They are also more frequent in warmer than in cooler countries. Second, low barometric pressures are associated with mental depression and an increase in suicides. It is a common observation in mental hospitals that patients become more restless or unruly just before a storm when the barometer is going down.

J. Russell Smith, who wrote *Industrial and Commercial Geography* (1913), believed that cool temperatures were a great stimulus to human activity and affected nations as well as individuals. Civilization, he wrote, is the product of adversity and thrives best where man must work hard or starve. Therefore, to an extent little appreciated, environment makes the race. Racial characteristics are not inborn but are determined by environment, or at least were initially so determined.

Edgar Lawrence Smith wrote a memorable book entitled *Tides in the Affairs of Men: An Approach to the Appraisal of Economic Change* (1939). "There is evidence enough," he states, "to warrant the preliminary conclusion that environmental change plays its part, possibly a most important part in the economic cycle. . . . We need to know much more than we do about these natural rhythms and about the means by which they influence the moods of men; their hopes, their fears, their energies and their lassitudes."

Henry L. Moore, another American economist, wrote in *Economic Cycles, Their Law and Cause* (1914) that an alternation of buoyant and depressed attitudes seems to be environmentally conditioned, and that economic cycles follow cycles in crop yields, which in turn depend on rainfall cycles.

In addition, there are four elaborate studies, each of many years duration. The first is Dr. William F. Petersen's four-volume work on *The Patient and Weather* (1938). This is an elaborate statistical study of the incidence of different diseases, mental and physical, under different weather conditions. In another book, *Lincoln and Douglas, The Weather as Destiny,* he traces Lincoln's depressed moods to weather episodes when it suddenly turned cold and dreary, and his spirited moods to the arrival of warm fronts. On the other hand, Douglas responded best to cooler temperatures. It is reasonably clear that sensitive, introverted people such as Lincoln stabilize and feel better on a rising temperature curve whereas extroverts like Douglas stabilize on a falling temperature curve. Dr Petersen also authored Man, Weather and Sun (1947), an elaborate study in medical meteorology.

The second study is written by another physician, Dr. Clarence A. Mills of the University of Cincinnati Medical School. His book with the greatest appeal to the lay reader, is *Climate Makes the Man.* Several of Dr. Mill's researches will be reviewed in Chapter 4.

The third study is written by Professor Ellsworth Huntington of Yale, an economic geographer and student of the effects of climate on man. Professor Huntington was the author of 28 books, some of which were: *Geographic Environment and Japanese Character; Civilization and Climate; Climatic Variations and Economic Cycles; What the Air Does to Us; Environment and Racial Character; The Pulse of Progress; The Season of Birth; and The Mainsprings of Civilization.* Huntington claimed that southeast England has the best climate in the world for human health, stability and advancement. Following this are the British Isles as a whole, New England, New York, western Europe, the Pacific Northwest, and southwest Canada. There should be cool but not excessively cold winters for mental stimulation and comfortably warm but not hot summers for physical stimulation. Properly clothed, people feel and *are* mentally most alert when temperatures are cool, and physically most efficient when temperatures are moderately warm, but not hot.

The fourth study was begun by this author nearly 20 years ago. The results of this study as it relates to business and commerce is summarized in this book. Other findings will furnish much of the material for later publications.

Thomas A. Blair, in a recent textbook, *Climatology,* has observed that differences in "climatic drive," as measured by temperature and changeableness of weather, result in differences in the rate of progress and advancement of civilization among different peoples. The most advanced and active nations today are those with a "stimulating" climate. In particular, they are those regions in the middle latitudes where annual temperatures are cool but not too cold, and where there is considerable annual variation in weather. (For a thorough discussion of this point, refer to Chapters 1 and 2 of this work.)

Summary

The conviction that human behavior is strongly affected by climate is an old one. Striking indeed are the agreements among observers who have given their attention to this problem through the centuries. Unless these observations were essentially correct, they could hardly have been so similar or so persistent among intellectuals of established repute. The main reason why ideas that have been known for so long are not now more widely appreciated seems to stem from an ingrained human aversion to any truth that, on the surface, would seem to reduce man's importance in the universe, or remind him of his subjugation to forces beyond his control. Not long ago the best informed men believed the earth was flat and occupied the center of the universe; and that the sun revolved around the earth. The discoveries of Copernicus, Kepler, and Galileo in the 16th and early 17th centuries were bitterly criticised and contested. Now their discoveries are common knowledge. The average student of today finds it easy to understand facts and principles that university professors could not understand in 1600 A.D. The broadened horizons furnished by these pioneer scientists made man feel insignificant, and he persistently does not wish to feel insignificant.

Man wants to feel free and be free. The fact that he is subject to natural laws and forces of nature does not mean that he is necessarily a victim of these laws or a slave to these forces. Man frees himself by discovering the laws to which he is subject and turning them to his own account! He has made use of the laws of gravity, electricity, and innumerable others to his lasting benefit.

If man is conditioned by climatic factors, as he undoubtedly is, it is to his advantage that he accept this fact. Only then can he make use of it. *Knowledge of any kind is a source of freedom.* It is ignorance of laws, not the laws themselves, that spells slavery.

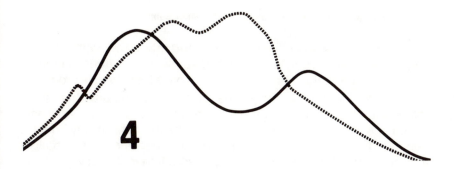

4

The Effect of Climate on Animals and Human Beings

According to Dr. Clarence A. Mills, man is far from a standard being of given proportions. From region to region he differs widely in body build, resistance to disease, and the urge to progress. Striking is the variation in his energy level and general vitality.

Energy as Biological Limitation

Man must have energy available to be active, to think, and to grow intellectually, morally, and socially. All of this requires exertion both of body and mind. All this energy comes from the food he eats and the air he breathes through the internal combustion of food. In this conversion process, there is much waste because the body is not an efficient engine. No more than 33% of the energy expended by a muscle results in physical work. A large percentage of the energy goes into things other than work and achievement, much of it into body heat. This is why a person soon feels warm when exercising vigorously. If this heat could not escape, the body would soon become overheated, and fever, illness, and ultimately death would result. This excess heat (there is always excess body heat) escapes by means of radiation. When temperatures are high outside the body, radiation is reduced. To help throw off heat, nature provides the process of perspiration. The evaporation of this moisture absorbs heat and in this way assists in cooling the body. When it is both humid and hot, air is slower to take on moisture and perspiration does not readily

35

evaporate. This is when we feel uncomfortably warm, lethargic, and depressed. There is only one thing to do under these circumstances — *slow down*. The body must do less work so that less heat is produced.

It is one of the provisions of a "wise" nature that, when temperatures external to the body are high, combustion processes within the body slow down. The heart beats more slowly (heat is generated with each heart beat), breathing becomes more shallow, and one's appetite lessens, causing a reduction in digestive work for the body. In other words, the body literally slows down.

Intellect as a Function of Physical Work

Because climate affects the ability of the body to create energy, it is easily seen why peoples living in hot climates are less energetic. They have less energy to spend and cannot, under these circumstances, build more. It is not their fault that they seem lazy and indolent. Nor is it their fault that they seem less intelligent. Intellectual problems create nerve tension; nerve tension increases muscle tension; and muscle tension creates fatigue and heat. Moreover, most problems that are intellectual have no meaning unless their resolution is associated with activity or achievement of some sort that sooner or later involves physical labor. And so, high intelligence and a high capacity for physical work complement each other. Where physical labor cannot be carried on, intellectual labor is useless. Therefore we find people living in warm climates adhering to "do nothing" philosophies. They stress leisure, solitude, and rest, while the philosophies of colder countries stress action, work, and achievement.

Resistance to Disease

The fact that internal body processes slow down when outside temperatures are high is evident in many ways. The human system consumes less oxygen, blood pressure is lower, growth processes are slower, and, contrary to popular belief, people are smaller and mature later in life. The body is also less disease resistant, and when infected, the white blood corpuscles are less responsive. Fertility, and hence the birth rate, is lower.

Dr. Mills found that, among persons dying from tuberculosis in Cincinnati, those who came from the Gulf states succumbed to the disease in half the time of people born and raised in the North. White immigrants from warmer, southern countries of Europe lived only 11 months as compared to 21 months for northern Europeans. In the case of blacks, those born and raised in the South resisted the disease for only 9 months while northern blacks survived 17 months.

The death rate from acute appendicitis increases as you move from north to south. On the other hand, certain diseases associated with hypertension such as diabetes, toxic goiter, arteriosclerosis, mental breakdown, and suicide are more frequent in more severe climates. From a health standpoint, climate can create too much mental and physical tension. This is especially true where the weather is exceedingly changeable with a combination of rapidly rising and falling temperatures, storms, and high winds.

Menstruation and the Onset of Maturity

The popular idea is that people living in the tropics mature earlier than those living in the temperate zones. This is a fallacy due, first, to a misunderstanding of the marriage customs and sexual behavior of tropical peoples, and second, to the fact that tropical people look much younger than they are. Actually, fertility develops later in life in the tropics than in the temperate zones, and many marriages are consummated long before childbearing can begin. The average Philippine girl, for example, begins to menstruate a year and a half later than the average girl in Minnesota, and she will not bear children until she is about 21 years of age. Maturity is also delayed when average temperatures are very cold. In Montreal, the average age of maturity in girls is 14.5 years; in Cincinnati, 13; in New Orleans, 13.5; and in Panama, 14. But in the tropics maturity in the sense of the onset of menstruation precedes fertility by from 3 to 6 years. Finnish girls are nearly 16 years old at maturity; German girls, 14; French girls 13.5. In Italy and Spain, the age of maturity rises again to over 15.

Dr. Mills found corresponding results in white mice reared in artificial climates. Mice that lived under temperatures ranging from 64° to 68° F matured in 33 days and first conceived in 59 days. Mice living between 70° and 80° also matured in 33 days but did not conceive until 64 days. Single days in the life of a white mouse are comparable to months for a human being. Mice living in a temperature of 86° to 92° matured more slowly, taking 37 days, and did not conceive before the 74th day, 15 days later than the cold-climate mice. Roughly this amounts to 1 or 2 years of human life. In the second generation, the mice raised in higher temperatrures did not mature until the 46th day, and few ever conceived.

This author (Wheeler) obtained similar results on white rats. First-generation litters born in a hot room (90°) F matured 10 to 14 days later than those living in a cold room (55°). The colony in the hot room would have died out completely after the fourth generation had it not been replenished with fresh stock

Climatic Influences on Human Stature

The climatic control of growth can also be seen in data obtained by Dr. Harold S. Diehl on the heights and weights of American college women as reported in *Human Biology*. College girls at the University of the Philippines averaged 4 feet, 10 inches in height as compared with 5 feet, 4 inches or more in the United States. Girls from Michigan, Minnesota, and Cornell on the one hand, and those from Kentucky, North Carolina, and Texas on the other, were found to be shorter than girls living in the in-between states.

In weight, the Philippine girls were again smallest, averaging only 105.6 pounds. Then came Texas girls, with an average weight of 116. In Kansas, they weighed 117.6; in Nebraska, 118.8; in Michigan, 120.5; in Wisconsin, 121.3; and in New York, 125.2 pounds.

During the 1920s and 1930s, the whole world experienced high temperatures. In the 1930s, long-time records were broken in many places. In 1934 the Midwest recorded 6 weeks of excessive temperatures with a high over 100° F nearly every day. For 2 weeks in Kansas temperatures of over 110° were experienced with a 118° maximum. During these same 2 weeks the thermometer failed to drop below 100° at night. Bed sheets were too hot to sleep on without being sprinkled with water; people lived in their basements; horses died in the fields.

Around 1930, according to Dr. Mills, stature began to decline in the United States. People were getting smaller and maturing later. Girls were slower in menstruating, and 20 year-old boys were on average less mature. They were "hot-house" babies compared with their fathers or grandfathers at the same age. Between 1830 and 1900, there were long cold periods, the climate during the age of Queen Victoria provided rugged conditions of living. Young men of 18 and 20 were already heads of families and in positions of responsibility. Among other things, they commanded clipper ships that sailed around the world and had tough crews with which to deal; these young men must have had mature personalities as well as mature bodies. Those were the days of large and lusty families.

Birth Rates and Death Rates

During the excessive heat of the 1930s, the birth rate declined everywhere. In normal times, the birth rate is higher than the death rate, but during this period the death rate increased while the birth rate decreased over much of the earth. Totalitarian nations became alarmed and tried various methods to increase the birth rate. In Germany, even single girls were exhorted to bear children "for the Fuehrer." According to the testimony of German physicians, even these extreme efforts failed to lift the birth rate to where they thought it belonged.

In the United States, only in the coolest sections, particularly the mountains, did the birth rate fail to decline. In parts of southern California it was reported that the birth rate dropped so much below the death rate that the population would have theoretically disappeared in a hundred years. All over the United States, the increase in childless marriages led to a wave of adoptions, creating difficulties when the demand for available babies outpaced the supply of adoptable children.

North temperate zone conditions in the 1920s and 1930s began to approximate those in the warm-dry areas close to the tropics, where the birth rate is always low. The lowered birth rate was not due primarily to economic reasons, although there was a serious depression at the time. It was not due to increased prevention, for a similar trend occurred in both the wild and domestic animal kingdoms.

Seasonal Variations in Conception

In harmony with these facts are others leading to the same conclusion: the lower energy level caused by excessive warmth affects brain, muscle, and reproductive tissue alike. These facts are relevant to normal conception rates where seasons are sharp and distinct as in the temperate zones. Montreal for example, has a peak in conceptions during May and June, when the average monthly temperature is about 60° F. There is a slight rise in conceptions when temperatures again reach this figure in late summer or early fall, but the trend is down until it reaches bottom in January. There is also a slight dip during the heat of July.

Further examples of seasonable variability in rates of conception are available. In Boston, a similar spring peak occurs, although it does not rise as far above the average as it does in Montreal.

The peak again comes in late May and early June. Then the curve declines through July, August and September, to rise again in October and November. Another drop takes place in late January, bottoming in February. In Chicago, a spring peak occurs in April and May following a steep late winter decline. The curve then drops in July, followed by a fall maximum. Farther south, in Wichita, Kansas, the winter level is relatively higher and there is a lesser but nevertheless appreciable decline followed by a spring peak. The conspicuous feature of this curve, however, is a strong decline extending from May through September, reaching a low in July, followed by a fall rise.

This same gap is even deeper in Charleston, South Carolina, and deepest in Tampa Florida. In all these curves, there is a conspicuous peak in the spring. In San Francisco we find a late winter drop and the usual spring peak, but only a small drop during the summer. This is because summers are cool in San Francisco.

Japan shows the same late winter drop followed by a tremendous peak during cherry blossom time, from March to June. Then a very sharp drop occurs in July and August, which are hot, followed by a sharp rise again in fall.

Note in all these curves a spring peak and another, usually smaller, peak in the fall. A decline generally occurs in late winter. It seems evident that human germ cells are strongest during a natural mating season in the spring, when physiological conditions in the female are best. Conditions are unfavorable for either male or female in the excessive heat of mid-summer. Moreover, the increased physiological load on the system caused by merely living through the winter produces another decline in late winter. The conclusion is that, even though sexual attraction in temperate zone humans is more or less steady throughout the year as compared with other mammals, nevertheless there are still mating seasons for human beings, the most important being the spring. That the conception rate is strongly associated with climatic changes of the seasons is demonstrated by the fact that *it reverses in the Southern Hemisphere.*

Aggressiveness in spring is not confined to sexuality. It also shows in curves of industrial production and mental and physical work. Wars are more likeley to break out in spring, which is generally a time of high energy level.

Life Expectancy Correlated to the Month of Conception

Huntington found that persons born in February or March — the results of May and June conceptions — in areas like New England live longer by 3 years or more than those conceived in July and August, when it is hot and the vitality of the parents is lower. He further argues that this difference in life span due to different conception dates is as much as 10 years in certain parts of the world.

Moreover, prolonged summer heat results not only in fewer conceptions, but these conceptions result in the birth of fewer scientists and leaders. Birth or conception in hot weather seems to result in a handicap from which the person never recovers. In the worst climates the average life span is 20 to 40 years less than among people born in the best climates and in the worst climates, Huntington concludes,scientists and world leaders constitute a negligible number of the subsequent adult population.

Effects of Climate on Intelligence and Productivity

We have examined the correlation between climate and physical health and work, but what about the effects of climate on the human mind and intelligence? Huntington found that conditions producing good health are also associated with better performance in civil service examinations and with an increase in business productivity, while conditions conducive to poor health, such as droughts and excessive temperatures, are accompanied by poorer performances on civil service examinations and by economic depressions.

Lifestyle Differences Between Northerners and Southerners

Assuming that the ability to read and write is a fair measure of the intellectual status of a people, and that the existance of well kept vital statistics in a region is a fair index of literacy, mental aletrness, and vitality, this same investigator notes that vital statistics in the southern United States are kept with far less accuracy than in the northern states. Many more ages in the South are reported inaccurately, perhaps merely to the nearest convenient number (such as ages ending in five or zero). This is particularly true of dates of birth.

The story is told of a famous admiral born and raised in the deep South who sent his son to Annapolis. As the admiral was bidding him goodbye, he remarked, "Son, you'll have to work hard to beat those damned Yankees. They're smarter than we are. You see, the sun's so hot down here that it bakes our brains." This fatherly admonition carried more than a grain of truth, for students from the cooler states generally find it easier to apply themselves than those from warmer states.

It should be emphasized that these remarks about the fine people of the South have nothing to do with their worth as human beings and constitute no reflection whatever upon their integrity. Southern people themselves are among the first to recognize that they are not, on average, as aggressive as northerners, that the greater heat requires them to live and move about in a more leisurely manner, that they were slower to adopt advanced methods of farming, that they were slower to industrialize, and that their educational system is behind that of the north.

Many southerners agree, too, that they are more sensitive than their northern cousins. They are easier to anger, more rash, and the incidence of crimes against persons in the white population is greater while crimes against property are more numerous in the North. Southerners also tend to be more religious. All of these are but *natural differences that exist everywhere* between the inhabitants of cool as opposed to warm countries. The same differences can be found between northern and southern Europeans, Chinese, Japanese, and Indians as well.

In justice to American southerners, however, it should be remembered that the War Between the States destroyed the type of economy on which their lives had been based and left them prostrate. In this connection, it should also be noted that a slave economy has never flourished in cool countires. (Incidentally, it might be added that the great slavery reform movements in history occurred during the cold phases of long climatic cycles.) Before the days of machinery, slave economies naturally developed in warm countries for the simple reason that the population could not maintain itself economically at a high standard of living with out slave labor; it was impossible to do the necessary amount of work. Wealth could be accumulated in no other way!

While it cannot be denied that southerners lack the "push" of the Yankee, they do possess other qualities not found to an equal degree in the North. Forced to take life more leisurely, the southerner lives more joyously, worries less, suffers less nervous tension, and, if he takes proper care of his health, has the capacity to live longer. He does not "burn himself out" to the extent that the northerner does. Moreover, a certain paradox should be noted in regard to certain types of "productivity," namely, those involved with the art of war. Southern soldiers and generals were uniformly superior to those of the Union Army in the Civil War. Personally they had more at stake, but they also made exceptionally fine fighters in both world wars. Why? They could "hate" more effectively, get more angry, and remain angry longer; they were not necessarily braver, but they were *more rash*. Dueling for the sake of preserving honor had always been a custom in the South. Translated into military effectiveness, this ability to *take more personal risks* is largely responsible for the ferocity of the South's soldiers and the brilliance of their commanders.

Climatic Experiments with White Rats

Experiments on white rats performed by this writer and a colleague, Dr. Leo Hillmer, at the University of Kansas succeeded in changing mentally sluggish rats into aggressive, alert animals in the short space of 40 days, and vice versa, by the simple procedure of alternating them from one "climate" to another.

In one experiment, a large number of litters were born at about the same time. When these litters were weaned at 3 weeks, they were divided into three groups. One group was put in a cold room where the temperature was a constant 55° F both day and night. Another group was placed in a hot room where the temperature was a constant 90° F. The third group, used as a control was kept under normal temperatures which varied from 85° in the summer to 75° in winter. Humidity was held as constant as possible. All three groups received the same food and all they would eat.

When the rats reached the age of 10 weeks, they were deprived of food for 24 hours. Then a simple maze or labyrinth was placed in their room. At one end of the maze was the starting box, at the other the food; it was constructed so that one direct route led to the food and six others led to blind alleys. The object of the experiment, of course, was to see how soon each rat could repeatedly reach the food by traversing the maze without making any false turns into the blind alleys.

Effects on Learning

One first-generation rat from the cold room learned the maze in 13 trials. The average was 21 trials. In contrast, a typical control rat required 31 trials while the typical hot-room rat took 56 trials to solve the same problem. There were several rats from the hot room that failed in 100 trials and were eliminated from the experiment because no one had time to bother with them any longer. Therefore, the actual difference in performance between hot-room and control rats was far greater than the apparent difference of 56 versus 31 trials.

In the second generation, the contrast between hot-room and cold-room rats was even greater. The efficiency of the cold-room rats remained about the same, but the hot-room rats' ability to solve the problem was greatly deteriorated; many more rats failed in 100 trials and were discarded, and the average for those that did finish was 76 attempts. In terms of maze learning, the cold-room rats of the second generation were more than six times as "smart" as their hot-room cousins.

The learning process of the cold-room rats was smooth and stable. They progressed more or less regularly from day to day. What they learned they retained. The control rats were not as good at retention; generally they could not traverse the maze for three consecutive times. Time after time toward the latter part of the experiment, the hot-room rats would make one perfect run, only to forget the path the next time. Their progress was extremely erratic.

Influence on Physiology

Already it was evident that the hot-room rats could not adjust to the demands of the maze. They were dying out. In the second generation they weighed half as much as the cold-room rats and showed many other striking differences. Even the hot-room rats of the first generation were much smaller than those in the control and cold rooms. The cold-room rats were the largest of all. (These results were similar to the findings of Dr. Mills in his white mice colonies.) The hot-room rats grew longer tails, hour-glass bodies, and longer ears. The tails and ears of the white rat are not covered with hair; these are the parts of the rat from which excess body heat can more easily escape. The hot-room rats were in effect trying to adapt themselves to higher temperatures by growing more radiation surface for the escape of waste heat. On the other hand, the cold-room rats grew fat, chunky bodies, with much heavier coats of hair, shorter tails, and smaller ears. Their radiation surface shrank in relation to their weight. The control rats were more like the cold rats in body size and shape but smaller.

Behavioral Patterns

The behavior of the hot-room rats was abnormal as compared with that of the cold-room rats. The latter were tame and docile and not seriously upset when placed in the maze. They accepted the situation as a matter of course and went about their business of searching until they found the food. If it took them a long time at first, they were none the worse for their frustration. The case of the hot-room rats was strikingly different. They were touchy and irritable; in humans we might call such behavior "hot tempered" or emotionally unstable.

Their behavior in the maze was extremely erratic. They were much more disturbed and frequently they would dash about the maze as if badly frightened. At other times they would sit in a corner motionless for several minutes unless prodded to move on. On the whole, they showed great lethargy. Obviously they lacked "push" as compared with the cold-room rats, which were seldom still in the maze.

In their cages, the behavior of the two groups was also strikingly different. The cold-room rats were much more active, more frequently engaging in play or climbing about the cage. They frequently would wrestle with one another in what was apparently a playful mood. The hot-room rats, until excited by one cause or another, moved more slowly and spent much of their time lying about the cage, apparently in an effort to keep as cool as possible.

Mating and Weaning

The mating and maternal behavior of the two experimental groups also showed marked contrasts. In the cold room, when a female was ready for conception, the male became at once interested. There was little or no sterility. These rats had four to five litters of healthy, vigorous offspring a year, with usually from 10 to 15 in a litter. Moreover, the cold-room mothers took excellent care of their young. Excelsior supplied for nests was freely used. Should one of the litter stray from the nest, it was promptly picked up and put back. The cold-room mothers showed a normal and healthy interest in feeding their young and possessed ample milk. Almost never did a cold-room mother lose a single member of her family, and almost never was there a runt among them.

The contrasting hot-room litters were small, generally ranging from four to seven. When the female was ready for cenception, the male was sluggish in taking notice. In the first generation there were seldom more than two litters a year, rapidly decreasing to one and then none in succeeding generations. Hot-room mothers were careless and indifferent, and frequently they practiced infanticide. The keeper might find a young rat minus a leg, or sometimes whole litters might be found half eaten by the mother. The mortality rate from other than violent death was also high. If a young rat crawled away from the corner of the cage where it was born (hot-room mothers did not build nests), the mother paid no attention; unless rescued by the keeper, the baby died of starvation. Frequently the mother had trouble giving birth to her young, a problem that almost never arose in the cold room.

"Neurotic" Tendencies

In general, the hot-room rats revealed many "neurotic" tendencies. They were far less docile than the cold-room rats and objected to being handled. Frequently they bit their keeper, something the cold-room rats never did unless handled too roughly. When placed in the maze, the hot-room rats were frequently upset, and their frustration resulted in many "fits" or "tantrums." The hot-room rats, especially the males, exhibited a good deal of superficial sexual behavior, yet they were less prompt when the female was ready for conception. In the cold room, none of this superficial behavior was noticed.

Reversing the Experiments

Having found the cold-room rat to be larger, healthier, stronger, more stable, and many times "smarter" than the hot-room rat, the next problem was to see if these qualities could be reversed by shifting each experimental group to the room previously occupied by its counterpart.

Dr. Kenneth Moore repeated the previous experiments and obtained essentially the same results. After 45 rats in each of three new groups learned the same maze, he divided each group into three parts of 15 rats each. In the case of the 45 cold-room rats, he kept 15 in the cold room and transferred 30 to the control room; after a week, he moved 15 to the hot room. Of the original 45 rats in the control room, he shifted 15 to the cold room and 15 to the hot room. Of the 45 rats in the hot room, he left 15 in the hot room, shifted 30 to the control room for a week, and then moved 15 to the cold room. After the rats had been in their new climatic environment for a month, he presented them with the same maze again to see how well they could relearn it. In this short period of time, the cold-room rats had been converted into hot-room rats and vice versa. Cold-room rats that had originally learned the maze best but had been in the hot room for a month did almost as poorly at relearning the maze as did those who had been kept in the hot room all the time. Conversely, hot room rats that had originally learned the maze so poorly but had been moved to the cold room relearned the maze almost as quickly as the original cold-room rats.

Complex Influences on Human Vitality

Returning now to a consideration of human beings, it is obvious that lower levels of culture found in the tropics and other warm locations result chiefly from a pronounced lack of energy, tracable to lowered food combustion and lowered body and nervous activity. Primitive human races that live where it is too warm or too cold never had a chance to advance. They lack the reserve energy necessary for "push," aggressiveness, and inventiveness. On the other hand, peoples living in cool countries are a direct product of a much higher energy level, which enables evolution to proceed farther and permits the growth of an intelligence, restlessness, and "drive" that creates advanced cultures.

But why do the highest civilizations cover so small a portion of the earth? Simply because only a small portion of the earth has the right kind of climate for maximum human activity, either mental or physical. These few areas accomodate less than one-third of the world's population. In many regions with the most beneficial annual temperatures, something else is wrong. For example, perhaps the differences in seasons are not great enough, or the region lacks the right kind of rainfall. The question of human adjustment to climate around the globe is naturally far more complex than are controlled experiments with white rats.

South America was explored and colonized before North America, but the explorers sailed from warm Spain and Portugal, not from cool Britain and northwestern Europe. Moreover, only small parts of South America are climatically comparable to the cooler regions of the northern hemisphere. Much of the continent is in the tropical zone. People living in Bogota, Columbia, boast about their perfect weather. It is excellent from the standpoint of physical comfort — always mild, never too hot or too cold — *but the human energy level is never as great at high altitudes* because of greater thinness of the air. In addition, this area is not frequented by *cyclonic storms.*

Much of the temperate region of South America is occupied by deserts and high mountains. Only a small area around Buenos Aires approaches the optimum, but here it is generally too warm. Paraguay is only barely within the tropics. There are summers like those in New Orleans and winters like those in Tampa. Like northern Florida, Uruguay has summer and winter seasons, but the range is insufficient. The climate is not unhealthy, but is only moderately stimulating. From Buenos Aires south to Bahia Blanca, the climate is like that of eastern Texas — subtropical marine. Along the coasts of Peru and northern Chile are to be found some of the driest areas on the earth. Inland in the north of Argentina it is semiarid. At the foot of the Andes, on a plateau 5,000 feet high, there are mild winters and cool summers where sugar cane, fruits, alfalfa, and grapes are raised with the aid of irrigation. But, again, cyclonic storms are absent. Much of southern Argentina is a desert.

Most of Africa is either tropical or subtropical; its climates are either too hot and dry or too hot and wet. Only in the mountains can Europeans live with comfort and maintain their level of vitality; but nowhere on the continent do cyclonic storms prevail as they do over North America and western Europe. In the Union of South Africa conditions are fairly good near the southern tip and on the east coast, but are not as stimulating as western Europe.

Much of Australia is too hot and dry or too hot and moist. A narrow belt along the east and south is favorable with abundant cyclonic storms, but the geographic area is too small to support a large population. New Zealand also has the right temperatures and variability, but the country is small and population growth is restricted by mountainous terrain.

India is much too hot except in the inaccessible mountains. Burma, Thailand, and Indo-China are too warm and often too humid, as is the south coast of China. The tropical monsoons along these southern coasts depress the population by constant low barometric pressures. High mountain ranges extending along the northern border of India into Burma and southern China keep the rainfall from moving inland and keep the cool winter winds from moving south. Hence, the climate has a monotony that provides stagnation.

The warm, humid climate reaches far north along the Chinese coast, much of which is in the lower latitudes. By the time we reach Peiping it is either too cold and dry or too warm and moist. Unhealthy dust storms blow down from the upper inland deserts during the winter. Much of China is either mountainous or arid, or both. Great areas are at high altitudes and are practically a desert.

Mongolia ia almost all desert. A few cyclonic storms manage to form in the Himilayan Mountains and traverse China, sometimes even reaching southern Japan. These storms make the upper Yangtze River valley a moderately favorable region. In Siberia, large areas are too cold and dry to support life. The vast inland portions of central Asia are swept by furious and unrelenting winds, blazing heat in summer, and freezing cold in winter. Other portions of central Asia contain the highest mountain ranges on earth, towering to heights of 28,000 feet. West of the mountains in Russian Turkestan, it is either semiarid or desert, too hot in summer and too cold in winter. Not until the Ural Mountains and the Ukraine is there a favorable climate with the right temperatures and essential cyclonic storms. A small portion of Iran has a good climate, but most of the country is a hot desert that produces extreme conditions as in Iraq and Arabia. Turkey's climate is generally unfavorable.

Central Japan has a favorable climate, but the southern part is affected by the depressing moist heat from summer monsoons. During the winter, cool winds with cyclonic characteristics move across from Asia, but Japan's climate is too warm and "easy" in the south, and too cold in the north.

Most of the eastern Mediterranean is hot and semiarid. Southern Italy is too warm and monotonous for a vigorous, industrialized civilization, but is a fair to good agricultural region. Industry has developed in the north where it is cooler. Most of the Mediterranean is subject to winter storms, but devitalizing heat prevails during much of the year. The winter dampness is often steady, continuous, and monotonous, and the sun often disappears for long periods.

This circuit of the globe leaves only North America and western and central Europe. Northern Russia, Finland, Sweden, and Norway are too cold and forbidding, as are northern Canada and much of Alaska. The Baltic states, Russia, and Poland have been retarded by too rugged a climate. The amazingly rapid progress of Russia in recent decades has been due to an exceptionally warm phase of a 100-year climatic cycle, so that the people of this ordinarily frigid land have had a chance to better their status. In the Balkans, the climate is more favorable, but other negative factors have interfered. This part of the world is a melting pot of diverse racial strains. Great progress requires both a unity of effort and an optimum climate. Unity has been lacking in the Balkans since the Middle Ages. Moreover, from the fourteenth through the nineteenth centuries, this region has been under the dominance of the despotic and backward Ottoman Empire. Czechoslovakia has developed rapidly since freed from the dominance of Austria, but her progress has been rudely halted by another despot, Russia. Once the Balkans find permanent peace and learn to pool their efforts rather than dissipate them in petty jealousies and quarrels, they should be able to make more rapid progress.

In addition to unfavorable climate, geographic limitation of habitable population areas, and lack of regional untiy, geographic isolation has always been a handicap to progress. Civilization develops first along the channels of least resistance — coasts and waterways that offer opportunities for commerce. But of two equally favorable harbors or waterways from a geographic standpoint, the cooler one will develop first and forge ahead of the warmer one, unless the warmer port is otherwise favorably positioned between strong markets or is developed by cool-climate peoples for imperialistic purposes.

Summary

In this chapter the results of statistical studies on human beings and experimental studies on small mammals have been examined.

The reason why warm-climate people remain primitive or backward is related to their energy level. The mere process of living, let alone working generates body heat. This heat must escape the body by radiation. If it accumulates too fast because of overwork or high temperatures outside the body, the body must slow down its activities in order to generate less heat. Failure to do so imperils health and even life itself. This is especially true where it is humid as well as hot. Dr. Clarence A. Mills demonstrated these facts both from studies on white mice and on human growth and health in different parts of the United States as well as in warmer countries of the world.

A study of the seasonal conception rate of humans revealed that human systems weaken in midwinter under the pressure of temperatures that are too cold, and again in summer when temperatures are too hot. Reproduction is at its best in spring, when climatic conditions are most favorable for vitality.

Studies by Professor Ellsworth Huntington show that intelligence is at its best when it is cool and when barometric pressure is not too low. His studies further demonstrate that cyclonic storms along with optimum temperatures are vital to optimum human achievement. *Areas of the earth where cyclonic storms are accompanied by the right temperatures are confined to North America, Britain, and western Europe.* These are the areas where civilization is at its best.

Contrary to popular opinion, high temperatures retard physical growth and delay the biological process of maturing. There is evidence that younger people in this country started to lose physical stature during a recent period of high annual temperatures which also witnessed a decline in fertility.

Experiments conducted on white rats by the writer and his associates demonstrated that high temperatures caused serious mental and physical deterioration but cool temperatures produced a superior strain. Animals reared at 55° F were larger, healthier, more intelligent, and more fertile than "normal" rats reared at seasonal variations of 75° to 85° and far superior in all these respects to rats reared at 90°. The latter were distinctly unhealthy, both physically and mentally.

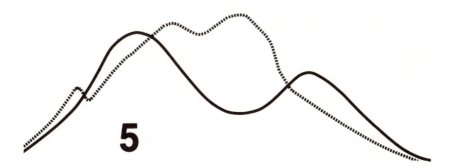

5

The Changeableness of Climate

The relationship of human achievement to climatic conditions has so far been examined only on the assumption that climate is steady and lasting in any given locality. To be sure, it is always warm in the tropics and cold in the far north. In some places, it is always dry; in others it is always wet. But over long periods of time, climate is not the stable phenomenon that superficial evidence seems to indicate.

Climatic Fluctuation in the Mediterranean World

From the time of Old Egypt to the fall of Rome in 476, the Mediterranean (as well as southeastern Asia, India, and southern China) was the truly vigorous part of the world.

Some students of the history of climate believe the earth was cooler then, that Great Britain and Europe were too cold and stormy in winter to support advanced civilizations. The Phoenicians, those great developers of shipping and commerce, frequently found parts of the North Sea frozen over in winter. It is probable that the races who found their way to the Mediterranean from the north were motivated by long periods of cold drought that made the northern latitudes too disagreeable for habitation.

Other authorities believe the chief difference between the Mediterranean climate of ancient times and today is one of rainfall rather than temperature. Whatever the answer, Mediterranean climate is evidently less favorable in modern times than it was in ancient times. Probably both groups of investigators are correct to some extent. That the Mediterranean once enjoyed a better rainfall than it does now can hardly be questioned. Traces of river beds are visible in regions both east and south of the Mediterranean coast. It is conceivable that temperatures were also more favorable because these two conditions are often associated with one another.

According to Huntington, the Mediterranean is not the only region where climate changed for the worse in the course of history. While this area lost rainfall, others gained too much, and, since they were warm, the result was a tropical humidity with which native populations were unable to cope. Changes of this kind were major factors in the decline of civilizations in Central America and Indo-China, where interesting and elaborate cultures existed until the Middle Ages. Great cities were either abandoned or wiped out. Disease, swamps, tropical vegetation, or encrouching deserts forced the populations either to migrate or die.

In ancient times Palestine was prosperous, as was Asia Minor in general. Palestine became prosperous again during the fifth and sixth centuries A.D. During the last glacial period, the Dead Sea was large enough to fill most of the valley of the Jordan. Glaciers existed on Mount Lebanon, and Syrian caves reveal both the remains of prehistoric man and leaves of northern trees such as oak and maple. Bones of animals whose usual habitat was much farther north have also been found. These facts support the hypothesis that for long periods of time the Mediterranean was cooler than in modern times and also enjoyed better rainfall. Moreover, the writers of the Old Testament mention forests that do not and could not exist in the present climate of the region. In the records of the third century B.C., known as a time of prosperity, five rivers are described as flowing in Palestine, where today not a single river exists. From the appearance and disappearance of wells and baths that can be dated, from architectural achievements indicating times of prosperity, and from the development of trade routes, Huntington concluded that climate has fluctuated several times in Palestine between wet and dry periods, and that recently the climate has again deteriorated.

Evidence From the Caspian Sea

Collecting accumulated evidence and adding much of his own, Huntington also found that the level of the Caspian Sea has not been the same throughout history. The Caspian Sea is a very large body of water. It would require a long and striking change in rainfall to alter its water level to any great degree for any great period of time. But beaches found high on the hillsides suggest that during the Golden Age of Greece in the fifth century B.C. the Caspian Sea was perhaps 265 feet higher than its recent levels. During the fifth century A.D., it must have been 40 to 50 feet below modern levels for there are ruins of forts, apparently built at that time, that are now under water as far as 18 miles from shore. The sea was again higher during the Middle Ages. There have been parallel lake level changes in Chinese Turkestan as well as corresponding changes in the expansion and contraction of oases in the African Sudan, along with periods of good and poor floods in the Nile Valley.

Historic Variations in the United States

The western United States must have gone through similar changes, based on evidence gathered from annual tree ring growth of the giant sequoias of the Sierra Mountains in California. During spring and summer, tree growth consists of whitish cells, but during winter, when growth has almost stopped because of cold weather, cells are much darker. Under favorable conditions, trees produce one ring per year. Thus the age of a tree can be determined. Furthermore, during years with plenty of moisture and a long, warm growing season, the rings are relatively wide. During droughts and years of short growing weather, the rings are narrower. Consequently, a great deal can be deduced about the climate of a region by measuring the width of the rings. The largest of the sequoias began growing a thousand years before the birth of Christ; they therefore provide a climatic record spanning many centuries. These trees tell much the same story about climate in ancient times as do the fluctuating levels of the Caspian Sea.

Prehistoric Fluctuations

Climate in the temperate zones has changed enough throughout history, to alter radically the habits, attitudes, thoughts, judgements, and actions of people down to the smallest facets of their lives, and to affect profoundly the nature of business production, prices, and markets — including stock markets!

Geologic evidence points indisputably to the fact that at no time has climate been a static thing. It is always in the course of changing, although the changes are of course slow. Both warm and cold periods are always progressing toward or away from a climax. The same is true for rainfall.

Geologists have long known that the earth has seen many upheavals, mountain building, and elevation of the continents, alternating with periods of erosion, the lowering of continental elevations, and encrouchment on the land surfaces by the oceans. It is further generally agreed that the earth has undergone radical drops in temperature during elevated times and has seen temperature rises during periods of low elevation, although these changes probably did not affect all areas of the earth equally. During periods of high elevation ice ages frequently occurred, and during periods of low elevation temperate zones became semitropical. There is little doubt that these fluctuations have been going on for at least a billion years. It is also well known that at the end of a long, cold period, perhaps following an ice age, and after climate had been dry for a long time, temperatures rose and, at the same time, rainfall revived over the earth. Again and again during this change in climate, and as soon as it became warm enough, plant and animal life revived. When warm-period rainfall declined and it became very hot, deserts expanded and plant and animal life thinned out in many areas, sometimes disappearing altogether. Reproductive powers declined and great "empires" of life vanished, to be replaced on the next recovery from a long cold period by new life, generally of a higher order.

The last cold period long enough to produce an ice age climaxed about 40,000 years ago. The return to a climate favorable to a plant and animal life was unsteady. According to one authority, Dr. Ernst V. Antevs, Niagara was uncovered about 9500 B.C. by the retreating ice that had previously spread over large parts of the northern United States. Dr. Gerard De Geer dates the close of the ice age in northern Europe at about 8700 B.C. Meanwhile, man joined in the great outburst that came with rising temperatures and increased rainfall.

Neolithic Conditions

Some experts say early Mesopotamian settlements showed signs of droughts as early as 8000 B.C. Block houses in Europe were made of pine instead of oak, indicating fluctuation from cold-wet to warm-dry conditions. By 6000 B.C. climate had again made a turn for the worse. Neolithic people were driven south by increasing cold and aridity. They took to caves again with the onset of increased glaciation. During the preceding wet period, certain races of people had become lake dwellers in parts of Europe. These habitats were now abandoned. Reindeer migrated to south Europe, and human migrations were numerous. American lakes dried up. The antarctic ice cap was thicker by some 600 feet before 4000 B.C. than it is now.

Recurring Outbursts of Civilization

Then came an outburst of civilizations in Egypt, eastern Asia, and China, indicating warmth and moisture again, but this cultural revival was not permanent. As climate became arid again, on the way to another cold-dry climax, new migrations began. Great hordes dispersed from the grasslands north and west of the Caspian Sea between 2300 and 2050 B.C. Around 2200 B.C., peoples from southeastern Europe and west central Asia started to move. Persia was drying up. North African cities were abandoned. By 1900 B.C., more hordes were moving from southern Asia down the coast of Syria. By 1800 B.C., a pastoral people known as the Hyskos moved into Egypt, conquering a decadent Egyptian civilization. Around the mid 1700s B.C., Chinese chronicles record an exceptionally severe drought accompanied by numerous invasions of the lowlands by peoples from the upper plateaus.

By 1600 or 1500 B.C., civilization was blossoming again, indicating the return of a favorable climate. Migrations dwindled or ceased. Lake dwellings revived, only to be destroyed by floods. Prosperity returned to China. This time the favorable period terminated between 1350 and 1300 B.C. The earth again seethed with migrations. The oldest known sequoias began to grow, sinking almost at once to their all-time minimum rate of growth around 1275 to 1250 B.C. Wave upon wave of migrations headed south from Europe. China suffered droughts and invasions from central Asia. The Hittite Empire collapsed under pressure from these migrating peoples. Traffic over the Alps lapsed to a minimum from 1300 to 1200 B.C. due to accumulating snow.

But by 1100 B.C., American lakes were rising again. The sequoias enjoyed luxuriant growth. Civilizations bloomed once more. After a temporary interruption, favorable conditions returned in the tenth century B.C., when numerous empires — including the Chinese, Mayan, Hebrew, Assyrian, Phillistine, Persian, Greek, and Etruscan — sprang up. Culture also reached a high level in central Europe where, according to British climatologist C.E.P. Brooks, Lake Constance in Germany, attesting to wetter conditions, rose 30 feet from previous levels.

Near 800 B.C., the sequoias record a long period of minimum growth, indicating a dry epoch. From 840 to 770 B.C., China suffered an extensive invasion and severe droughts. By 882 B.C., inhabitants from the middle Danube were spreading westward into Europe. These migrations were repeated around 775 B.C.

By 700 B.C. the sequoias recovered and a period of maximum growth resulted around 670 B.C. Brooks reports a rainfall maximum in Europe between 690 and 660 B.C. There were cultural revivals at this time also, notably in Assyria. But all this was over by 600 B.C., at which time Brooks believes there was an Asiatic and European rainfall minimum. European and Asiatic races migrated again. At this relatively recent point in history, a date has been reached where a more intensive analysis of the history of climate can begin, namely, 600 B.C.

The Flowering of Ancient Civilization

It is important to become accustomed to the concepts: first, of the continuous fluctuation of climate; second, that these fluctuations have in the past been sufficient to cause life to bloom on the earth in rich abundance and then, periodically, to decline and even disappear; and third, that *man has not been immune to this influence.* Ever since the last ice age, man's fortunes have fluctuated with the climate. During periods of sufficient rainfall and optimal temperatures, man has prospered, built cities, and forged empires. On the climatic recovery following 3000 B.C., there dawned the first of the brilliant Egyptian cultural epochs initiated by the pyramid builders. This civilization then sank into a long Dark Age, which coincided with a climatic turn for the worse - long droughts and the return of cold temperatures. During this time, there were numerous migrations and interminglings of races. With the revival of a favorable climate around 1500 B.C., another prosperous Egyptian "epoch" dawned — the age of the temple builders. This civilization in turn became decadent; there was another period of droughts, another period of migrations, and another long period of colder climate. As we shall see over and over, civilizations rise and fall on tides of climatic change.

The Sun and the Nature of Climatic Change

The next question is: Are climatic changes of this sort still going on, and are they still affecting the behavior, energy and achievements of mankind? As we shall see, the answer is yes!

But first we must accustom ourselves to another idea, namely that these climatic fluctuations are world wide. Evidence has been accumulated to this effect, although some contemporary climatologists are inclined to dispute this point.

Essentially, the climate of the earth is controlled by the sun, and the relationship of the sun to the earth affects the whole earth, not just parts of it. Other things being equal, temperatures on earth are dependent on the degree to which the sun's rays approach the vertical. Where sunlight penetrates the earth's atmosphere at close to 90°, it is the warmest. This relationship results in the seasons of the year, and the seasons are not confined to limited areas but are coextensive with all the regions affected in the same manner by the sun.

The sun is also responsible for the positions of permanent high- and low-pressure areas that are so important in determining global rainfall. There are numerous complicating factors, to be sure, but nevertheless the evidence bears out the existance of a world climate that fluctuates as a whole, although to a varying degree according to local conditions.

Sunspot Maxima and Minima

The heat of the sun also fluctuates. This variation is associated with sunspots, or storms in the gaseous envelope of the sun similar to cyclones in the atmosphere of the earth. They symptomize increased instability of the sun's energy, causing variations in the amount of heat emanating from it. These storms that we see as sunspots cause electrical disturbances in the earth's atmosphere, sometimes to the extent of interfering with telephone, telegraph, and radio communication. Connected with these electrical disturbances are the aurora borealis or "northern lights" of the arctic and its counterpart the aurora australis of the antarctic. During periods of increased sunspots, there are also more aurora, but not necessarily at the same time or in exact proportion to the number and size of the sunspots.

Now it happens that there are sunspot rhythms. Every so often there is a sunspot maximum, lasting for a year or two and sometimes more, when an above average number of storms occur. Sometimes these storms are so extensive that the spots can be seen without the aid of a telescope. Sunspots reach a climax in number and generally in size approximately every 11 years. Between sunspot maxima come minima, or periods when spots are fewest and smallest, and when frequently none can be seen for months at a time.

It has long been known that the world is colder during sunspot maxima and warmer during sunspot minima. This does not mean that temperatures invariably fall everywhere on earth at maxima, or invariably rise at minima, but discounting local conditions, the sunspot rhythm has global effects. In the 11-year sunspot cycle, the differences in temperature are not great, but as we shall see, they are significant.

Paradoxically, when the sun is hottest, which is at sunspot maxima, the surface of the earth is coolest; when the sun is coolest, the earth is hottest. One theory is that the electrical disturbances associated with sunspots increase atmospheric turbulance, thus removing heat from the earth's surface. Another is that these disturbances interfere with the earth's precipitation / evaporation cycle so that the atmosphere becomes "clogged" with clouds that do not break up. At any rate, during maxima there are many more cloudy days during a year, but there is not necessarily more rainfall. This cloud blanket keeps out the sun's heat. On the other hand, there are more days of sunshine during sunspot minima, and more direct sunlight produces more heat. So again we see that there has to be a world climate; when it fluctuates, it must of necessity do so over the entire earth.

The Argument for a World Climate

Huntington was convinced that climatic variations were in this sense world-wide, although their precise form differed from place to place. Specifically he noted that rainfall in Scandinavia and the Mediterranean region corresponds to similarly placed areas in Canada and the American Southeast. In the interior of Europe and northern Asia, there is an area where rainfall decreases corresponding roughly with a similar area in the interior of the United States, and there is an almost uniform decrease in rainfall along the equator at times of increased solar activity. He observed further that periods of prosperity and decline of the Roman Empire corresponded with growth maxima and minima of the California sequoias.

World-wide climate has been hypothesized and argued by many other researchers. O. Pettersson, a Swedish climatologist, thought these variations in climate must be of cosmic origin. Brooks, in his *Climate Through the Ages,* is impressed by the widespread character and simultaneity of climatic fluctuations. H.H. Clayton, an American weather expert, observed that there is something in common in the weather in widely separated parts of the earth. Bruckner, a Swiss glaciologist, also observed the remarkable similarity of climatic fluctuations. Throughout the world, with the single exception of New England, he discovered a maximum rainfall from about 1845 to 1850, a minimum between 1860 and 1870, another maximum about 1880, and a subsequent decrease until the end of the century. A.J. Henry, another American weather expert, assumed a world climate, as did Albert W. Giles. Warm periods, he said, alternate with cold periods, and the fluctuations are world-wide. De Geer agreed. He noted that conditions producing glaciation affect the whole earth simultaneously. Arctowski found that world wide fluctuations in weather could be as short as two years in length in areas as scattered as Peru, South Africa, Java, Ceylon, the eastern United States, central Russia, and the Arctic Ocean. Simpson declared that temperatures rose and fell over all parts of the world at much the same time.

Therefore, the results of the present investigation, contained in the next few chapters, need not be surprising. They constitute only a more detailed account of general assumptions, theories, and facts that have been discussed for a long time.

Summary

The temperature of our environment is not and never has been stable. It has always been in the process of moving toward or away from a warm or cold climax, and it is still doing so, although in short, mild fluctuations compared with those of geologic time. In regard to rainfall, climate has shown a corresponding instability, always moving toward or away from a wet or dry climax.

Evidence points to the fact that, in many parts of the earth, climate deteriorates for long periods of time due largely to changes in the type of rainfall. This has happened around the Mediterranean several times, in Central America, Indochina, and central Asia.

The evidence so far considered points to a definite succession of stages or phases that regularly repeat themselves in climatic fluctuations. As it turns warm after a cold period, it is at first very wet, but eventually turns dry. The heat climax comes during the drought. Then as it turns cold rainfall picks up. Before it turns warm again, there occurs another era of droughts during which the cold climax is reached.

In historic time, the transitions from cold to warm periods have been attended by cultural revivals and eras of prosperity. For centuries migrations reached a climax during the cold and dry phase of the climatic cycle, and great civilizations declined. In geologic time, during transitions from cold to warm phases, great waves of new life sprang up both in the plant and animal kingdoms, only to decline during the long hot-drought periods and to reach their lowest ebb during cold periods, several of which were cold for periods long enough to produce ice ages.

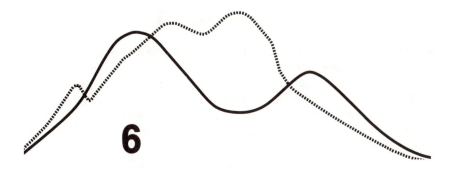

Evidence Dealing With the Climate of Historic Time

Three sources of evidence concerning the climate of prehistoric times have already been mentioned: lake levels, tree rings, and sunspots. It is important to examine the latter two sources in more detail.

Tree Rings as Indicators of Historic Climatic Conditions

Professor A.E. Douglass of the University of Arizona was the first to intensively study and draw conclusions from tree rings. He founded the famous tree-ring laboratory at the University of Arizona. Among its accomplishments is the dating of early Pueblo ruins through examination of the rings in the log rafters used to construct these buildings. Douglass and his associates also developed a tree-ring "master key" for the southeast United States, back almost to the time of Christ, using successive generations of trees. He was the first to study the rings of the giant California sequoias. Douglass also inspired Professor Ellsworth Huntington to utilize sequoia rings in his long-range studies of climatic fulctuations.

This is not the place for a technical discussion of the problems involved in counting and dating tree rings. Suffice it that when the proper safeguards and corrections are employed and the width or area of the ring for each period is plotted against time in years, a curve is obtained indicating the relative rate at which the tree grew each year. Large numbers of these curves are now available for different parts of the United States and Europe. By comparing them with measured temperature and rainfall as far back as weather records go, it is possible to obtain some idea of how the trees grow under different climatic conditions. Figures 4 and 5 show the results of such a comparison.

It seemed reasonable to suppose that if trees grew slowly during dry periods and rapidly during wet periods, then tree minima (periods of slowest growth) obtained from large numbers of trees over widely separated regions ought to be reasonably accurate indicators of the dry periods, and tree maxima (periods of fastest growth) indicators of the wet periods. Huntington, Douglass, Antevs, and others have long since made such deductions with evident success. Huntington thought tree growth was a valuable indicator of prevailing temperatures as well.

It further seemed reasonable to suppose that a combination of warm temperatures and abundant rainfall would produce the fastest rates of growth and that, other things being equal, a combination of cold and dry conditions would produce the slowest rates of growth. It seemed reasonable to assume that tree growth curves would show their highest maxima during the warm-wet phase of the 100-year cycle; that minima immediately following these maxima would be indicative of the warm-dry phase; that as temperatures were falling and rainfall was returning to normal in the formation of the cold-wet phase, there would be secondary maxima; and that the trees would register their longest and lowest minima during the cold-dry phase of the cycle. In this manner, tree rings ought to locate successive phases of the climatic cycle, even to the drops in temperature (often with lowered rainfall) during the long warm phases, and the rises in temperature (usually with increased rainfall) during the long cold phases.

Huntington and Antevs measured the sequoias in terms of 10- and 50-year running averages. Would it not be that ascents to the peaks in these curves represent the warm-wet phases of long weather trends; that the descents to periods of average growth represent the warm-dry phases; and that the minima represent the cold-dry phases? All these expectations are indeed born out by the facts.

As many different tree ring curves as could be found (about 100 in all) were examined by varying methods five different times over a period of 20 years. Each of the five investigations showed the same results. (Figure 4 shows the results of the first study and Figure 5 the results of the second.)

Deficiencies of Using Averages

A word should be said here in regard to the use of averages and smoothed curves. In investigations of climate and its relationship to tree growth, human behavior, death, conception rates, and so on, the traditional and accepted procedure is to use averages. For certain purposes this is the best procedure but for others it is not because averages, either stationary or running, may distort and hide important facts.

For example, consider the temperature and rainfall curves of Figure 5. It took one assistant 10 hours a week for 9 months to obtain the data on this figure, based on 100 stations as evenly scattered over the earth as possible. About half the data were originally given in Centigrade and millimeters, and half in Farenheit and inches. It was necessary to convert the former into the latter. After 1860 the curve was smoothed by a 5-year running average. The amplitude of the curves represents percent departures from the general average. *If the climatologist relied on such curves as these, he would never arrive at the basic facts regarding long-time weather trends because the method of treating the original data has obscured the facts.* The figure reveals that, in the long run, temperature and rainfall fluctuations tend to parallel one another, but it obscures the equally important fact that, following a warm-wet maximum, there are almost sure to be some dry years with maximum temperatures. (Figure 7 presented later in this chapter suggests correctly that before it turns cold and dry there is a cold-wet period; it also shows that the anchor points of the climate curve are the warm-wet and cold-dry maxima, not the warm-dry and cold-wet combinations, as Bruckner and many others seemed to imply. It does not show, however, the occurrence of warm-wet years ahead of the cold-wet.)

We spent an enormous amount of time calculating 10-year smoothed temperature and rainfall curves. For a correct understanding of weather trends they turned out to have very little value. *They were too artificial.* Similarly, we found that essential facts were hidden or distorted by comparing tree curves with smoothed temperature and rainfall curves. We are not disputing the usefulness of these smoothed curves for certain purposes. But unless the false conception that good scientific method always demands the use of averages is abandoned, many basic facts will forever remain unknown. This is why our figures are not always expressed in averages.

Tree Growth Maxima and Minima

Figure 4 covers the 200 years from 1730 to 1930. The upper half of each row of figures indicates tree ring peaks or maxima from various parts of the world while the lower half shows the years these same curves reached their bottoms or troughs, indicating years of slowest growth. The height of the column above or below the center indicates the number of available curves whose maxima or minima occur in a particular year. Successive half decades are numbered along the top of each Figure. The bottom of the Figures indicates periods when the world as a whole was cold and dry, warm and wet, and warm and dry.

Generally, when the upper half of each row indicates relatively fast growth, the lower half shows few, if any curves registering minima and vica versa. If trees from different areas corresponded in their periods of fast and slow growth, this confirmation is exactly what would be expected.

A warm-wet maximum occurred in 1750. Notice that where data are available for this date there are verticle bars above the various horizontals. This means that the trees were growing relatively fast at that time. Around 1755 it was warm and dry; the bars are below the horizontals indicating relatively slow growth. In the mid 1760s it was cold and dry; most trees were growing slowly. The 1770s were warm; the first half of the decade (column 9) was wet, but the second half (column 10) was dry. Notice how the trees were generally setting peaks of growth during the warm-wet periods and troughs during warm-dry periods.

During the 1780s, world weather was generally cold and dry. Notice in column 12 how the various areas were showing minima. There was a strong warm-wet phase in world weather during the early 1790s, again enabling trees to grow quickly. It was dry from 1795 to 1800 with the trees laying down minima, some a few years ahead of others. And so it goes across Figure 4.

Curves for individual trees do not *always* agree with one another even when the trees are only 50 miles apart. Many different factors affect growth, but when large numbers of curves are considered together, there is about an 85 percent agreement between tree-ring maxima and minima and the phases of climatic cycles.

Tree Rings in Relation to Climatic Cycles

Figure 5 was obtained in the following manner: The highest peaks and the lowest troughs of the available sequoia curves were chosen as standards of reference. Their amplitudes in millimeters were divided into three equal parts. The central points of the peaks and troughs falling within the third next to the midlines were given a value of 1; those falling within the second third, a value of 2; and those within the outer third, either above or below the midline, a value of 3. Long secular trends, where the tree curve remained at a given level for a long time, or where a particular curve deviated from the usual performance by rising or falling steadily over a long period of time, were ignored. (These uncommon features of the curves were studied in another part of the investigation to be reported in another volume.)

In developing Figure 5 we wanted to know if a more refined method than that used in Figure 4 would reveal the same results. Five years elapsed between the two studies. A composite curve of pines by Douglass will be represented by the sign x, a smaller sequoia curve by the sign =, and an unsmoothed sequoia curve by the symbol o.

The bar diagrams locate the positions of maxima and minima of about 55 different tree curves. It can be seen, as in Figure 4, that the majority of the maxima coincide with warm-wet phases in the weather trends, that tree minima next to the maxima locate the warm-dry phases, and that the tree minima midway between the higher peaks locate the cold-dry periods. In order to help the reader locate the briefer warm-wet maxima, short arcs are drawn just above the clusters of tree-ring peaks. The long, major, warm-wet periods are marked by longer arcs. The W's indicate the positions of the warm years, the "C's" the positions of the cold years.

As will be seen, Figure 5 covers a 200-year period, 1730 to 1930. World weather data for this period are in the bottom row. Prior to 1800 each little black square represents one weather station, showing rainfall above or below the long-time average, or it represents a single report of excessive rain or excessive dryness for that year because there were insufficient rainfall and temperature curves to permit any other procedure. After 1800 the amplitude of the curve is proportional to the percentage of weather stations showing above average temperatures for a given region, in excess of stations showing below average temperatures. Hence the temperature represents relative area, not intensity. *For the purpose of this chart, ignore the absolute amplitude of the rainfall and temperature curves and use their relative amplitude by means of which to locate the phases of the world's weather trend fluctuations.*

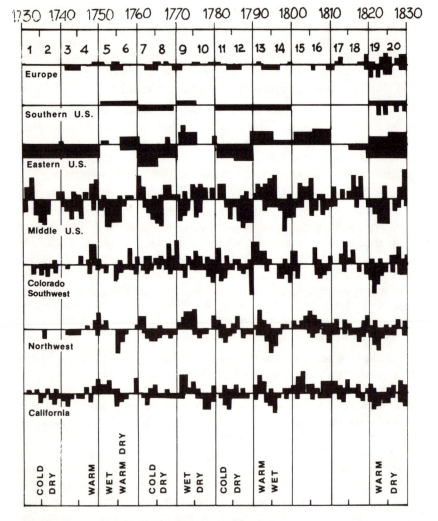

Figure 4.   Tree Growth Maxima and Minima

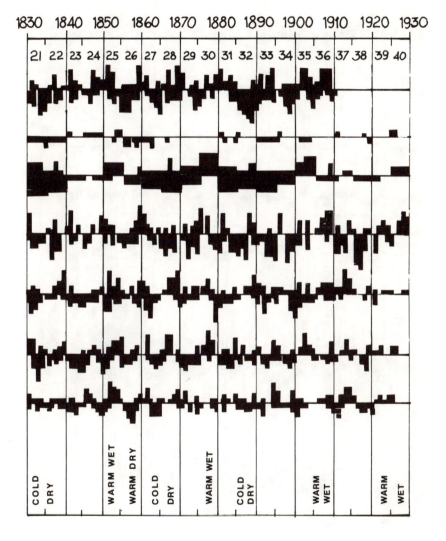

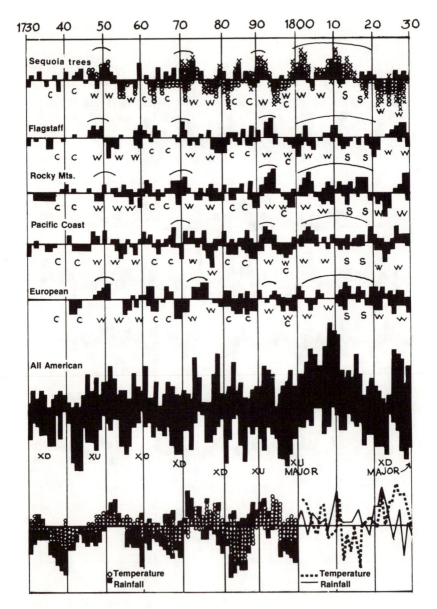

Figure 5. Tree Rings in Relation to Climatic Cycles

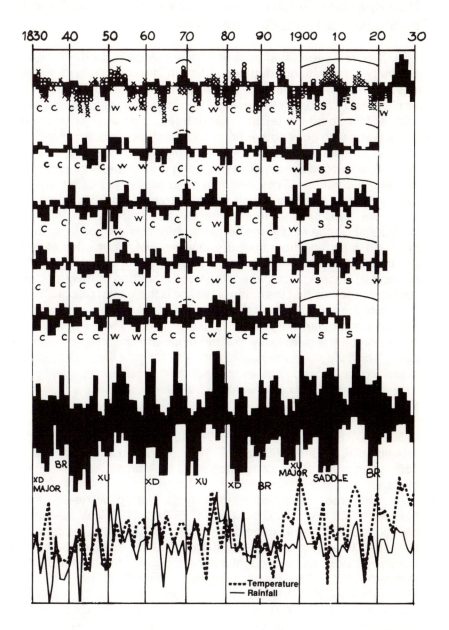

1830 40 50 60 70 80 90 1900 10 20 30

Discrepancies Between Tree Rings and Cyclical Patterns as Signals of Climatic Transitions

Figure 5 shows that trees of different kinds from different areas generally agree with one another, although in some cases with certain lags and leads. The next to the bottom row (a summation of the amplitudes of the upper five rows) was added in order to demonstrate another fact about the relationship of tree growth to weather trends: Trees agree with one another better at some times than at others. The periods of best agreement occur during warm-wet and cold-dry maxima, with good agreement also during the warm-dry phases of the climatic fluctuations. They disagree most when the weather itself is most erratic or unstable, which is during transitions from cold-dry to warm-wet maxima and from warm-dry to cold-dry maxima. The symbols XU in the next to the bottom row locates the positions where the trend is shifting from cold-dry to warm-wet. Notice that at these positions some trees are growing quickly, some more slowly. The symbols XD locate places where the trend is shifting from warm-dry to cold-dry. It seems that the cold-wet phase is the least stable of the four phases of the cycle. Just before formation of the warm-wet maximum, a short run of warm-dry years is likely. This is an unstable period during which trees are likely to differ in growth. *In short, those periods during which the trees disagree with one another most are just as valuable in locating the transition phases of the climatic cycle as the places of best agreement are in locating the warm-wet, warm-dry, and cold-dry phases of the cycle.*

The widest ring growth occurred during warm-wet maxima at 1750, 1770-1775, 1790-1795, 1800-1815, around 1830, 1850-1855, around 1878, around 1900, and 1915 with short peaks around 1760 and 1868 when much of the world underwent a 2-year period of warm-wet climate.

The trees recorded narrow rings during warm-dry times between 1755 and 1760, between 1775 and 1780, and during the droughts (some warm, some cold) from 1795 to 1800. European and California trees registered a warm drought from 1825 to 1830; other trees registered warm drought during the preceding 5-year period. Warm-dry 1855-1860 is evident in tree growth in all but the Rocky Mountain area. Note the long minima during the cold-dry 1830s and 1840s, the cold-dry 1760s, and the cold-dry 1780s. The cold-dry early 1890s, the dry middle 1860s, as well as cold-dry 1873 show in all tree groups. Very seldom did the trees fail to identify a dry period. Thus we see again that, while estimating climatic trends from tree rings would result in some errors, they would be few, especially if enough trees from several geographically separate areas were used. By calculation, the sequoias agreed with the expected climatic cycle pattern at least 90 percent of the time; all trees except sequoias agreed 83 percent of the time; and all trees including sequoias agreed 85 percent of the time.

In addition to tree rings, lake level data, going back varying lengths of time, are available from California, Oregon, Utah, Europe, the Caucasus, Palestine, central Asia, Australia, and South America. Data on river levels are also available, including seasonal floods of the Nile.

Sunspot Cycles

Sunspot cycles go back almost to the time of Christ. The Chinese kept records of these phenomena for hundreds of years — those spots, of course, that could be seen without telescopes. They also recorded aurora. Similar records were also kept from time to time by various agencies and organizations in Great Britain, including monastaries during the Middle Ages. A study of these sunspot chronologies, of their relationship to weather data, and of sunspot occurrance since 1755 (when telescopic daily records were started) reveal some very interesting facts. That sunspot maxima are associated with lowered temperatures and minima with higher temperatures has already been discussed in Chapter 5.

The Length of Sunspot Cycles

While the sunspot cycle averages 11.2 years, it varies greatly from time to time, and these variations show a definite relationship to climatic changes on earth. As it is about to turn cold, that is, when long climatic cycles are shifting from the warm to cold phase, the sunspot cycle shortens, sometimes to only 8 years in length, and averages shorter than normal throughout the cold period. At the same time, the maxima contain more and larger spots and the spots continue to be more numerous throughout the cold phase. Just before it turns cold, solar storms large enough to identify with the naked eye are likely. Such an occurrance is excellent evidence that the warm phase of a long climatic cycle is about to end.

Then, as the climatic cycle starts shifting from cold to warm, the sunspot cycle lengthens, sometimes to as many as 18 years, and the size and number of spots decrease. During warm times there are rarely spots large enough to see with the naked eye. The sunspot cycle averages longer than normal throughout the warm phase.

Because aurora are associated with solar storms, the frequency of aurora is a pretty good indication of the current phase of the climatic cycle.

Sunspot Maxima Since 1755

In the years since 1755, sunspot maxima have been associated with temperatures in the following manner:

1761 — Temperatures are dropping; a cold decade begins.

1769 — Temperature minimum occurs in a long, cold phase.

1778 — At the end of a short warm period, temperatures are again beginning to cool.

1788 — A temperature minimum occurs during the latter part of a cold phase in a long climatic cycle.

(Notice the shortening of these cycles to 9, 8, and 10 years, respectively. 1760 to 1790, with the exception of a few years in the 1770s, comprised the second half of the cold phase in a 100-year climatic cycle.)

1805 — The cycle is suddenly lengthened (1788 to 1805 is 18 years). The warm part of a 100-year cycle begins in 1790. Temperatures during 1805 drop only temporarily.

1816 — An 11-year cycle ends. The 1810s are a cold decade centered on this maximum. 1816 is famous as the year without a summer. (It was reported that frosts occurred during all 12 months in New England and Europe.)

1829 — The cycle lengthens again. There is a return to the warm phase of the climatic cycle, and temperatures reach a maximum in the 1820s. Right after 1829 the next cold phase begins.

1837 — Another cycle of only 8 years ushers in a cold phase.

1848 — A temperature minimum occurs.

1859 — An 11-year cycle ends. The 1850s are warmer but not excessively so. 1859 precedes a return to the cold side of the cycle; this year marks the middle of a cold period lasting from shortly after 1830 to nearly 1900.

1871 — 1871 is immediately followed by some very cold years.

1884 — The cycle is stretched out to 13 years. The last half of the 1870s is very warm all over the world. 1884 records a temperature minimum during the cold phase.

1894 — A 10-year cycle terminates. We have just returned to a long run of cold years; we are now at the bottom of a cold phase.

1905-1907 — A 12- to 13-year cycle. Another long warm phase begins. A peculiar phenomenon occurs, a double sunspot maximum with one climax in 1905, another in 1907. 1907 is especially cold. The cycle stretches out again at the beginning of the warm period.

1918 — A temporary drop in temperature during a warm phase.

1929 — Another temporary drop in temperature during a warm phase.

Sunspot Reports Since 51 A.D.

Wider historical surveys confirm the correlation between sunspot maxima and the onset of a cold climatic phase. Sunspots and aurora were reported in 51 A.D. Severe cold was reported in Britain the year before. From 85 to 120 A.D. aurora were fairly frequent. These factors, along with other evidence, confirm that shortly after 85 A.D. it turned cold for several decades.

Negative evidence also seems to be significant. Thirty warm years, from 135 to 165 A.D., lie in the center of a long period during which no sunspots or aurora were reported in the chronicles of the times. But in the 180s and 190s reports appear again. In accordance with other data, we are once more in a long cold period.

Aurora were seen in 249 A.D. during a decade in which there were many reports of severely cold winters and heavy snows in Europe and Great Britain. From 200 to 375 A.D., the chronicles contain many reports of meteorological phenomena associated with sunspots large enough to be seen with the naked eye. Most of this interval was cold, with frequent reports of excessively cold winters in Britain.

In the 440s A.D. there was another outburst of sunspots and aurora. Evidence indicates that they occurred just before the beginning of a 30-year cold phase. The year 499 A.D. seems to have been a major sunspot year; if so, it occured where one might have been expected, at the beginning of a cold decade. Similar results are to be found throughout history.

There is little doubt, therefore, that where evidence is strong for particularly large numbers of sun spots and aurora, it is reasonably certain that a cold phase is either occurring or about to occur. Throughout history there is direct confirmatory evidence for this phenomena.

Miscellaneous Sources of Weather Data

There are many other sources from which to obtain evidence regarding the climate of the past. For years the Russian government kept a record of ice-forming and ice-breaking dates on the rivers of European Russia and Siberia. Grape harvesting dates were recorded for many generations in France and southern Germany. There are also records of years during which extremely heavy snowfalls cut off travel through the passes of the Alps and other mountains. Records exist of advancing and receding glaciers. Chronicles of one kind or another, official documents of many kinds, records from military posts, and accounts of battles and campaigns frequently report extreme cold or heat waves, droughts, crop failures and famines, and excessive cold and snow. It is surprising how many descriptions of extreme weather exist in the annals of military history. The annihilation of an army by excessive cold and snow while on a campaign, the failure of a campaign because of drought and famine, the suffering of marching troops because of excessive heat, difficulties encountered because of storms and floods, or the particular agonies of a siege army in the trenches mark the dramatic climax of many military narratives. In addition, locust plagues prove to be particularly good indicators of hot droughts. The Chinese scrupulously kept records of their droughts, floods, and famines for centuries. Floods, serious famines, heavy snows, untimely frosts, and so forth, are likely to be recorded because they profoundly affect human economy and comfort.

Dr. C.E. Britton assembled weather reports from varied sources in Great Britain covering the time from the Roman conquest to 1450 A.D. This chronology contains an elaborate list of general storms, floods, droughts, excessive heat and cold, freezing and thawing dates, sunspots, aurora, famines, and reports of "good" or "pleasant" weather. Other chronologies are available for various parts of Europe. Professor M.A. Hosie collected considerable data for China and India, and in 1890 Bruckner published a lengthy monograph assembling in one place the different kinds of miscellaneous information available to him from throughout the world. Every now and then a private diary is found with information about the weather. Comparisons of diaries with tree rings or official rainfall and temperature records indicate that diaries are reasonably reliable.

Information on long-time climatic trends can also be deduced from pollen analysis of soil. Data of this sort point to changes in the types of forests existing at different times in a given area.

Reliability of Miscellaneous Data

How reliable is this miscellaneous information? Reports of climatic conditions that made a sufficient impression on populations to have been recorded are associated with conditions that vitally affected human welfare — food and water supply, general health, crops and herds, commerce, military exploits, or simply personal comfort. There are reports such as would be recorded in annual almanacs as part of a chronology of world events.

In order to ascertain how reliable this information is, weather events mentioned in the chronologies of the New York Herald-Tribune World Almanac from 1918 to 1935 were compared with actual temperature and rainfall records in the United States. Reports of excessive heat waves and droughts were found to cluster during known hot-dry years; reports of storms and floods clustered during known rainfall maxima; reports of excessive snow and blizzards occurred during years of low annual temperature. Thus it is reasonable to conclude that a pool of such reports makes it possible to detect the phases of climatic rhythm through the centuries.

In another experiment, miscellaneous data of various kinds were collected and compared with measured temperatures and rainfall back to the 1730s. Again, there was a striking agreement. It seems safe to assume, therefore, that when clusters of reports occur, especially in several countries at the same time, these reports identify the various phases of the climatic rhythm. Moreover, miscellaneous reports so consistently parallel tree-ring growth patterns that the validity of the tree-ring interpretations also seems beyond serious question.

Of course, as one goes back in history, miscellaneous reports become fewer; the researcher may find only a single isolated report for an entire decade. But because that report usually describes some very extreme phemenon, it agrees with tree-ring readings in almost every instance. In 500 A.D., dated reports run about 20 per decade; by 1000 A.D., about 30; by 1600, about 40; and after 1700, 50 or more. In item-years, which are years within which a given item occurs or is repeated, a conservative estimate puts the number of information units well over 20,000. (If ten different items of information are available during a given year it amounts by definition to 10 item-years.)

Consolidating Miscellaneous Weather Data

Figure 6 shows the extent to which incidental information from around the world agrees with measured temperatures and rainfall from 1800 to 1940. Row 1 reports epidemics; the heights of the black columns are proportional to the number of epidemics reported in a given year. The horizontal lines in Row 2 indicate decades or years of high water levels for individual lakes. Notice how, for the most part, they agree with one another. In Row 4, the blackened circles and other symbols indicate individual reports of excessive warmth. Row 5 consists of individual reports of heavy storms or rain. The horizontal lines in Rows 5 and 6 locate periods during which various trees were growing fast. The heavy horizontal lines in Row 7 indicate warm decades. The open symbols between Rows 7 and 8 are the positions of tree maxima in the southwestern United States. The solid symbols in Row 8 indicate tree maxima from California tree curves. Row 9 is a temperature curve representing relative world temperatures, and Row 10 pictures the ups and downs of rainfall. The distance of the curves from the midline is proportional to the percentage of warm stations around the world in excess of cold stations in a given year, of cold in excess of warm, of wet in excess of dry, and of dry in excess of wet. The maximum amplitude is 75 percent. The solid symbols just below Row 10 indicate California tree minima; the open symbols show southwest tree minima. Row 12 indicates cold decades. Row 13 illustrates years or decades when trees grew slowly. Row 14 shows individual reports of droughts. Row 15 designates positions of more tree minima (horizontal lines) and reports of excessive cold; "s" means a report of heavy snow that year. Row 16 shows the positions of sunspot minima and maxima, the minima represented by small squares and the maxima by the double circles; aurora are shown by "x". Row 17 depicts years or decades when lake levels were down.

Row 18 shows years during which extensive migrations occurred, mostly in China and other parts of Asia. Each square represents one migration.

In Figure 6, the symbol "=" indicates a report from Britain; "o" from Europe; "•", the United States; "x", southern Asia; "‖," South America; "■", China; "L" locust plague; "cf", a famine so bad as to result in cannibalism; and "s", heavy snow.

Analysis of Miscellaneous Weather Data

The first decade of the eighteenth century, according to Figure 6, was warm and wet. Note that lake levels are high and individual reports of excessive warmth and moisture are abundant. Notice how these reports drop off during the next decade when both rainfall and temperature declines, and notice how reports of drought and cold increase. Notice also how miscellaneous reports of warmth and dryness agree with the rainfall and temperature curves for the 1820s. Reports of extreme cold almost disappear. In the 1830s, reports of cold increase while temperatures remain low. Both temperature and rainfall revive in the late 1840s. In the early 1850s, when it is warm and wet, lake levels are up again while reports of droughts and extreme cold fall to a minimum. The second half of this decade undergoes falling temperatures and increasing dryness. Note again the conspicuous decline in records of dryness and cold during the late 1870s, when it is warm and wet. Heat waves usually occur when it is dry; few reports of warm weather enter the records in the late 1870s, presumably because rainfall is then at a maximum. Note the increase in reports of cold and drought in the 1880s, when temperature and rainfall again decline. Notice how the clustering of warm and cold reports on one hand and wet and dry reports on the other tend to alternate. The extensive hot droughts of the 1930s show up in the miscellaneous reports, as do temporary cold-dry phases in 1920 and 1930.

Figure 7 is a similar chart covering the years from 400 to 600 A.D. In this figure, however, the dotted and solid lines in the center of the page representing relative temperature and rainfall, respectively, are *deduced* from the miscellaneous data, including tree-ring minima and maxima. The various horizontal rows represent the same classes of data as in Figure 6. The symbol = represents data from Great Britain; o, from Europe; ■, from China; and X from India. Sunspots are represented by o, aurora by x. Where miscellaneous data other than tree rings are few in number, then tree rings comprise the brunt of

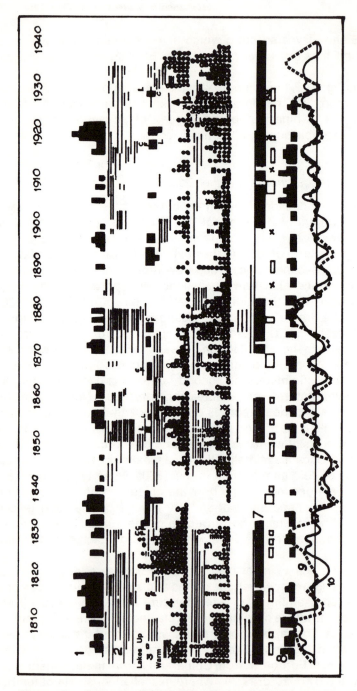

Figure 6. Extent to Which Miscellaneous Reports of the

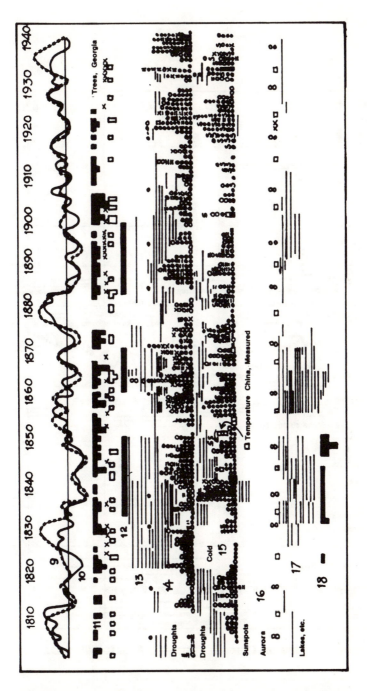

Weather Agree with Measured Temperature and Rainfall.

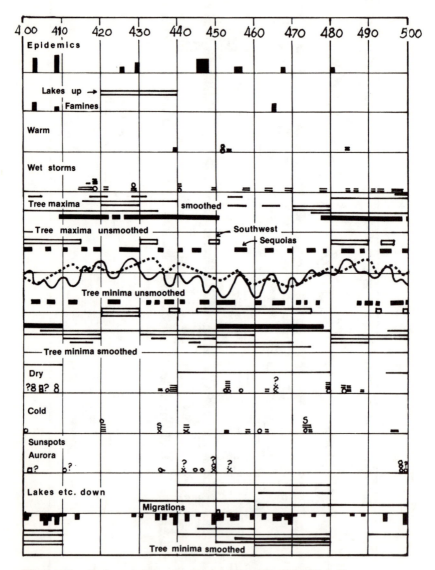

Figure 7.   Data on Climate From 400 A.D. to 600 A.D.

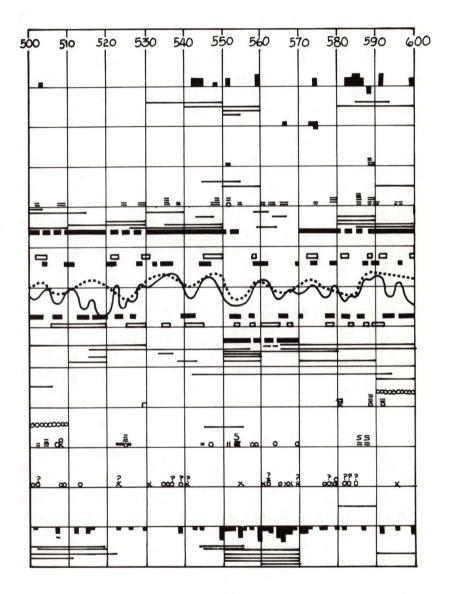

evidence. Note how conspicuously migrations cluster during times which are deduced as cold. The consistency of this relationship can only mean that a regular correlation of some sort exists between migration and climate.

One important factor that has not yet been explained is the regular manner in which hot droughts follow warm-wet maxima with a temperature drop in between; a similar regularity with which cold-wet conditions follow hot droughts, and cold droughts follow cold-wet periods. (More detailed explanations of these variations will be presented in Chapter 7.)

For times prior to temperature and rainfall records, it is impossible to state just how warm, cold, wet, or dry it was at any given time. For the purpose of this study, such accuracy is not essential. Departures of the deduced temperature and rainfall curves from the midline of "normal" signify only that the trend was in a certain direction at a given time; that a certain decade or half decade was warmer or colder, wetter or drier than the preceding; or that certain years appear to have registered rainfall or temperature maxima or minima on a world-wide basis.

Mass Migration as a Climatic Indicator

It has been fairly well established that mass migrations seldom occur except under severe climatic conditions. When an area is prosperous, the population settles down to a life of agriculture and commerce; even if invaded, they will somehow manage to remain in or near their home territory despite heavy taxation by a conqueror or reduction to slavery. There are exceptions but the vast majority of extensive migrations throughout history have occurred during long cold-dry periods. Not infrequently, these migrations begin during the preceding hot droughts, especially in semi-arid areas. Many historians are reluctant to believe that migrations have been caused mainly by climate. They point out that civil wars frequently stimulate such movements of whole peoples. We shall see later in this volume, however, that civil wars of consequence do not occur during prosperous times, which happen also to be times when it is warm and wet, but during cold times when greater vitality, combined with a condition of economic insecurity or political tyranny, provides the catalyst for action. Tyrannies have lasted for decades at all cultural levels throughout history, but as long as climate stays warm, there are no consequential rebellions, revolts, or migrations resulting from that tyranny. Willingness to accept subjugation has consistently been part of the human behavior pattern during periods of prolonged high temperatures and lowered energy levels. Therefore migrations can be used as good climatic indicators once this important distinction is understood.

Summary

This chapter has summarized the various studies that show how tree growth is related to climatic fluctuations. When conditions favoring growth prevail, such as ample rainfall and long warm growing seasons, the annual growth rings of trees will be relatively wide, but when it is both cold and dry, tree growth is slow and the rings are narrowest.

Various types of information are available with which to deduce the various climatic periods in history. Some 20,000 individual items constitute the accumulated miscellaneous evidence used in this volume to determine climate at different times in history.

Certain characteristic features of the sunspot cycle and their significance in relation to prevailing climatic conditions have been discussed. The emergence of sunspots large enough to see with the naked eye is a fairly safe indicator that the cold phase of a long climatic cycle is about to begin. The sunspot cycle is shorter than normal during cold periods and longer than normal during warm periods. At the beginning of a cold period the cycle will shorten; at the beginning of a warm period it will lengthen. During cold periods, sunspot numbers are relatively low during warm times, and seldom do any spots large enough to see with the naked eye appear, except as it is about to turn cold again.

A study was made of the accuracy of miscellaneous reports on weather, and it was found that, when accumulated in large numbers, such reports point to the successive phases of the climatic cycle with a reasonable degree of accuracy. That is, by their clustering during different years, half decades, or decades, it is possible to determine the phases of the climatic cycle during those times. Tree-ring data and miscellaneous weather records agree with one another sufficiently well to conclude that one set of data generally confirms the story told by the other.

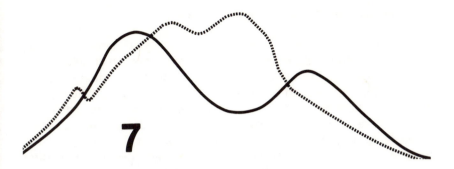

7

The Successive Phases of Climatic Fluctuations

Climatic Patterns Relative to Area During the Nineteenth Century

The fact that temperature and rainfall behave in a regular manner with respect to one another in the course of a climatic cycle was apparently not known until a study of Clayton's two volumes of *World Weather Records,* supplemented by early nineteenth century records, was made by this writer. This study pertained to *area,* and revealed the following climatic trends: Both Europe and eastern North America were warm and wet during the first decade of the 19th century. Beginning in 1810, Europe was cold and wet but getting drier; the eastern United States was cold. The second half of the decade shows a continuation of these conditions, with the end of the decade becoming warmer and wetter both in Europe and in the eastern United States. There was more dryness in this half decade in both regions. In the decade 1820-1830, Europe and the United States are out of phase with each other, but averaging warm, with conditions generally dry except for the first part of the decade in Europe. India seems to be fairly wet until the end of the decade. Large areas on North America, Europe, and Asia suffered from droughts during this period. But the 1830s were very dry in Asia, Europe, the United States, and Africa as well if the few obtainable entries can be trusted as being representative. Europe and the United States were extremely cold. Europe descended into this severe cold-dry "valley" ahead of the United States.

Tree-ring curves from throughout the United States, Scandinavia, England, Germany, and Austria show fast growth during the first decade of the century, generally confirming temperature and rainfall data. The growth of American trees continues in the second decade, indicating that moisture remained adequate and cold temperatures were not severe enough to impede growth seriously. These facts confirm evidence that Europe was wet at this time. But the trees show slower growth than in the preceding decade, indicating some increase in dryness. Miscellaneous data from Bruckner show evidence of high temperatures and dryness in the 1830s, with dryness spreading to the Ukraine, south central Asia, and Australia. Trees in the western United States grew slowly throughout the decade, a condition that spread to the eastern trees before the decade's end. Lake levels were low in Europe, south central Asia, Australia, Venezuela, and central Africa. Siberia and the Ukraine were reportedly very cold. Bad droughts occurred in China, Japan, and India.

The data from the 1840s while showing less homogeneity, reveal a continuation of low temperatures in four continental areas. There is a slight tenedecy toward rainfall and temperature recovery in Europe and the United States around 1845. Trees in the United States continued to grow slowly but began to recover in the late 1840s as temperatures rose and rainfall began to pick up. Bruckner's data and other miscellaneous information leave no doubt about the fact that there was a widespread revival both in temperature and rainfall toward the end of the decade, especially after 1848.

There is good confirmation on three continents regarding the 1850s. During the first 5 years, temperature and rainfall averaged above normal in Europe and the United States. Rainfall and temperature recovered in Asia. The second half of the decade was generally dry on all three continents. According to Bruckner's data, the years 1850-1855 were warm and wet in most of Siberia, the Ukraine, India, and southeastern Australia. Africa was wet in areas. American trees grew rapidly. The second half of the decade was dry in the Ukraine, central and western United States, Spain, India, China, and Australia, and temperatures were falling in the United States.

In the 1860s trends are mixed. Nevertheless, general trends can be discerned: Bruckner's data reveal that most of the world was cold from 1861 to 1865, and moisture was generally below normal. In the second half of the decade, dryness increased and temperatures began to rise. The United States closed the decade cold and wet. Asia, Europe, and South America ended dry.

The 1870s, following temporary warmer and wetter conditions just as the decade opened, was at first cold and dry. Then climate turned warm and very wet. Low temperatures were general on four continents during the first half of the decade. The widespread character of the warm-wet maximum in the second half of the decade was very striking. Between 1876 and 1880, it was also warm and wet in Siberia, India, Australia, and New Zealand. The level of the Caspian Sea was high.

The 1880s were cold the world over except for Africa. In the Western Hemisphere conditions were cold and wet at first. The middle of the decade was dry except for Africa where climate was only relatively drier.

In the middle 1890s came a strong, universal cold-dry climax. World temperatures rose sharply in the latter half of the decade, generally preceding increased rainfall. By 1900 all continents were experiencing a mild rainfall recovery, strongest in Africa and South America.

The years 1900 to 1910 showed a world wide shift toward cold-dry climate, especially in the second half of the decade. Then, all continents fluctuated to the warm-wet from 1913 to 1916, rainfall lagging in some places and leading in others. The year 1917 centered on a world-wide, but only temporary, shift to cold-dry, which was associated with a sunspot maximum. After that, the general picture is one of a return to warm and wet conditions. Asia, Africa, Europe, and the United States remained warm through the decade, and South America stayed warm during the second half, but climate was slowly becoming drier on a world wide basis.

Around 1932 there was a slight revival of rainfall, after which the world passed through the hot drought phase of the 100-year cycle. Temperature records were broken on many continents and over vast areas, droughts were extreme. Around 1942 to 1944 the warm-dry phase shifted to the cold-wet phase. This transition occurred in the United States in 1944.

Thus it turns out that world-wide rainfall and temperature tend to fluctuate together between warm-wet and cold-dry maxima. Just preceding a warm-wet maximum, and especially shortly afterwards, there is a hot-drought era. Once this is over, there comes a recovery of rainfall on falling temperatures until climate becomes cold and wet.

Climatic Patterns Relative to Intensity

An example of these patterns can be found in Figure 8, based on a hundred stations evenly scattered across the world. This study, in contrast to the investigation based on Clayton's World Weather

Records, involves intensity not area. The departures are percent fluctuations from long-time mean annual data, with all temperatures converted into degrees Farenheit and all rainfall converted into inches.

Figure 8 represents the labor of one research assistant working 10 hours a week for an entire academic year and is extremely disappointing. Compared to the amount of work involved, it reveals little about the interaction of temperature and rainfall except for one highly important fact: In the long run, temperature and rainfall *follow one another up and down.* In other words, it rains the most when it is moderately warm, and it is driest when it is the coldest. Of course, this is what one would expect since cool air carries less moisture than warm air. Thus it is that the poles of a climactic fluctuation are warm-wet and cold-dry maxima. The two other combinations (warm-dry and cold-wet) are secondary and may be considered as transitional stages in the climatic cycle.

Because all continental areas do not shift from one set of climatic conditions to another at exactly the same time, the process of employing averages obscures many of the actual facts. However, Figure 8 shows the temperature curve's tendency to cross the rainfall curve as the warm phase is shifting to the cold phase (around 1882 and again around 1906). This crossing of rainfall by temperature occurs on the transition from the warm-dry to the cold-wet phase of the weather cycle. The curve also shows the fact that on the shift from the cold to the warm phase, temperature crosses rainfall again, rising to the warm side before rainfall rises to the wet side. Events like this can be traced back through history. Because temperatures rise ahead of rainfall following a cold-dry climax, a period of warm-dry years generally ushers in the warm wet phase of the cycle.

Figure 8 also distorts the facts because the original rainfall and temperature curves were smoothed by a 5-year running average. The smoothing process results in an artificial and displaced value for any given year, which may be quite misleading. The overreliance on averages has obscured basic facts about the weather trends ever since measuring the weather began.

Climatic Cycles Around the World

Let us now return to the discussion of this writer's study of climatic patterns relative to area based on Clayton's Records. This study shows the *extent* to which a given condition prevails in a given region at a given time.

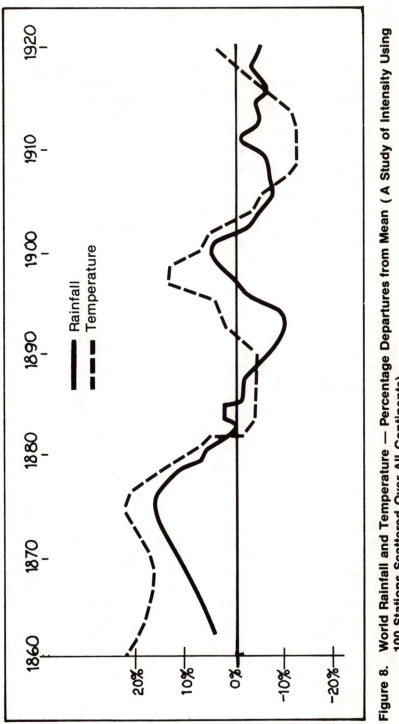

Figure 8. World Rainfall and Temperature — Percentage Departures from Mean (A Study of Intensity Using 100 Stations Scattered Over All Continents)

The Asian Cycle

Specifically, the study shows that in Asia temperature recovered ahead of rainfall at 1877, from a cold-dry climax. The descent into the cold-dry climax of 1844 was through the cold-wet year of 1882. In 1896 the rise in temperature preceded the rise in rainfall. Following four warm-dry years, a shift to the cold side occurred while dryness continued. This time the return to the combination of cold and dry did not pass through the cold-wet stage.

The next recovery followed the same pattern. Temperature rose first to 1906 and rainfall increased 3 years later. The descent to the next important cold-dry climax was preceded by a hot drought, but the cold-wet years are missing. The later recovery into a long warm-wet period in the 1920s repeated the pattern once again — temperature ahead of rainfall — this time by 5 years. Toward the end of the decade, the expected warm-dry phase following the warm-wet period began.

The African Cycle

In regard to Africa, the ascent to the warm-wet peak in 1883-1886 occurred through the warm-dry year of 1882. There was a subsequent drop in temperature during the cold-wet phase with rainfall still high. Next came a variation in the pattern. Instead of normally passing directly to cold-dry from cold-wet, a minor fluctuation occurred with warm-dry conditions ushering in a warm-wet phase (1889-1900). Then came a cold-wet year again, followed by an expected cold-dry period. Another minor rhythm occurred in 1895. Temperature did not lead rainfall this time, but underwent a strong recovery. A warm-dry year, 1896, then followed a cold-dry year. The poles in these short, minor fluctuations continue to be warm-wet and cold-dry, as are the major fluctuations. On the way to the strong warm-wet period at 1900, the usual warm-dry phase appeared first. As temperatures were about to drop again, there was another trend toward warm-dry, although rainfall did not fall below average until it had turned cold. There were some cold-wet years in the cold-dry period from 1905 to 1910. A strong 3-year warm-dry period preceded the warm-wet phase around 1915; then followed the descent from the warm-dry years to the next cold-dry period. The year 1918 (a sunspot maximum) was cold and wet. The return to the warm-wet maximum of 1924-1925 went through a strong warm-dry phase, followed by four out of five warm-dry years from 1926 to 1931.

The European Cycle

Turning to Europe, where more data are available, we find the pattern — cold-dry, warm-dry, warm-wet, warm-dry, cold-wet, cold-dry — holds up quite well. Beginning in the late 1840s with a cold-dry maximum, the weather changed briefly to warm-wet in 1852, with a cold-wet year intervening. But the return to the next cold-dry climax was through a warm-dry phase. Similar shifts into cold-dry years in 1864 and 1870-1871 were preceded by warm-dry years in 1863 and 1868-1869, respectively. The upswing to the warm-wet years of 1866-1867 was through warm-dry 1865. The long, warm-wet maximum in the 1870s was interrupted in 1875 by a cold-wet year. (We shall discuss these interruptions again later in this volume.)

The next cold-dry climax came in the late 1880s, preceded by the warm-dry years 1882-1884 and the cold-wet year 1885. This intense cold-dry period continued, with minor interruptions, to 1897. Then the warm-dry year 1898-1899 preceded a long, warm-wet epoch. There were two interruptions in this period, one from 1907 to 1913, the other from 1917 to 1921 when the years 1908, 1912, and 1919 were cold-wet. These cold-wet interruptions during warm-wet phases are very common. Many are discernible through the centuries, and they invariably have had a profound influence on political and social events.

The ascent from the valley of 1917 to the peak of 1922-1930 passed through warm-dry 1919-1920 with one cold-wet year intervening between the warm-dry phase of the upswing and the peak itself. In general, then, climatic changes have followed the same pattern in Europe as in Asia and Africa.

The North American Cycle

In North America, beginning in 1860, the pattern varied for a time. Between cold-dry 1863 and warm-wet 1865 came warm-dry 1864. An unusual number of cold-wet years then fell between 1866 and 1874. While this abberation may be due to an insufficient number of reporting stations, runs of cold-wet years interspersed between warm maxima that are fairly close together seem not to be uncommon. A conspicuous warm-wet peak in 1878 was ushered in by one warm-dry and two cold-wet years. Between this peak and later cold-dry years came some expected cold-wet years. This phase was also found in Europe and Asia. The late 1880s and the 1890s underwent a long ,cold-dry period throughout the world. The subsequent temperature recovery preceded the recovery in rainfall, as usual. 1896 was warm-dry; 1897 and 1898 were warm-wet. The usual warm-dry stage on the way to a cold-dry period took place from 1899 to 1901 and occurred near the sunspot maximum of 1905-1907.

The long, warm-wet period so prominent in Europe was cooler and drier here, but North America shared in the warm-wet recovery of 1912-1915. The interruption in 1917 was world-wide. The recovery in 1926 and 1927 was preceded by a warm-dry year while 1929 was cold-dry again, a sunspot maximum. The fall in temperature was preceded by the warm-dry year 1928.

The South American Cycle

South America developed cold-dry conditions in 1871, preceded by warm-dry 1870. The advance toward the warm-wet 1880 peak passed through warm-dry and cold-wet years. As elsewhere, the shift to the cold-dry late 1880s and 1890s passed through some cold-wet years.

A strong warm-wet peak developed in 1900 preceded by warm years from 1895 to 1897, two of which were dry. The drop to cold-dry 1907 passed through the transitional warm-dry stage in 1906. Then the warm-wet upswing in 1914 went through warm-dry 1912-1913. Leaving this peak, we pass through warm-dry 1915 to cold-dry 1916 and 1917. The years 1918 to 1922 can be called a warm-wet peak but with cold-wet trends before and after instead of the usual warm-dry trends. But the approach to the next warm-wet peak between 1925 and 1930 was through warm-dry 1924.

Characteristics of Climatic Fluctuations

It is the rule, rather than the exception, that climatic changes follow a repeating pattern. Regardless of length, the fluctuations reveal the same basic characteristics. There are local variations, but these do not ordinarily extinguish the pattern's basic features. Both in the case of fluctuations too short to be interrupted by a sunspot maximum or minimum, and of long cycles susceptible to the influence of sunspots, the basic patterns are those depicted in Figure 9. In general, the climatic pattern is characterized, in the absence of interruptions, by the stages cold-dry, warm-dry, warm-wet (rainfall maximum), hot-dry (temperature maximum), cold-wet, then cold-dry

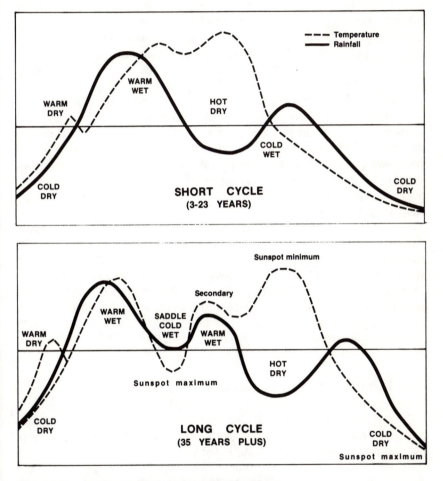

Figure 9.   Patterns of Climatic Fluctuations

again. In the case of interruptions, a minor cycle tends to repeat the pattern of the longer one, but on a smaller scale.

World climate, as reported by weather stations alone, cannot be ascertained prior to the 1860s for the lack of sufficient stations. Since then world trends were as follows. Dryness and, in most regions, low temperatures prevailed in the 1860s; this is a period within the generally cold era that began around 1830 and lasted until nearly 1900. The early 1870s were unstable, but a warm-wet maximum formed between 1875 and 1880. A cold-wet trend then occurred, followed by a cold-dry period through the rest of the 1880s and early 1890s. Instability, marked by temporary trends back to the warm-wet side, occurred in 1890. There was a world-wide rise in temperature by 1900, accompanied by an improvement in rainfall. The mid-1900s underwent a drop in temperature with increased dryness. Between 1910 and 1915 came a revival both of temperature and rainfall until a warm-wet maximum was reached. A short downtrend in both variables centered on the sunspot maximum of 1917, followed by a rise to another warm-wet maximum around 1925. After that dryness again became universal.

Prior to 1860, where data cover smaller areas, what would appear to be world-wide trends occurred as follows. The warm-wet decade 1800-1810 was preceded by a hot drought. A warm-wet to warm-dry 1820-1825 ensued followed by a hot drought. A long, cold, mostly dry period followed during the 1830s and 1840s, with a slight recovery in 1845. Another temperature drop and decline in rainfall occurred, then a warm-wet maximum in the early 1850s, with somewhat warm-dry conditions prevailed from 1855 to 1860.

The Intensity of World Climate

The world climate data so far has been presented in terms of area. Let us now examine the picture using criteria of intensity of rainfall and temperature. Results are presented in Figure 10. In this part of the investigation marine stations were separated from continental stations. Stations located on islands or along coastlines have been defined as marine, others as continental. Stations in South America and the tropics were not so divided. The open symbols represent temperatures at a given station; solid symbols represent rainfall. Each entry depicts a station that during the year departed 25% or more above or below its own long-time average. Thus a cluster of open symbols above the midline represents a year of high annual

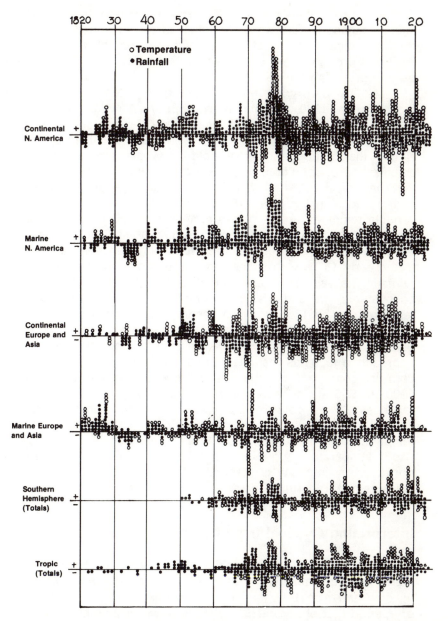

Figure 10. Rainfall and Temperature Departures over 25% from Mean (Actual Number to 1870; then One-Half of Actual Number)

temperatures at many stations. A cluster of open symbols below the midline means a cold wave. A cluster of solid symbols above the midline indicates very wet years; solid clusters below the midline designate drought years. (All of Clayton's *World Weather Records* were used in preparing Figure 10.)

Notice the dryness and evidence of high temperatures in the first half of the 1820s in continental Europe and Asia. Marine climate in Europe and Asia was warm-wet; the tropics were apparently drier than usual. Warm-wet conditions prevailed in the second half of the decade. Notice the preponderance of cold-dry years around 1835, the stabilization of conditions in 1840, the cold-dry combinations in the first half of the 1840s, then the universal change to warm-wet combinations in the early 1850s. Droughts in 1855 accompanied variable temperatures. A rise in temperature and rainfall occurred temporarily at 1860, with a decline in both variables approaching 1865. In 1868 a rainfall maximum occurred, followed by unsteady conditions in the early 1870s with widespread drops both in temperature and rainfall. The year 1878 saw an extraordinary warm-wet maximum, conspicuous in stations the world over. The return to cold temperatures by 1855 was also general across the world. Even the tropics were cooler. Near 1890 climate was warmer and wetter in most places. 1893 centers on another stretch of cold-dry years. The approach to 1900 was unstable with warm-dry years in many areas and cold-dry conditions in others. A warm-wet maximum centered on 1900. In 1905, at a sunspot maximum, there was instability but with a tendency toward cold-dry conditions. The approach to 1915 was characterized by a return to warm-wet years, followed by a drop in temperature accompanied by dryness centering on 1917 and another rise in temperature and rainfall in 1920. So the picture of climate as portrayed by intensity is essentially the same as that obtained by measurement in terms of area.

Interpreting Cyclical Irregularity

Climate has a way of stabilizing over the largest area at three points in the climatic rhythm: at warm-wet, and subsequent warm-dry maxima, and at cold-dry maxima. There is less uniformity in the warm-dry period that often precedes the warm-wet phase. More variation occurs between the warm-dry and subsequent cold-dry climax where one might expect the cold-wet phase.

We find the greatest instability during the transition from cold to warm and vice versa. During the transition from cold to warm, temperature rises ahead of rainfall. As rainfall increases, temperatures may fall temporarily and a cold-wet year may intervene. During the transition from warm to cold, at the end of the hot-drought, rainfall increases and one can expect another period of erratic weather. Sometimes a warm year intervenes; then temperatures keep falling and climate becomes drier until a cold-dry phase is fully evident.

On these transitions, sharp contrasts are common; it is likely to be warm in one place, cold in another, dry in a third, and wet in yet another. These are also times when floods, tornadoes, and hurricanes are most likely to occur. It was during such transition periods in geologic time that the earth's crust showed its maximum instability, and when it was probably the most stormy. It was during these climatic transitions that a majority of the great volcanic eruptions and earthquakes occurred. Volcanic eruptions seem particularly common on swings from warm to cold, for these were mountain building times. Earthquakes seem more likely on swings from cold to warm. In short, climatic conditions share the instability of our whole environment at these times.

It is during these same periods that the greatest contrasts are manifested by tree rings both from tree to tree and region to region. (Tree-ring evidence for temperature and rainfall is most uniform at warm-wet, hot-dry, and cold-dry maxima.) Some trees will grow faster than others, reflecting erratic conditions. But far from being a source of confusion, this irregularity helps to determine times of climatic transitions. In other words, *the irregularities of growth have a regularity of their own,* which makes them just as useful as regular growth patterns.

There are all sorts of minor variations. None, however, wipe out the general features of the overall pattern. In some regions the rainfall recovery occurring at the end of the hot drought as temperatures fall is as great, or greater, than the recovery on the transition from cold-dry to warm-wet times. This variation is most likely in China and the American Southwest. In some regions the rainfall recoveries or droughts will last longer, or the temperature extremes will be greater. There are other complications in the climatic picture. Probably at no time is there not some place where for years or even decades, one region is not losing rainfall while another is gaining. For example, at this writing, rainfall on the North American Pacific Coast has been dropping since the 1870s while the North Atlantic states have experienced a gradual increase during the same period. These are long term secular trends, however, and they do not extinguish the basic pattern of climatic fluctuations because the Pacific Coast also shares in world-wide climatic fluctuations which are more basic in character than are the secular trends.

For the most part, however, rainfall and temperature tend to swing back and forth together despite the times during hot drouhts and cold-wet periods when they are out of phase. Generally, when it is warmer it is wetter, and when it is colder it is drier because of the elementary principle that cool air does not carry as much moisture as warm air.

Constructing and Interpreting the Cycle Curve.

Figure 6 helps to explain further how the climate curve was obtained. First, the sequoia tree-ring curves published by Antevs were used to determine the fluctuations of the climate curve. (The original curves were given as 50-year running averages.) These were refined with Huntington's figures based on 10-year running averages. That is, the faster fluctuations of the 10-year averages were superimposed on the 50-year averages. The mid-points from maxima to minima of the fluctuations were chosen to indicate the approximate time when the climate curve should pass from warm to cold and back again. That is, these points were assumed to represent the long-time climatic average. A section of the curve constructed in this manner can be seen as the "First Stage" of Figure 11.

Next, because almost all ascents to major peaks in the two curves were associated with the warm-wet phase, and the descents with the warm-dry phase, and because the trough between peaks was generally associated with cold-dry conditions, it was assumed that any time the smoothed tree curve was ascending to a peak, it was mostly warm and wet. When the smoothed tree curve was descending into a trough, it was presumably mostly warm and dry. The mid-point of the trough was assumed to center in the cold-dry phase.

Subsequently the tree curve was segregated into temperature and rainfall curves. The dotted line in Figure 11 represents temperature; the solid line, rainfall. This deduction is illustrated in the "Second Stage" of Figure 11.

Now turn to Figure 12 (a type of chart explained in Chapter 6). In Row 8 the black entries position individual peaks in an unsmoothed sequoia tree curve plotted from Douglass's tables. These maxima were used to determine when rainfall fluctuated to the wet side. The amplitude of the swing was determined by the size and height of the peak. Row 11 shows the tree minima in the same curve, which were used to determine the time and extent of individual fluctuations of the rainfall curve to the dry side.

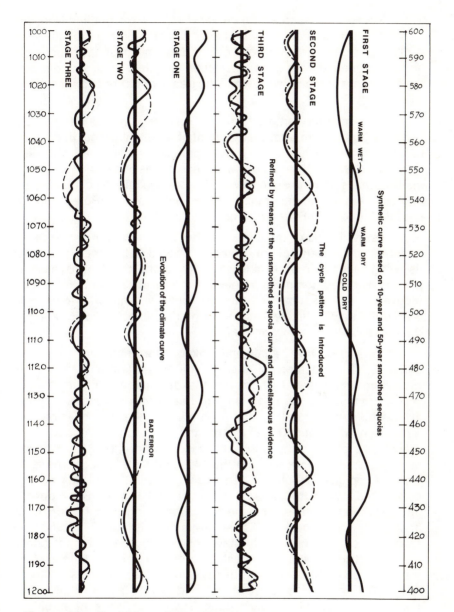

Figure 11.   Evolution of the Climate Curve

Notice that the tree-ring curve was below the midline from 600 to 555 B.C. In accordance with the relationship of tree growth to the cycle pattern, the weather trend during this time must have been cold and dry. Because trees grow least when climate is coldest and driest, the curves are at their lowest when the tree minima are strongest (Row 11).

Tree minima centered on 590 B.C. and the 560s indicate a recovery both in temperature and rainfall. Remember that in the long run rainfall and temperature curves parallel one another, diverging only during warm-dry and cold-wet times. It was because of these tree maxima that secondary cycles were introduced into the climate curve at these points. The generalized cycles are shown in Row 2 and the final deductions in Row 3 of Figure 11.

Many details of the climate curve were in conformity with the general cyclical pattern. For example, in 555 B.C. the tree curve starts its swing back to the warm side where it remains for about 20 years. As previously noted, temperature generally rises ahead of rainfall during recoveries. It is practically certain that for a few years prior to the next wet period in 550 climate was warm and dry, so between 555 and 550 the curve is shown as warm and dry.

Turn to Figure 12 again and look for a tree minimum from 543 to 545 B.C. The position of this minimum right after a warm-wet maximum is an excellent indication that during the minimum, climate was warm and dry. We know further that warm-dry years are almost always followed by cold years. Tree minima after 540 bear out this interpretation, so at 540 both rainfall and temperature dropped. Here, then, was a break in the warm phase like that of the 1810s. Notice a succession of minima through the 540s and 530s. This is where the warm-dry phase should be. The basic 50-year curve has not yet descended into its trough, so it is not yet cold and dry. See Figure 11 again for the two stages in these deductions. Note also the horizontal lines in Row 13, Figure 12. These are minima in the 10- and 50-year smoothed sequoia curves of Antevs and Huntington. Their position in the cycle through 490 B.C. speak for a cold-dry period following the warm-dry phase. After that more peaks in the tree curves (see Rows 5 and 6, Figure 12, and "First Stage", Figure 11) tell us to swing the rainfall and temperature curves back to warm-wet while the amplitude and length of the tree curve peaks tell us of prolonged warm-wet periods.

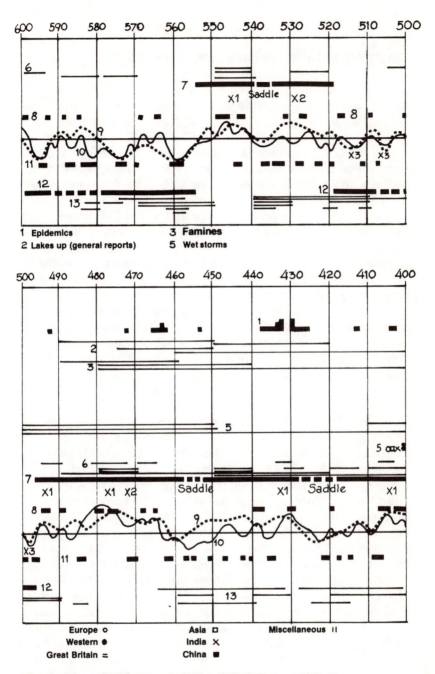

Figure 12. World Climate from 600 B.C. to 400 B.C.

Verifying With Miscellaneous Information

Miscellaneous information for the period 600-400 B.C. is sparce, but what is available seems significant. Although we did not know it when these curves were first drawn, we found out later that many migrations occurred between 600 and 650, when it was cold and dry. Migrations are recorded during cold-dry periods throughout history. For example, they occurred in Asia on a large scale in the very cold dry 1830s and 1840s. According to Griffith Taylor in *Environment and Nation,* there were migrations to Great Britain from Europe near 600, and Polynesians probably migrated to the East Indes about the same time. Taylor also points out that, near this time, primitive Ainu tribes moved into Southern Japan from the mountains and colder regions of the north, and Greeks pushed westward to the Rhone. All this *indicates* that our interpretations of tree curves were generally either correct or at least reasonable.

Brooks has mentioned that Scandinavian climate deteriorated between 650 and 600 B.C., implying drought conditions. Evidently several waves of Teutons were driven out of Scandinavia about this time. That Babylonia was dry in 540 is indicated by the fact that Cyrus was forced to divert the water of the Euphrates for irrigation. (This area was wetter than it is now.) There is a record that in 530 Polycrates built an aqueduct in Greece.

Very little is heard about migrations until the next phase which tree-ring studies indicate should be interpreted as cold and dry. While a single entry, independent of other information, would have no value, the report of severe cold in Britain at 539 B.C. happens to fall exactly in the position designated in the climate curve as a time when cold-wet conditions temporarily prevailed. Such coincidences occur throughout the centuries. Recall that severe cold waves cluster during cold-wet periods, where severe cold and drifting snow induce deep psychological impressions on the population. Just as these events make news today, they made news then, and were entered into the chronologies and other historical documents of the times. The chances are very high that single occurrences agree with other evidence of weather trends much more often than they will disagree.

It hardly seems necessary to take more time explaining the derivation of the climate curve. It is known that most of the short fluctuations in weather trends defined by the California trees are world wide in scope. The curve has been reviewed so many times during the last 15 years that the author has lost count. It is not pretended that the curve is accurate in all respects; rather, the curve simply seems the most accurate picture we have at present. Since the curve was made, many different kinds of cultural data have been plotted against it. The consistency with which known cold-phase behavior occurs only during times deduced as cold, and known warm period behavior occurs during times deduced as warm, permits no other conclusion but that the climate curve is fairly accurate as to *trends.* For example, international wars consistently occur during periods deduced as warm, and civil wars are regularly fought during periods deduced as cold. In fact, the warm and cold periods could have been located almost as well by researching recorded military battles as by studying tree rings.

Return for a moment to Figure 11; notice that the lower half shows the deduced climate curve from 1000 to 1200 A.D. Figure 13 shows the corresponding miscellaneous evidence. Observe how consistently mass migrations occurred within this 200-year period during the cold phases of the long cycle. Observe, too, how many reports of excessive cold and snow there were in the 1040s. According to the tree rings, this should have been a cold-wet phase with heavy snows and severe cold over much of the country during the winters. The reports of snow came from England "=" and Europe "o".

A Word of Caution

One cannot always be right in deducing weather trends from tree rings as can be seen from the serious error made between 1130 and 1160, Stage Two, second row from the bottom in Figure 11. Because the warm-dry phase always follows the warm-wet phase, a 25-year warm-dry phase was indicated to be followed by the usual cold-dry phase. Yet the miscellaneous evidence showed a very long cold period began in 1135 rather than in 1170. A warm-dry period followed the warm-wet peak at 1120, as it should have, but it was only 10 years long. Figure 13 charts reports of cold and snow through the 1140s and 1150s. Also, there were sunspots large enough to be seen with the naked eye in the 1130s. These reports indicate without question that the decades following the 1830s were cold. In the late 1930s large sunspots also appeared. Almost invariably, therefore, within a few years after such sunspot maxima a cold phase begins. Furthermore, there were migrations during the 1140s and 1150s that also indicate a cold trend. And so, in Stage Three of our research, the error in deduction made in Stage Two was corrected. Errors of this sort were made three times in the course of developing the climate curve.

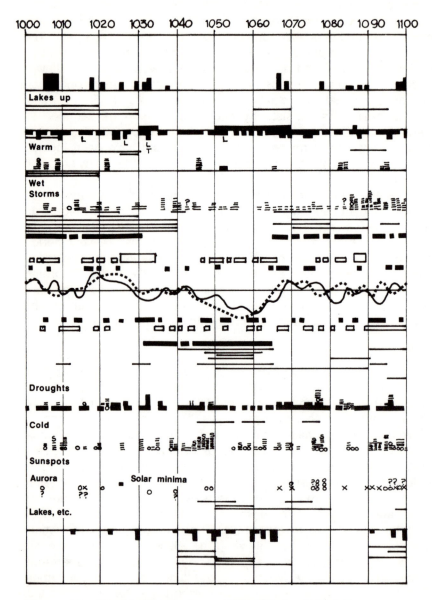

Figure 13. World Climate from 1000 A.D. to 1200 A.D.

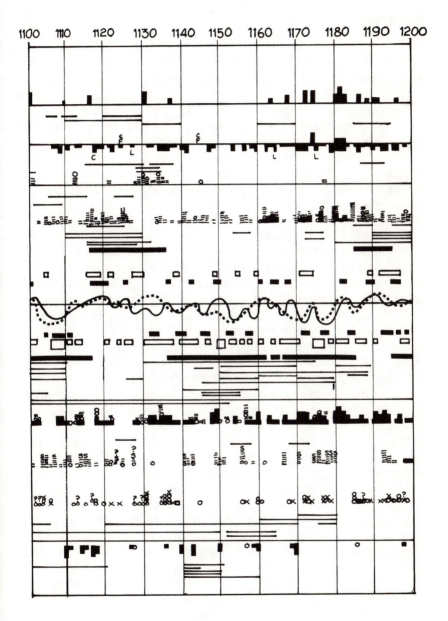

Summary

In this chapter rainfall and temperature data have been presented from stations scattered throughout the world. These data were obtained from Clayton's two volumes of *World Weather Records* derived from 250 stations and supplemented by other sources. In the earlier time periods, especially prior to 1871, the number of stations is less than in later years when the United States and other governments began keeping systematic records on a large scale.

An analysis of these data made with both area and intensity as criteria reveals that climatic fluctuations, whether long or short, follow the same pattern, which is a repeated succession of phases where temperature and rainfall always occupy the same positions with respect to one another.

In the long run, temperature and rainfall follow one another back and forth between warm-wet and cold-dry maxima. In between these maxima, the curves separate in a fairly regular manner. As temperature moves from a cold-dry maximum, it tends to rise ahead of rainfall, thus creating a short warm-dry phase. Following a warm-wet maximum, and barring complications, a period develops where climate is dry and temperatures reach a high point. Then temperatures begin to drop and rainfall recovers. This process develops into a cold-wet phase. Then rainfall declines in conjunction with temperatures, creating a cold-dry phase, thus completing the cycle.

In cycles where the warm and cold phases last longer than the sunspot cycle, the pattern is more complicated. During the warm phase, whether climate is wet or dry, temperatures frequently drop below average at sunspot maxima. Sometimes this interruption lasts several years, during which time many cold-wet years are likely to occur. Invariably, in the second half of the warm period, before the next cold phase begins, there is a conspicuous, often severe hot drought phase.

Similarly, during long cold phases, there may be interruptions during which temperatures briefly rise to above average, usually at sunspot minima. This happened in the 1850s and 1870s in the midst of a long cold period. During these minor rhythms superimposed on the longer ones, the same pattern of successive stages or phases are repeated, but they are of short duration.

It has been further explained how the regularity of the climatic pattern made it possible to deduce from tree-rings how a given decade fit the phasese of the cyclical pattern.

Finally, this chapter has explained how the climate curve was deduced and refined through successive stages, using both miscellaneous and tree ring data.

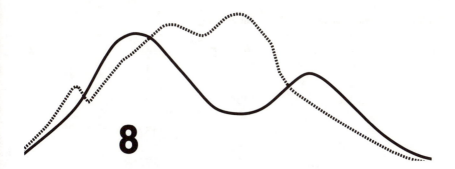

8

The Principal Climatic Cycles in History

It is important to remember, before we begin discussion of the three basic climatic cycles, that the amplitude of the fluctuations in our deduced climatic curve represents a subjective estimate of relative conditions at a given time in history, and pretends to be only a device by means of which to locate the probable positions of successive phases of the climatic cycle. The curve should be interpreted as meaning *only* that during certain periods climate was probably warmer or colder, or wetter or drier than in the preceding period of time. The curve is meant to provide a picture of the probable long-time trends. The evidence, prior to measured temperature and rainfall, does not permit stating precisely what the average was at a given time, nor does it permit giving an exact definition of the amplitude of the fluctuations. Everything must be interpreted on a "more than" and "less than" basis.

The Major Cold-Dry Maxima in History

If this volume contained charts of the climate curve for its entire length, it would be seen that every so often there was a conspicuous cold period varying considerably in length. The first centered on 575 B.C., the next on 505, the next on 420, and so on. These were also dry periods. Our studies show that the most outstanding cold-dry periods of history have centered on the following dates:

575 B.C.	190 A.D.	1055 A.D.
505	285	1175
420	340	1295
300	460	1400
235	560	1475
170	650	1570
90	745	1655
30 A.D.	845	1765
115	955	1865

The time periods between these cold-dry maxima average 94.6 years. We have generalized and called this the 100-year cycle. In the earlier centuries of history it averaged shorter than it has since 400 A.D. Since then it has averaged 101.6 years in length. Twice in ancient times the cycle shrank to 65 years; it was 70 years long once; 75 years three times; 80 years once; 85 years three times; 90 years once; 95 years three times; 100 years four times; 105 years once; 110 years twice; and 120 years five times. There have been 26 such cycles between 575 B.C. and 1865 A.D. with the 27th scheduled to be completed about 1975. Ever since the fall of Rome the cycle has maintained an average of approximately 100 years.

During each of the 26 cycles the sequence of phases has been the same: cold-dry, short warm-dry, warm -wet, long warm-dry, cold-wet, then cold-dry again. In each cycle the first part of the warm phase was the wettest while the second part contained a major hot drought. The first part of the cold phase was also the wettest, and was where most of the cycle's cold-wet years occurred. Since cold-wet years are the most difficult to detect from miscellaneous evidence, it is very likely that our curve does not show as many of these years as actually occurred.

During the warm half of each of these 26 cycles there were occasional interruptions when temperature dropped to the cold side; each time, there was also a drop in rainfall. Each major cold period was interrupted by a temporary shift of temperatures to the warm side accompanied by an increase in rainfall. In the long run, rainfall and temperature fluctuate together. These minor fluctuations are secondary cycles that obviously follow the same pattern as do the longer ones but whose phases are much shorter. The secondary cycles do not obliterate the pattern of the longer, major cycles.

The Major Warm-Wet Maxima in History

Warm-wet maxima have also occurred with rhythmic regularity throughout history. At first, the rhythms were rapid. Apparently it has never been as wet as it was from 550 to 320 B.C. based on evidence from California, Europe, Egypt, and Asia. A strong warm-wet maximum in 545 was followed, after a double sunspot cycle, by another maximum that was not quite so wet but considerably warmer. Immediately thereafter came a hot drought. The approximate dates of history's more prominent warm-wet maxima (with secondary maxima indicated in parenthesis) are as follows:

545 B.C.	305 A.D.	(1120) A.D.
480	385	1215
(430)	(430)	(1260)
375	485	1335
(330)	(540)	(1375)
275	590	1420
205	(620)	1495
150	690	(1525)
(105)	775	1610
70	885	1675
70 A.D.	(920)	1805
145	995	1925
235	(1020)	
(270)	1070	

During the warm phases of the 100-year rhythm, there are frequently two major warm-wet peaks, one near the beginning of the period and the other in the second half. After an interruption to the cold side, a second warm-wet maximum generally forms. When this happens, the second maximum is usually weaker than the first. The great hot droughts of history have occurred after the second maximum. The peaks listed in parenthesis constitute part of a secondary cycle and are omitted in calculating the time intervals between major warm-wet phases. The average duration of time from one warm-wet maximum to the next in the 100-year rhythm is 95.8 years. The average interval between the first and second peaks of the warm periods is a little over 44 years or approximately the fourth multiple of the sunspot cycle.

The Major Hot Droughts in History

Turning now to the major hot droughts, we find much the same thing. They almost always occur toward the end of the warm phase just before it turns cold. There seem to be a few exceptions when droughts did not develop at this time. The years when major hot droughts have occurred (with secondary peaks in parenthesis) are as follows:

525 B.C.	265 A.D.	1135 A.D.
470	320	1225
(375)	435	(1355)
325	(490)	1395
250	550	1455
195	(595)	1530
115	(625)	1630
(45)	695	1695
15	805	1825
95 A.D.	900	1935
160	1025	

The average interval between major hot droughts is close to 90 years; but there are several variations to be noted. In 625 A.D., there was a trend in the direction of a hot drought but it did not fully materialize. A hot drought did develop in 695, early in the warm period, but the expected drought in this cycle came 10 years later, just after temperatures turned cold, and even then the drought was not of major proportions. Another variation of the pattern occurred with the drought of 900 A.D., which was early and was followed by a moderate drought in 925 when a major drought was expected. Finally, the drought in 1225 A.D. also occurred early while a cyclical drought expected in the 1260s never occurred.

Owing to these variations in the pattern, the hot-drought rhythm is not as regular as the cold-dry and warm-wet maxima. This is not surprising because the hot drought is a transition stage between warm-wet and cold-dry maxima. Climate is more stable when both temperature and rainfall are in phase with one another.

The Major Cold-Wet Maxima in History

The most variation in cyclical pattern seems to occur with cold-wet maxima. The major cold-wet periods of history (with secondary peaks again in parenthesis) have centered on the following dates:

515	B.C.	270	A.D.	(1230)	A.D.
(540)		325		1285	
425		445		1395	
315		555		1460	
240		630		1545	
185		720		(1595)	
100		820		1645	
10		940		1715	
105	A.D.	1040		1830	
175		1145		1945	

Again discounting the secondary peaks, the average time interval between cold-wet maxima is approximately 95 years.

The 1000-Year Cycle

By correlating all four major maxima — warm-wet, warm-dry, cold-wet, and cold-dry — since 575 B.C., one can discern four distinct climatic cycles which seem to have paramount historical significance. These are the 1,000-, 500- and 100-year cycles. The long cold periods during the Dark Ages and the long warm period in the Middle Ages belong to the 1,000-year cycle. These rhythms terminated at 575 B.C., 460 A.D., and 1475 A.D. The current cycle is not due to terminate until around 2475 A.D.

At each termination of this 1,000-year rhythm, something very extraordinary has happened. *An old world has vanished each time and a new one has begun.* At 575 B.C. the older civilizations in the Ancient World — Egypt, Babylonia, Assyria, and China — vanished, to be replaced by a new world dominated by Greece, Rome, and fresh empires in Persia, India, and China. A little over 1,000 years later these civilizations vanished to be followed by the Middle Ages again lasting approximately 1,000 years until around 1475 when they were replaced by the Modern World. The modern world, in the sense that we know it, is not due for a major shake-up until around 500 years from now, if this climatic pattern keeps repeating itself although fairly significant changes can be expected with the imminent birth of the new 500-year cycle.

The 500-Year Cycle

The 1000-year cycle tends to break down into halves of about 500 years each. Centering on the dates of 575 B.C., 30 A.D., 460 A.D., 955 A.D., and 1475 A.D. climate was dry and colder than usual. The warm periods were short and were often disrupted by drops in temperature. Midway between these dates, the warm periods stretched out; the interruptions were not as long, and the cold periods shortened. The result is an intermediate cycle averaging 510 years in length.

The beginning of the first of these approximately 500-year rhythms marks an important place in the history of climate. Prior to 575 B.C. climatic cycles were longer and more extreme than they have been since. In the two centuries immediately following, from 550 to 320 B.C., it was warm much of the time. Two 100-year cycles were almost fused into one. The cold period between them, at 420 B.C., was very short. After that, the cold periods lengthened. By the end of this 500 year period, at the time of Christ, there was an exceptionally long, cold period. The cold phase centering on 460 A.D., at the end of the next 500-year cycle, was also exceptionally cold. Mass migrations were extensive, and all the ancient civilizations collapsed. There was a long-term down trend in rainfall. Although there were long cold phases in the 600s and 700s A.D., they were frequently interrupted by shifts to the warm side and did not seem exceptionally bad. The cold phases of the 800s and 900s were extremely severe, causing many migrations, from the northern countries,especially when conditions began to deteriorate approaching 955, near the end of a 500-year rhythm.

Subsequently temperatures warmed suddenly. The 1000s were so warm that trees grew in Greenland. This was the period when Vikings crossed the Atlantic. One of the most severe hot droughts in history occurred in the 1130s. The thirteenth century saw a long, warm period. Then climate began to deteriorate again. While the fourteenth century was warm much of the time, there were frequent and sharp drops in temperature; often it was very stormy. During several winters the straits between Denmark and Sweden froze over solid enough to support horses and sleds. Greenland began to freeze. In the fifteenth century there was no long, warm period. The next 500-year period terminated in 1475. Subsequently temperatures warmed up again. The seventeenth century was so warm that the next 100-year cycle had but a short cold phase, centering on 1655, and this was quickly interrupted by a shift back to the warm side. During the 19th and 20th centuries climate deteriorated again, but that is a story to be told in later publications.

Events of great importance occur every 500 years. Midway between 575 B.C. and 460 A.D., the Roman Empire began its decline, as Christianity rose. There were no strong European civilizations for a long time. On the other hand, there were very strong Asiatic empires such as that of the Huns. Midway between 460 A.D. and 1475, in the ninth and tenth centuries, a vast change occurred, again involving mass migrations. These events divided the Middle Ages into two halves. In the first half there were brilliant empires like those of Justinian with its capital at Constantinople, Charlemagne in the West, and the Arabs in the East. The Arabs moved into Spain and India, developing brilliant civilizations first at Bagdad and later at Cordova. Following 975 A.D. the feudal period developed, with the growth of the principalities that were to form modern European states. Amazing empires were built by the Mongols in Asia, the Incas in South America, and the Mayas in Central America. In India and Japan new empires also were born. The Balkans achieved their Golden Ages during this period as well.

All this came to an end in the 15th century. The Medieval World, with its economy, customs, and modes of thought disappeared. With the new 500-year climatic cycle came the Renaissance, the Reformation, and the building of modern nations, first under absolute monarchs and then under constitutional governments. This most recent 500-year cycle has witnessed the awakening of modern art, science, and economics. In these more advanced civilizations, the common people have for the first time in history come into their own under democratic political and economic systems.

The 500-year period beginning in 1475 is drawing to a close. We are witnessing many of the same types of events that have occurred under similar circumstances with almost clocklike regularity five times before in history. These events, to be explained later in this book as well as in later publications, are of the utmost significance for the businessman and student of today — and tomorrow.

The Short Cycles

The next, and perhaps most important cycle in this heirarchy, is the 100-year cycle. Because of its importance, Chapter 11 is devoted in its entirety to illustrating the interplay of this 100-year climate on business conditions in the United States since 1794.

This 100-year rhythm also tends to break down into halves. The short rhythm of warm-wet maxima averages 43.5 years. The short intervals between droughts is close to 45 years. Calculating the time between the crossings of temperature from cold to warm, the average is a little over 45 years for the shorter rhythms. The rhythm of the major drops in temperature is about 46 years. Many of the shorter rhythms are 35 years in length; others range up to 55. A 35-year rhythm was discovered by Bruckner, who regarded it as a fluctuation between warm-dry and cold-wet maxima. There are many other rhythms. Short rainfall cycles 7 years in length are conspicuous throughout history. These are of great value in making predictions a few years in advance. Both in temperature and rainfall, there exists an 11-year rhythm, identical to the short sunspot cycle. There is also a rhythm similar to the double sunspot cycle, a rhythm of about 22.5 years both in temperature and rainfall. There is a fairly conspicuous 18-year rhythm of the crossings of temperature back and forth across the average line, as well as a fairly stable 6-year rhythm in temperature and also a common 60 year cycle. These rhythms are not, however, the basic features of the climatic cycle, for in the long run rainfall and temperature fluctuate together. The basic features are the warm-wet and cold-dry maxima.

Summary

Throughout history the general pattern of climatic fluctuation has been the same, regardless of length of the cycle. Historical cycles range from 1,000 years down to 7 years and even less. *The picture is that of rhythms within rhythms.* Although the pattern of a climatic fluctuation is always the same, there are many variations to the pattern; therefore no two rhythms are exactly alike. *Nevertheless, with a knowledge of these cyclic patterns, trends can be predicted long in advance.*

There is a 1,000-year fluctuation dating from antiquity. If we define this rhythm as beginning and ending in a cold-dry maximum, we are about half way through the current cycle. Prior cycles have terminated around 575 B.C., 460 and 1475 A.D. *At each termination of this cycle, a distinct historical epoch has ended and another began.* A deterioration in climate characterizes the years immediately preceding these key dates, while favorable climatic conditions appear early in the new cycle to signal its arrival.

The 1,000-year cycle breaks down into halves, with both resulting 500-year rhythms ending in exceptionally cold and dry phases. *Each 500-year cycle termination throughout history has also marked significant upheavals or turning points in society.* The dates of these terminations are 575 B.C., 30 A.D., 460 A.D., 965 A.D., and 1475 A.D. Moving forward 500 years one can easily see that the next 500 year cycle is scheduled to begin around 1975. The significance of this transition will be discussed later.

The 500-year rhythm, in turn, breaks down into five cycles each averaging 100 years in length, although these may vary from 80 to 120 years. Prior to 400 A.D. they were as short as 65 years at times, but since the fall of Rome they have averaged very close to 100 years. The most recent termination of this cycle occurred around 1865. The next termination should occur around 1975, coinciding with the termination of the 500-year rhythm. The 100-year cycle has invariably had a profound effect on history, on the behavior of human kind, on economic and business trends, and on the conduct of government including the occurence of wars. *Nothing of any consequence in the way of human affairs has escaped the influence of the 100-year climatic cycle* as is evidenced by the chapters that follow.

The 100-year cycle itself breaks down into halves, sometimes thirds or other harmonics, and the halves frequently break down again into further halves. In all these rhythms, the same pattern prevails — cold-dry, warm-wet, warm-dry, then cold-dry again. The overall effect of these brief rhythms is to provide variation with the profoundly significant 100-year cycle.

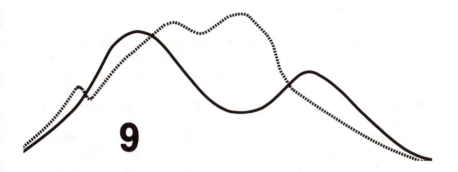

9

Climatic Conditioning in History

The Effects of Climatic Cycles on Human Achievement

When our climate chronology begins in 600 B.C., the golden ages of Egypt had long since passed and Homer of Greece and Helen of Troy were but memories. Just prior to the earliest period in our study, in about 700 B.C., the Assyrians, who once before had ruled a formidable empire, rose anew. Through their introduction of the horse and chariot, they conquered Syria, Palestine, Babylonia, and Egypt; which they organized into a provincial empire. Under this system their subjects were ruled by Assyrian governors and, as long as they paid their tribute (now known as taxes) and did not revolt, they were otherwise allowed to go about their business. So much of the empire's income (now known as the Gross National Product) went toward maintaining the huge military force that agriculture and other domestic activities suffered. This generated a great deal of discontent until eventually the provinces rebelled.

600 B.C. came during one of history's major periods of rebellion and civil war. Governments throughout the world were weak and their people wandered from one region to another. Among these wanderers were the Medes and Persians, who between them broke up the now declining Assyrian empire, thus permitting the Chaldeans to capture Babylonia and overrun Jerusalem. *Our climate chronology distinguishes this period as the middle of a long cold-dry phase.*

119

Early in the same century, the Greek nobility went through a period of struggle with underpriviliged farmers and small merchants. Coinage had been substituted for barter but only the rich could secure coins. This was all happening at a time of slow growth for the California sequoias, again indicating cold-dry conditions on a world wide scale.

In Egypt, the armies could not agree on a new ruler. In Italy, the Celts roamed at will. The Phoenicians in Carthage and Cadiz were having difficulties with the native tribes. There is evidence that Polynesian races migrated from the Asian mainland to the East Indes, as did Mongolian tribesmen to southern Japan. From 600 to 550 B.C. governments were weak and crumbling. *Everywhere during this cold-dry phase, there was a lack of unity and loyalty.* People quarreled among themselves, especially about religion. Hostility and strife prevailed between rich and poor, rulers and subjects. Savages everywhere successfully raided the very centers of civilization.

Then in 550 B.C. the picture suddenly changed. *Climatically, there was a strong though temporary rainfall revival accompanied, as is usual after a long cold period, by rising temperatures.* Under these conditions, storminess and more variable temperatures must have prevailed; just the sort of thing — as we have noted in earlier chapters — that is necessary to maintain optimum human vitality. Suddenly civil strife came to a halt, and just as suddenly, strong new governments with capable and energetic leadership appeared throughout the world. In some cases this new energy was directed toward international "nation-building" wars, while in others it was directed to more enlightened national purposes. Within 10 years the Persians created an empire that stretched to the Mediterranean. The Spartan League was formed in Greece at a time when such leagues and alliances became the order of the day.

There seems to have been an outburst of scholarship at this time, for the chronicles describe famous jurists in early Rome and China and a famous Hindu physician in India. Thespis performed the first tragic drama in Athens. Famous schools for philosophers and mathematicians sprang up; this was the time of Pythagoras. Order was restored in Egypt, where commerce reached impressive proportions. There was an industrial revolution in Athens and manufacturing fluorished. *All this spells the nation-building energy of a warm-wet climatic phase.*

But this particular warm-wet phase of the climatic cycle was short lived. By 540 B.C. California tree growth rapidly declined, indicating a hot drought phase. Within the Persian Empire, Cyrus was forced to divert water from the Euphrates for irrigation, while in Greece Polycrates built an aqueduct to supply drinking water for the population. Paralleling this abrupt climatic change, human behavior suddenly and drastically changed throughout civilization. Good governments, scholarship, unity of spirit, and the democratic way of doing things all disappeared. So many despots sprang up in the Greek city states that this period in history is referred to as the Age of Tryants. From what is recorded, the conclusion is inescapable that the new empires recently formed on the transition from cold-dry to warm-wet phases now rapidly declined. With the deterioration came a period of decadence. There are no longer reports of scholarship, no longer noted jurists or dramatists, no longer chronicles of economic prosperity. Instead, everything points to tyranny and a public apathy. As we shall see later in this chapter, *all these phenomena are characteristic of hot drought phases.*

Following a recovery, the California trees again show rapidly declining growth at 520 B.C., at precisely the point in time when one would expect a cold-wet phase lasting about 25 years to intervene between a hot and cold drought. With this change of climate, reports of international wars almost ceased while migrations, rebellions, and civil wars begin to crop up once more. Revolts occurred in Persia, Athens, Rome, Scythia, India, and China. The drive toward democracy was again on the rise, largely through the struggle of the common people. As climate grows colder, there is a revival of energy that, although undisciplined and characterized by a lack of political untiy and national spirit at first, eventually brings freedom back to the people and extends the franchise. These are periods of chaos, but also of emancipation.

From 500 to 450 B.C. occurred one of the greatest nation-building epochs in history, with the birth of many new states. This was also an outstanding period of invention and revival of learning, with one of the most striking flowerings of commerce and prosperity. Just a few of the many nations that rose at this time were: Illyria; Syracuse on the island of Sicily; Thrace and Macedonia north of Greece; Bithynia and Cappadocia in what is now Turkey; Numidia south of Egypt; the Caledonian empire in Scotland; and the region of present day Belgium. From excavated art objects and tools, one is led to suspect that there were also strong warrier states in Central and South America, central Asia, and Japan.

None of these new states seems to have reached the high level of culture enjoyed by the ancient Greeks, but then, the level of scholarship — philosophy, history, medicine, science — in Greece at this time was extraordinary compared to almost anything the human mind had created up to this point. (And of course it has been argued that the Greek architecture, sculpture, and tragic drama of this period have never been surpassed.) *All this reflects vitality.* This was the Golden Age of Greece — the age of Pericles, Aeschylus, Sophocles, Euripides, Herodotus, Hippocrates, Socrates, Plato, and Aristotle.

It is of paramount importance to recognize that, climatically, beginning in 500 B.C., the California sequoias began one of their longest and most rapid spurts of growth in several thousand years. At this same time, sea levels of the Caspian and Baden Seas rose much higher than normal, as did Owen's Lake in California (180 feet above its present level) and numerous lakes in western China. Egypt enjoyed a long period of immensely abundant floods along the Nile, and oases in the Sahara blossomed and prospered greatly. During the Golden Age of Greece, *it is quite evident that the world was experiencing a major climatic recovery from a cold-dry phase to a long, mostly warm, abundantly wet period.* Yet the evidence is that it was *not excessively warm* because north Europe was having its share of cold winter weather.

Eventually, following such an invorating warm-wet phase, the rains cease and temperatures soar. As they do, climate becomes drier and the energy level of people declines. With this decline they lose their initiative and turn over the responsibility for governing their own affairs to an increasingly bureaucratized or militarized government, within which the greedier and more aggressive members of society are waiting to seize power. Government ownership and control increases, so does regimentation, causing various forms of communism and socialism to spring up. These are typical behavioral phenomena during the hot drought phase of the 100-year cycle. Then, as climate shifts from warm-dry to cold-wet again, as it did in the second half of the 300s B.C., activity, accompanied by civil strife, picks up once more. The wars that come at this phase of the cycle, like those of Alexander the Great and, in our day, of Hitler are nation—falling wars because they are fought by a nation or empire just before it is about to collapse through internal disintegration.

The entire social pattern changes once more on the move toward colder weather. A prolonged cold-dry phase began about 330 B.C., a wave that lasted about 40 years. Throughout this period there was no international fighting of any consequence, although there was an abundance of civil war. Migrations from central Asia became so troublesome that the Chinese were forced to build great protective walls in the north. In Rome, class struggles between rich and poor reached a bloody climax.

These patterns can be traced through all the climatic cycles up to the present day. However, it is not our intention to do so at this time. Our intention here is to introduce the reader to the concept of climatic cycles and to show how climate has affected human activity for the past 2,600 years. For those interested, more detailed evidence of material introduced here will be presented in forthcoming volumes.

Historical Behavior During Hot Droughts

So far we have observed that whenever a prolonged warm-dry phase has developed in the climatic cycle, governments have become reactionary and tyrannical, and civilizations everywhere have become decadent. An examination of a few such periods in history will enable us to see how well this pattern of behavior holds up.

Climate was warm and dry in the 150s and 160s A.D. when Marcus Aurelius ruled Rome. Although himself interested in mystical philosophy, he permitted a cruel persecution of Christians during which several prominent martyrs were killed. In China, drought and famine became so serious that people ate human flesh and a number of provinces were required to "relieve" (kill) the poor and the weak.

One hundred years later in Rome, the Christians were again persecuted. This time all bishops were removed and all asemblies were forbidden.

During the warm-dry phase that occurred shortly after 1000 A.D., Basil II of Constantinople, victorious in a war with Bulgaria, deprived 15,000 war prisoners of their sight. At about the same time the then residents of England perpetrated a frightful massacre of the Danes who had earlier invaded the country while Mahmud, a Ghanzi prince who conquered India, burned an enormous number of captives at the stake.

During the 1360s and 1370s, when several short hot droughts followed one another in rapid succession, tyranny reached a point in England where the wages of a laborer were set and had to be accepted by him under penalty of the pillory or the loss of an ear; if he did not comply, he was branded with a "V" for vagabond; if he attempted to escape, he was branded with an "S" and made a slave for life; and if he protested this, he was hung.

Jews in Toledo, Spain, were exterminated in the 1530s, as were the Moslems in Granada. There were holocausts in the low countries. Free thinkers were burned at the stake. Henry VIII executed Anne Boleyn and Sir Thomas More and sacked the monasteries. In Austria and Germany, minorities of all kinds were persecuted in the 1550s.

During the hot droughts of the 1670s and 1680s, Almagir I in India destroyed the temples of the Hindus, killed their priests, and transferred their treasures to his capitol. The armies of Louis XIV burned the homes of the Hugenots and destroyed their crops. Coffins were dug up and looted. Protestants could bury their dead only after nightfall. In the American colonies, South Carolina adopted Indian slavery. In Hungary the execution of ministers, priests,and teachers by the Turks was an almost daily occurrance.

In 1816, England again during a hot drought, repealed the Habeas Corpus Act. In Germany liberal ideas were suppressed. In Poland the liberty of the press was completely nullified. Massacres were committed on both sides by the Egyptians and Sudanese. In 1821, the Turks massacred Greeks at Smyrna. This was also a period of commercial depression throughout the world.

The most recent hot drought era occurred in the 1930s, when an epidemic of dictatorships broke out all over the world. Of the more than 20 republics organized after World War I, only Czechoslovakia survived. Fanaticism, persecution of minorities, and decadent nationalistic movements along with swings toward socialism and communism became the order of the day. The birth rate declined, health suffered, and economic systems all but collapsed during one of the most severe economic collapses in history.

All this has happened time and time again in history, each time under the influence of debilitating temperatures and a sharp reduction in cyclonic storms and precipitation. This is not to say that these historical events could not happen of themselves, but the fact remains that only in isolated instances have they ever reached world-wide proportions and reached such tyrannical political climaxes *except under conditions of hot drought in the warm-dry phase of the 100-year climatic cycle.*

Cold Phases and the Growth of Democracy

To trace the growth of the democratic pattern of behavior through all the cold climatic phases of history would require many more pages than are available here. As with hot droughts, an examination of a few such phases should enable us to appreciate the general consistency of this phenomenon.

It is highly significant that Christ was born and lived during a long cold period and founded the most democratic of the world's great religions. It is also significant that throughout history the spread of Christianity and democracy has been simultaneous. On the other hand, when governments have become reactionary during warm-dry phases, churches have instituted their own inquisitions and persecutions. It is significant that the best leadership in religion and in government have come at the same times, and that church and state have been weak,and frequently immoral and corrupt, simultaneously. Moreover, missionaries have always spread the gospel during cold periods characterized by international and interracial tolerance, during which nationalism has run low. These have been periods of migration, immigration, cultural mixing and borrowing. The orient has frequently welcomed Christianity during cold periods and resisted it during warm times. During these warm times the emperors of China and India have turned to Buddhism, making it the state religion, only to repudiate it and force the Buddhist priesthood back into the laity on the next turn to cold.

From the time of Christ until around 100 A.D., the California trees suggest a cold-dry climate. Both India and Ireland reported grain failures, famines and droughts. Aurora, as well as sunspots, both of which indicate low temperatures, were frequently seen. During this unusually long cold phase, citizenship was extended throughout the Roman Empire.

The most recent cold phase of unusual duration began around 1135 and lasted until 1185. It was at this time that an important step was taken in the direction of democracy when Henry II established trial by jury. He also established a grand jury of men selected in each neighborhood to give his judges information about crimes committed. In Scotland there was a long civil war, an important characteristic of cold times. In France the communes repeatedly revolted against the nobility. In the Holy Roman Empire there was continuous fighting between the followers of the Pope and those of the Emperor. The Swedes were fighting with the then less civilized Finns. In Japan the emperor was forced to abdicate. In spite of all this, Europe was becoming economically prosperous. As always happens during cold times when hostility between nations is at a minimum, there is a revival of foreign trade and commerce. This time it was intensified by the Crusades. To finance them great banking houses arose, promoting the growth of city republics and hence the principles of democracy. Having spent their fortunes on the Crusades, the barons were forced to borrow from groups of bankers and merchants, who lent their money only on condition that they be granted local freedom and independence in case of default.

During a brief but historic cold period in the thirteenth century, British barons forced King John to sign the Magna Carta in

1215 although it was soon repudiated during the next warm spell. During the cold 1260s, the barons again revolted, this time forcing Henry III to establish the Oxford Parliament. This was the first time in English history when untitled people shared in the deliberations of government. Although the representatives dealt only with matters of taxation, this was the real beginning of the House of Commons and modern representative government.

In 1295, during the next cold period, for the first time middle class representatives of English society were included in the deliberations of a parliament that had a hand in establishing the laws of the land. About the same time, in 1302, a French national assembly, the Estates-General, was established composed of the three classes or estates, the nobility, the clergy, and the townsmen or merchants. In Switzerland, Lucerne joined with Zurich and Bern to form a union that, in a sense, developed into the first modern republic.

During the major cold period in the fifteenth century, the Polish legislature adopted one of the first acts of habeas corpus, which promised not to let any property owning Pole be imprisoned for a crime (unless he had been caught red handed) until he had first been given a trial. This was one of the great emancipation periods in history, with patriots everywhere rising up to espouse the cause of democracy, religious freedom, and the elevation of the status of serfs. People began to abandon Latin as the universal language of the educated classes and began to write literature in their own native tongues. In many places the cities had no rulers, the emperors no power. This great awakening, with its demands for independence, came more in the religious, intellectual, and commercial areas than in the political arena. A great wave of exploration burst forth that was to result in the discovery of the New World. Perhaps most important was the invention of printing, which itself did much to promote the spirit of freedom.

In the cold 1640s, the first written constitution of modern times was drawn up during the war between Parliament and the Crown at the time of Cromwell. Later, during a short cold period in the 1680s, the British Bill of Rights was signed. At about the same time in the colonies, the Quakers of Pennsylvania voluntarily emancipated their Negro slaves.

During the cold decades of the eighteenth century, labor troubles developed almost everywhere. In one of the first strikes in history, bakers and journeymen left their work in protest for higher wages in New York. They were arrested, tried, and convicted, but there is no record that they were sentenced. Slave riots developed at this same time in New York and New Jersey. The American Revolution was paralleled throughout the world. In France the third estate usurped power in the National Assembly on behalf of the common people. Egypt declared herself independent of the Turks, while Austria abolished serfdom.

The march toward democratic reform continued during the cold years of the nineteenth century as Texas and California rebelled against Mexico. New constitutions were adopted in Australia, Austria, Hawaii, and Sicily. A civil war was fought in the United States involving issues of states rights and the emancipation of slaves, while agitation for equality between men and women became increasingly frequent. In Italy, the right to vote was extended to all adult male taxpayers who could read and write. These are only a few of the hundreds of events that advanced the cause of democracy universally.

As the twentieth century dawned within a cold phase, a constitutional government was adopted in China. Bulgaria achieved complete independence from Turkey and, as the other Balkan states tried to free themselves from Turkish domination, their quarrels triggered World War I. In a brief cold period after that war, Germany, Austria, Czechoslovakia, Turkey, Greece, Poland, and the Baltic states all underwent revolutions of one sort or another, on their way toward founding new republics and adopting democratic constitutions. Even the Russian Revolution, at its very beginning, was democratically oriented. Most of these countries promised equality of opportunity, religious freedom, freedom of speech and of the press. Privileges due to birth or rank were abolished. Many countries extended suffrage to women. At this time the Irish established a Free State in southern Ireland.

But as climate became warmer, the whole world rapidly headed in the same direction of socialism, communism, decadence, and fanaticism — as it had done 26 previous times in 26 different 100-year cycles since the sixth century B.C. Democratic constitutions were thrown to the winds, freedom of speech was curtailed or eliminated, states' rights were set aside, open trials were discarded, the church gave way to the state, and hardly a nation escaped the havoc of the world's worst commercial depression in modern history.

This historic hot-drought depression further undermined the confidence of the people in the old economic system and the old patterns of government. Even the most democratic countries made sharp turns to the left, and in an effort to help the economic situation, clamped on one form of regimentation after another. Private cooperatives emerged for the purpose of buying and selling or for the ownership of production. Social insurance of many kinds came into being. Freedom of action was curtailed everywhere and the bureaucratic powers of government increased.

The most interesting fact concerning this socialistic movement in the United States deals with the far-reaching extension of federal power by the Democrats. What makes this so interesting is that the Democratic Party was founded in the early nineteenth century to curb exactly the same trends during the previous major warm period that they themselves, as a majority party, so aggressively extended during the twentieth century's hot drought. And it was the minority Republican Party, descended from the Federalists (who in the early days advocated more federal power) that was now endorsing more individual freedom and initiative, more states' rights, and less federal authority. When it is cold, a political party, to be successful, must initiate democratic reforms and stress individual initiative, freedom, and fair competition because society is conditioned to be capitalistic. But when it is warm, a party in power, in order to succeed, must stress federal control and assume more responsibilities for the common good because now the human energy level is lower, initiative is poorer, individual self-interest and assertiveness are less, and *human nature is conditioned to perform its functions in a complex society in a less individualistic way.*

The Paramount Lesson of History

So it is that the change to a colder climate leads people to discover their individual worth as well as the value of freedom, initiative, and ways to keep the interest and vitality of the individual alive through competitive enterprise. On the other hand, warm times lead to the rediscovery of cooperation, of unification into organized societies, of disciplining greed, and of impulses to provide for security from societal hunger and want, eventually on a scale beyond that of society's then current capacity. In his ignorance, greed, and intemperance, man has continually gone from one extreme to the other. He has moved toward anarchy, exploitation of the underprivileged, unfair competition, and weakened government during cold times; toward excessive regimentation, reaction, persecution, communism, fascism, fanaticism, and the crushing of freedom and individual initiative during warm times. *During both phases of the cycle man has made important and necessary discoveries, but he has not yet learned to apply them moderately. This is the great problem of the future — to find the elusive "golden mean."*

Not since the purges, persecutions, and massacres of Louis XIV and Ivan the Terrible had Europe witnessed the disintegration of human nature on the scale that prevailed in the late 1930s. Not since Tamerlane and the Turkish atrocities in the Balkans had warfare by a supposedly civilized nation become so depraved. Once more, for the 26th time, a fiendish, nation-falling war erupted after the moral tone of society had been lowered by excessive temperatures. Nothing like the atrocities that were committed had ever happened in the memories of living men *because no one was alive who could remember back to the end of the last epoch that had terminated in a similar outburst of degenerate behavior.* If there had been, they would have remembered similar incidents, time after time again, always at their worst on the transition from warm to cold times. To blame human degeneracy on climate, of course, does not excuse either the people or the atrocities they committed. But realizing that climate is in vital ways responsible for these forms of behavior may ultimately lead to doing something about them.

Summary

It was previously explained how an elaborate investigation of the correlation between climatic fluctuations and human achievement was undertaken. The existance of cultural fluctuations throughout history had already been worked out by others before it was suspected that they were climatically conditioned. This demonstrates that the conclusions we reached could not have been the result either of a preconception or of wishful thinking.

The story of the main trends of history as they have repeated themselves down through the centuries on tides of climatic change is herein summarized. Although space is not available in this volume for a complete summary, the rise and fall of the Greek city-states was traced in some detail, together with certain main events in the history of Rome up to the birth of Christ.

A definite human behavior pattern was found to repeat itself as the 100-year climatic cycle moved through its successive stages. The cold phases of the cycle are dominated by various kinds of civil strife — civil wars, class struggles between rich and poor and between conservatives and liberals, religious wars, democratic reforms, emancipations, broadening of the franchise, colonization, migration, and piracy. This is a time of weak governments and generally, but not always, of poor leadership.

During the transition from the cold to the warm phases, profound nation- and empire-building events occur. This period is characterized by an outburst of: nationalism; nation-building, imperialistic wars of conquest; generally good to great leadership; strong governments that are initially democratic and benevolent; industrial revolutions; the sudden expansion of trade and commerce; the revival of learning; the appearance of great geniuses in philosophy, science, and the arts; and the rise of a new aristocracy.

As the warm-wet phase terminates, climate becomes drier and hotter. As it does other phenomena manifest themselves: creativity declines; reaction and decadence set in; governments become despotic; minorities are persecuted; general health declines along with the birth rate; economic systems collapse; socialistic and communistic regimes rise under an epidemic of dictators; individual freedoms vanish; and the moral tone of society reaches a low level. Toward the end of this period comes another series of wars we call nation-falling wars because many of the governments initiating them during this period are either tottering or about to collapse internally. These particularly savage conflicts occur on a falling temperature and a rising rainfall curve.

The next climatic phase is a transition back to cold-wet. As soon as this happens, reinvigorated populations rise up in rebellion against the excesses committed during the hot-drought phase just past. Civil wars break out and the cold pattern of behavior that we have already summarized returns with its emphasis on democracy.

We then briefly examined the human behavior patterns that prevailed during several exemplary hot-drought phases of past 100-year cycles. In each example we found a consistent pattern of reaction, totalitarianism, and decadence. Each time, there was an epidemic of cruel despots, persecutions, massacres, and degenerate wars.

In contrast, we briefly examined human behavior patterns during several of history's cold periods. We consistently found that cold periods are characterized by civil wars, riots, rebellions, revolutions, democratic reforms, and the extension of the franchise. For centuries during these periods, migrations and piracy have returned again and again to harass a weakened civilization.

Finally, we have deduced what may well be the paramount lesson of history. Man, in his ignorance of the profound degree of social conditioning effected by climate, has always overreacted to climatic change. In cold times, he has carried his natural inclinations beyond benevolent individualism and democracy to the point of nihilism and anarchy. In warm times, he has carried his natural tendencies beyond benevolent cooperation and stability to the point of socialism and tyranny. If man could but *recognize* and *temper* his reactions to climatic change, and *apply in moderation* the best inclinations of both cold and warm times as they occur, he is capable of generating that ultimate golden age of world civilization of which philosophers have only dreamed.

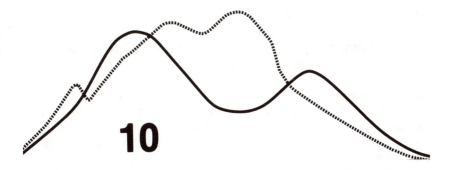

10

The Golden Ages of History

Correlating Superior Leadership with Climatic Phases

Suppose we were to consider those political leaders throughout history who have been endowed by posterity with the title, "the Great," and we were to add to them the obvious names such as Julius Caesar, Justinian and Napolean. We would have 53 rulers of this class. Undoubtedly there were more, but these probably include most of the more familiar examples from history.

Suppose, then, that we add those rulers whom modern historians generally characterize as "good" rulers because they unified their kingdoms, kept their vassals and people under control, formulated and enforced with equity and justice new, more democratic and constructive laws, improved the condition of their country economically, were enlightened and tolerant, (relative to their time), and tried to improve the intellectual, moral, and physical status of their subjects. We would have 253 of these rulers.

Suppose, finally, that we were to consider those rulers whom historians agree were neglectful of their government or people; who were spendthrifts, treacherous, murderous, and tyrannical; who were voluptuous to the extent that their conduct was a public scandal; who were profligates; who carried on senseless wars at great sacrifice of life; who failed to try constructively to limit civil war; who ordered or permitted massacres and pogroms; who permitted the wholesale use of torture; or who for any other reason incited a profound and memorable bitterness and hatred among their own people. Using these criteria, we would have 342 "bad" rulers.

133

Combining "great" or "good" rulers with distinctly "bad" ones, we arrive at a total of 648, 47% of whom we classify as "good" and 53% of whom we designate "bad." This total by no means includes all of the rulers since 600 B.C., but it is presumably a large enough sampling to justify a conclusion regarding trends in government in relation to climatic fluctuations. Also, by proceeding in this manner, it is clear that there has been no selecting of rulers in the interest of demonstrating a preconceived theory.

In the subsequent correlations, all these rulers were grouped into three classes in relation to the 100-year climate cycle. The first consisted of those who ruled on the transition from cold to warm phases and into or through the warm-wet phase. Most of the rulers whose reigns began during the transition lived through the subsequent warm-wet phase, for, as has been seen, this is the time when governments have been the most prosperous, when human longevity and health have apparently been best, when the moral tone of society has been the highest, and when society has been most stable. Hence the total situation at these nation-building times, not only permits but is conducive to long reigns. The great majority of the rulers were young men when they assumed office or became sovereign, owing to the fact that the cold-to-warm transition always falls at the end of a period of civil war during which previous rulers have been liquidated. We will call this group the "warm-wet rulers."

The second group will be called the "warm-dry rulers," many of whom reigned during the transition from warm to cold until either the people or revolutionary parties were strong enough to remove them from office or throne. In many instances the rebellions that burst out when temperatures turned cold either deposed or killed these rulers before they had a chance to die a natural death.

The third group is classified as "cold rulers" and includes heads of state during both cold-dry and cold-wet phases. Only a small number of sovereigns or elected heads of state have ever ruled through both a major warm and a major cold period. There are two main reasons for this. First, it is ordinarily impossible for them to live long enough; and second, the cultural changes that occur during the climatic transitions generally bring with them changes in government. In the instances in which a ruler covered both phases of a secondary or short cycle — the warm and the cold — the ruler was classified in accordance with the phase occupying the larger part of his or her term of office. Thus, while Queen Victoria reigned through four and a half cold decades and one and a half warm decades, she is classified as a "cold" ruler. Frederick the Great reigned through the cold 1760s as well as the warm 1750s, but, because the most active part of his reign occurred during the 1750s, he is classified as a "warm" ruler.

The following table shows where on the climatic cycle these 648 heads of state ruled. They include the better known dictators, kings, emperors, presidents, and prime ministers of history, oriental as well as occidental.

Quality of Ruler	Cold-to-warm transition and warm-wet		Warm-dry		Cold	
	No.	No.	%	No.	%	No.	%
Great	53	48	90.6	2	3.7	3	5.6
Good	306	205	67.0	34	11.0	67	22.0
Bad	342	14	4.0	136	40.0	192	56.0

As shown on the table, 90.6% of the world's finest heads of state ruled during the transition from cold to warm and during the warm-wet phase. Only 3.7% ruled during the warm-dry phase, and 5.6% during the cold phases.

Of the 306 good heads of state (which includes the 53 finest leaders discussed above), 67% ruled during the transition from cold to warm, 11% during the warm-dry phase, and 22% during cold times. The 22% are mostly cold-wet rulers who instituted democratic reforms, although most of them ruled into cold-dry times as well. (Cold-wet periods tend to be broken up badly, although the major part of the cold-wet period generally occurs immediately following a warm-period. Because of this overlapping it was not considered feasible to separate cold-wet from cold-dry rulers.) Many cold-wet rulers were not good, but when good rulers did appear in cold times, they were likely to have done their best work during cold-wet periods.

Of the 342 bad leaders, only 4% ruled on the transition from cold to warm and during warm-wet times, while 40% ruled mainly through warm-dry periods, and 56% during cold times. The reason that more rulers came during cold than during warm-dry periods is the fact that, owing to civil wars (when it is cold) reigns are of generally short duration. Moreover, the cold period as a whole is always longer than that part of the warm period which is dry.

Stated in other language, of the 219 rulers who lived during the transition from cold to warm, 93% were good or great and only 7% were bad. Of the 170 rulers who lived during warm-dry times, only 20% were good while 80% were bad. Of the 259 cold rulers, 26% were good and 74% were bad. (The fewer number of warm-dry rulers is due to the fact that some of the good rulers of history have lasted into or through warm-dry periods from the warm-wet. However, in many instances they turned from good into poor rulers as it became hot and dry. In other words, they deteriorated along with the climate. If they were good during warm-wet times, however, they are represented in the table as good rulers. Hence, the actual number of bad rulers during warm-dry times is somewhat more than the table indicates.)

The "Golden Transitions" of Climatic History

Our table of rulers clearly points to the position on the climatic cycle where the majority of Golden Ages in history have occurred, where civilizations have usually been at their best, and where the vast majority of great and enlightened rulers have lived. This conclusion is verified when we correlate our historical climate curve with the periods in history which historians generally characterize as those richest in vitality, brilliance, and prosperity.

Golden ages throughout history have almost invariably occurred within every second 100-year climatic cycle beginning at the transition from cold-wet to warm-wet. All such golden ages (perhaps an equally approximate term would be "golden transitions") reveal the same general pattern regardless of location on the earth. This pattern consists of:

1. Illustrious leadership from sovereigns likely to be designated "the Great" by posterity.
2. Prosperity; expansion of commerce and development of industry.
3. Upturn in building — public works, roads, bridges, whole cities.
4. Improvements in agriculture.
5. Industrial revolutions.
6. A golden age of art, science, and literature; a concentration of genius producing intellectual and artistic awakening.
7. Emergence of a new aristocracy.
8. Upsurge of nationalistic feeling; nation building.

9. Imperialism; international wars of conquest pitting the strong against the strong; the creation of great armies and navies; exploration and colonization.
10. Reorganization and centralization of government; constitutional reforms.
11. Maximum participation of the population in political and social life.
12. Reorganization of taxation and financial systems (In recent centuries, the emergence of new international banking systems).
13. High birth rates.
14. Improvement in health and longevity.
15. Peak in moral tone of society.

A brief review of the golden-age rhythm in history follows. Golden ages occurring during primary climatic recoveries are differentiated from those occurring during secondary recoveries with the latter being indicated by parentheses.

450 B.C.   Periclean age of Greece; great dramatic poets and sculptors, philosophers and scientists; recoveries all over the world.

(380 B.C.   The time of Plato.)

270 B.C.   Ptolemaic period in Egypt; outburst of learning; first Alexandrian School; many brilliant empires, including India and China.

(150 B.C.   Second Alexandrian School; revival of learning; Roman conquests.)

50 B.C.   Golden Age of Rome; Augustan Age of literature; the Caesars; revivals generally including the Han dynasty in China.

(70 A.D.   Roman empire strengthens; Pliny Persia; revival of learning in India; Josephus.)

(160   Marcus Aurelius)

(250   Rome regains vitality;Persia; second-ary revival of learning; Plotinus.)

380   Theodosius, a strong Roman ruler; conspicuous revival of learning; Basil the Great; St. Augustine.

(480   Clovis, first of the French monarchs; Old Mayan kingdom in Central America; majestic cities; astronomy.)

570   Justinian,beginning of Greek empire at Constantinople; large Avar empire in central Europe; birth of Japan; Pope Gregory the Great; Caedmont.

(700   Arabs; Venerable Bede; China; Japan)

780   Charlemagne; brilliant Arabian culture at Bagdad, Haroun-al-Rashid; birth of Denmark.

(890   Alfred the Great, England; birth of Russia; Bulgaria.)

980   Arabian culture at Cordova, Spain; great universities; Denmark, Cnute the Mighty; Holy Roman Empire, Otto the Great; Navarre, Sancho the Great; Venice; the musician Guido; the Persian poet Firdausi.

(1080   William the Conqueror;St. Anselm; Omar Khayyam; the Islamic scholar Al Ghazzali.)

1220   France, St. Louis; scholastic philo-sophy; cathedrals, universities; Thomas Aquinas; amazing Mongolian empire of Genghis Khan; Inca Empire; Seljuk Turks; Roger Bacon; Frederick II; Serbia; Bulgaria.

(1320   Dante; Hungary, Louis the Great; numerous strong states.)

(1410 Chaucer; universities; humanism; Turks.)

(1500 One of the greatest golden ages of history — the Renaissance; exploration; Spain; Portugal; Poland, Sigismund the Great; Ottoman Turks, Suleiman the Magnificent; Mogul Empire in India; Russia, Ivan the Great.)

1600 Shakespeare, England under Elizabeth; Spanish dramatic poet, Lope de Vega; France under Henry IV; Japan; Mogul Empire in India at height; Cossacks in the Ukraine; Sweden, Gustavus Adolphus; science from Galileo, Francis Bacon, Kepler; art by El Greco, Cervantes, Rubens.

(1690 Louis XIV; Moliere; Racine; Isaac Newton; Leibnitz; Iroquois Indians; Peter the Great in Russia.)

1800 One of the great golden-age periods in history. the Age of Napoleon; nascent period for United States; founding of many new sciences such as chemistry, geology, physiology, paleontology; great poetry by Goethe, Wordsworth, Coleridge music by Mozart, Beethoven; art by Goya, Ingre; great mathematicians and non-Euclidian geometry; great architecture and design by Sheraton, Chippindale; great philosophers such as Hegel, Schopenhauer; inventions and the Industrial Revolution.

(1910 Powerful nations; another industrial revolution, the assembly line; automobiles, airplanes, and radio; Einstein; functionalism in art; grand opera and Caruso; literary revival; great financial empires.)

Summary

We began by objectively selecting those rulers which modern historians have designated as the finest and worst rulers in history and correlating their periods of leadership with warm-wet, warm-dry, and cold (including cold-wet and cold-dry) phases of the 100-year climatic cycle. We found that over 90% of the world's great leaders and almost 70% of its most enlightened leaders have governed on the transitions from cold to warm climate and the subsequent warm-wet phases, whereas these same climatic conditions have coincided with the reigns of less than 5% of history's worst tyrants and incompetants. On the other hand, 96% of those rulers regarded by historians as being poor rulers have governed during the warm-dry and cold periods of history. These correlations provide a powerful argument on behalf of the climatic conditioning of human behavior on a world-wide scale.

Because a highly detailed presentation of the historical effects of climate on human societies will appear in a separate volume, we have only briefly outlined the almost invariable correlations found by comparing the historical climate curve with periods which historians generally characterize as golden ages. This exhaustive investigation has again clearly identified transition periods from cold-dry to warm-wet as harbingers of ages of societal excellence and dynamism.

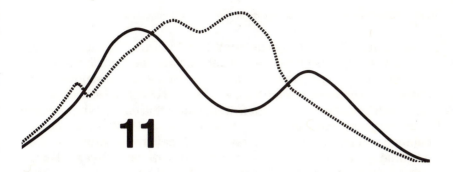

11

Weather and Business Trends in the United States, 1794-1950

Climatic Phases and Business Cycles

Warm-wet, warm-dry, cold-wet, cold-dry: These, as we have discovered, are the essential building blocks of climatic history. We have seen how the golden ages of history, noted for their vitality and cultural achievement, good government, and economic prosperity, have generally occurred on the climatic transitions from the cold-dry to the warm-wet phases of the 100-year cycle. Vitality, brilliant leadership, and the creation of wealth are inseparable. The cold-wet phase is the second best time in history. Golden ages and good government sometimes prevail during this phase, especially in the orient, but not nearly so often as during the warm-wet phase. However, the evidence is clear that cold-wet phases, like the warm-wet, tend to be times of economic prosperity.

Both dry phases, on the other hand, have consistently been times of economic stagnation and depression. The warm-dry phase has been characterized by dictators, absolutism, statism, socialism, communism, and cultural, moral, and economic decline. During the cold-dry phase, which is usually long and drawn out, all the evidence points to a correspondingly long, or at least recurring, depression. These have been the dark ages of history when entire civilizations have completely disintegrated. Chaos, anarchy, and piracy prevailed. The world seethed with migrations. There was no orderly government or commerce anywhere. Throughout history, lack of vitality, decadence, and economic depression have been inseparable.

From all this it can be seen that the question of whether a consistent relationship exists between business and weather trends is not an isolated problem. It is part of a larger question of the relationship between human behavior and the weather. Not one aspect of human behavior and productivity escapes this relationship. Trends in government, wars, scientific and philosophical thinking, invention, painting, music, design, literature, education, religion — even costume — shift predictably with the phases of the 100-year climatic cycle. Were business trends exempt, it would be fantastic. However, they are evidently not exempt.

The fact that human behavior is conditioned by weather trends should, from a logical and factual standpoint, play a large part in the theory of the business cycle. If it does not, the conclusion of necessity follows that the basic, as opposed to the secondary and derived causes of the business cycle have not yet been found. Stated deductively, it is obvious that whatever explains the relationship of the human behavior pattern to weather trends must also explain the relationship between business and the weather. Stated inductively, whatever relationship is found to exist between specific kinds of human behavior, studied individually, and weather trends, would probably be found valid in connection with business trends and the weather. If the weather has any effect at all on human behavior and productivity, it is logical to suppose the effect would be the same on all types of productivity for all types of people in all types of places. The facts bear out this assumption.

The correlation between human behavior and the weather (suspected since ancient times and established by many investigations in recent years) grows out of the effects that temperatures and storminess combined have on the metabolism of the body or, in simpler language, on the level of energy available for work. It has been found that cool temperatures and cyclonic storminess, phenomena that generally occur together, is the best combination for human vitality. These conditions also produce the greatest yields per acre, assuming, of course, proper soil and agricultural care. Experiments on animals show there is an optimum temperature for the development of size, behavioral stability, fertility, and intelligence. There are optimum temperatures for the most economical conversion of energy from food into meat in hogs and other animals. Why should there not also be optimum weather conditions for the conversion of man's energy into the kind of work we call business?

Evidently there are such optimum conditions. They are to be found on the transitions of the 100-year climatic cycle, from cold-dry to warm-wet and from warm-dry to cold-wet. Civilizations are at their best during these times, especially on the transition to warm-wet.

Just before the transition from warm-dry to cold-wet, civilizations pass through a period of decadence. The old aristocracy becomes reactionary and despotic as it goes into decline; the only acceptable leadership now comes from the lower classes and the younger generation but it as yet lacks experience and calibre. Social, economic, and political forces all work in the direction of decentralization. Governments are unstable. Insurrections and revolutions dominate the scene as the underprivileged begin to acquire power. These conditions are not conducive to the brilliance, vitality, and innovation of nation—building times which occur on the transition from cold-dry to warm-wet.

Now people are invigorated and hardened. Having just lived through a long cold period, they are in the best possible state of health. Social, economic, and political forces are now all trending toward centralization. The people are becoming more unified and better organized. This in itself makes more energy available for work and achievement because the energy is now being constructively focused rather than destructively dissipated. Nations now have definite goals which adds to the power and efficiency of their populations. All this generates individual aspirations as well. This is the "springtime" of the climatic cycle, and people have the same vitality and enthusiasm now that they have each spring when conditions are exactly the same, only for a shorter period.

It might be argued that greater prosperity and vitality at these wet times are simply products of abundant crops. It is undoubtedly true that good health and great strength require a bountiful food supply. However, this argument breaks down when we consider that the food supply of people in the tropics can be excellent, yet they invariably lack vitality and aspiration. Using another example, the abundant rainfall of the southeastern United States produces an excellent food supply, yet the high annual temperatures make it necessary to live more slowly than in the northern states. Recall for a moment our experiments with rats in Chapter 4. Rats reared at a constant 90 degree temperature may be offered the choicest, most nourishing rat food available but they eat relatively little of it. They are half the weight of "cold-room" rats reared at 55 degrees. In the first generation these "hot-room" rats are less than one third as fertile as "cold-room" rats; they are almost completely sterile by the fourth generation.

There are other reasons why climatic cycles and prosperity do not correlate simply with periods of good food harvests. Abundant crops are associated with two opposite trends, one on a rising, the other on a falling temperature curve. The two wet phases, equally good for crop production, produce opposite types of business trends and cultural patterns generally because temperatures are shifting in opposite directions. One economic and political trend is toward centralism, the other toward individualism. Leftist trends occur on rising and rightist trends on falling temperatures.

This material has been presented by way of introduction for the purpose of placing the relationship between business and weather trends in its true and natural setting. The more perspective with which to see a limited, specialized problem, the more likely will the problem ultimately be solved.

The Present Study and Its Results

The results of correlating weather and business trends in the United States from 1794 to 1950 are summarized in the accompanying 16 charts. In each chart a verticle column represents a year. There are, therefore, 10 years to a chart. The top row on each chart depicts climatic conditions in the United States for the year in terms of the variables — warm, cold, wet, and dry. Warmth and moisture are measured above the median line while cold and drought are measured below the line. From 1791 to 1890, the scale represents the estimated percentage excess of reporting weather stations in terms of cold versus warm and wet versus dry. Looking at the year 1791 on Chart 1, the interpretation is that the year was cold and wet. The degree of wetness is almost 30%. That is, of all stations for which weather data was available in 1791, almost 30% more stations reported above average annual mositure as compared to those who reported below average annual moisture. At the same time, almost 20% more stations reported colder than normal annual temperatures compared to those reporting temperatures warmer than normal. Moving over to 1794, the interpretation is that it was warm and wet with about 20% more stations reporting above average warmth and 10% more stations reporting above average moisture.

The bottom row represents the percentage amplitude of fluctuation above and below normal in the Index of American Industrial Activity prepared for the Cleveland Trust Company by Col. Leonard P. Ayres and updated to the year 1950.

A simple validation of these early estimates can be found in the fact that the estimated temperature and rainfall for the earlier decades covered by the charts correlate practically to the same degree with business trends as do the rainfall and temperature data from 1890 to 1950 for which more numerous temperature and rainfall curves are available. If the early decades correlated more poorly than did the last 60 years, it would be reasonable to suppose the estimates made on the basis of the more scanty data of earlier decades were lacking in accuracy. This is not the case. It is unlikely this relationship between business and weather trends would change from one century to another. Similarity of correlation, therefore, between the earlier and later decades, tends to confirm the weather estimates of the earlier decades, at least as to the estimate that a given year was warm or cold, wet or dry.

Beginning with 1890 the verticle scale needs to be interpreted differently. As before, the midline represents the median. But now each verticle unit represents 25 temperature degrees (not actual degrees of temperature) above or below the median totaled United States temperature. For example, the average temperature in Arizona for the year 1900 was 64 degrees; for Minnesota it was 44 degrees; and for southern New England it was 49 degrees. The average temperatures for the entire country for each year, state by state, were added, making a total of temperature degrees ranging from around 2,200 to 2,400. The median figure for the years 1890 to 1949 was 2,337 temperature degrees. After 1890, the length of the column represents the total number of temperature degrees accumulated in a given year to a given amount above or below the median value.

The same interpretation holds for rainfall after 1890, except that the verticle distance representing 100 temperature degrees now represents 200 inches of rainfall, accumulated by adding the rainfall figures for the separate states.

Because the median was used, fewer years from 1890 to 1949 fall on the warm side as would be the case if the weather data were based on the average; and not quite as many years fall on the dry side as when the average is used. But what constitutes a wet or dry year depends on one's definition, and is a relative, not an absolute, matter. The median is just as much "normal" as is the average.

The overall year-by-year correspondance between prosperity and wet years on the one hand and depression and dry years on the other was 74%. The correspondance between warm-wet and boom years was 79% and between cold-wet and boom years 85%. The correspondance between warm-dry and depression years was 75% and between cold-dry and depression years 56%. In the case of the cold-dry years, however, business declined or else wars cut across the expected relationship in two thirds of the exceptions.

(Continued on Page 178)

Chart 1. American Weather and Business Trends, 1791-1800

The top row in these charts depicts climatic conditions in the United States for the year in question in terms of the four variables — warm, cold, wet, and dry. The degree of relative warmth and wetness is measured above the median line while cold and drought are measured below the median. The interpretation of the chart for the year 1791 is as follows: First the year was cold and wet. Of all the reporting stations, approximately 20% more reported colder than normal, as opposed to warmer than normal, temperatures in 1791 while about 30% of the stations reported wetter than normal conditions. Moving over to 1794, the interpretation is that it was warm and wet with about 20% more stations reporting warm than cold and 10% more stations reporting wet than dry.

The bottom row represents the percentage amplitude above and below normal on an Index of American Industrial Activity prepared by Col. Leonard P. Ayres for the Cleveland Trust Co. and updated to 1950.

As you study these charts, notice the high correlation between booms and wet years on the one hand and depressions and dry years on the other. Whatever reasons may be offered for the occurrence of a boom or a depression at any given time, the weather always seems to be an underlying, predisposing cause, without which no explanation of a boom or depression is complete or adequate. No other single factor so successfully accounts for the timing of booms and depressions.

The warm-wet phase of the 100-year cycle begins in 1794. This is a nation-building and golden age time in history, and is always an era of prosperity. Good years outnumber poor years in business. There was a renaissance in literature, art, and science — one of the most brilliant epochs in history. All human behavior, including business, demonstrated that man was living at a high energy level.

The boom ended with the onset of several dry years. While the depression was attributed to French hostilities, the chances are eight out of ten that, whatever the economic reason, the depression would have occurred anyway.

The boom of 1794-1796, conventionally attributed to "sea-borne commerce prosperity", would undoubtedly have occurred in the absence of any particular economic incentive. We may presume that the weather trends, especially rainfall, promote the findings of incentives by increasing human vitality and aspirations.

In this chart, the principle of wet-year booms and dry-year depressions works for 6 out of 7 years, and in the seventh year, 1796, although business conditions remained good, they were declining from the previous year's peak during a year of cold-dry conditions.

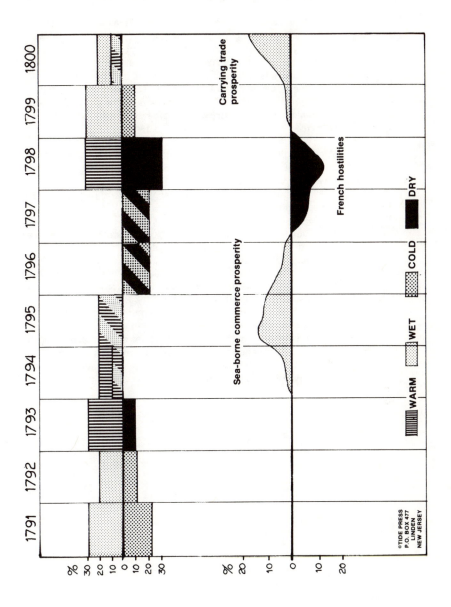

Carrying trade
prosperity

Sea-borne commerce prosperity

French hostilities

WARM   WET   COLD   DRY

©TIDE PRESS
P.O. BOX 477
LINDEN
NEW JERSEY

Chart 2. American Weather and Business Trends, 1801-1810

In the weather cycle the sequence of the main phases of all cycles, whether long or short, is usually: cold-dry, warm-wet, warm-dry, cold-wet. Although the warm-dry phase of this 100-year cycle occurred in the 1820s, there were a number of dry years in this decade. It is interesting that during the dry spell from 1801 to 1803, there was a lull not only in the Napoleonic Wars, but in fighting the world over. The rainfall revival in the early 1790s was world-wide, as was the dry wave just mentioned, the wet climax at 1810-1811, and the cooler years, 1808-1809.

The boom that started in 1799 continued into dry 1801 before the dry years "took hold." Again the chances are that there would have been a depression at this time, anyway, whatever may have been the economic or political reason assigned to it.

Warfare, business, commerce, and general human activity picked up as it turned wet again in 1804.

Note the tendency for business volume to fall during dry 1806, but the boom had enough vigor to recover, reaching its climax during wet 1807. Thereafter it declined rapidly as climatic conditions turned dry.

The year 1808 is associated with a depression. Notice that when the dry period is short, so is the depression. With the revival of rainfall came a revival in business.

In this chart the principle of wet-year booms and dry-year depressions works for 8 of 10 years. In warm-dry 1801, the direction of the boom that began in 1799 was down after peaking in mid-year but not enough to reach depression levels while in 1806, the boom then in progress seems to have been moderated by the warm-dry climate conditions.

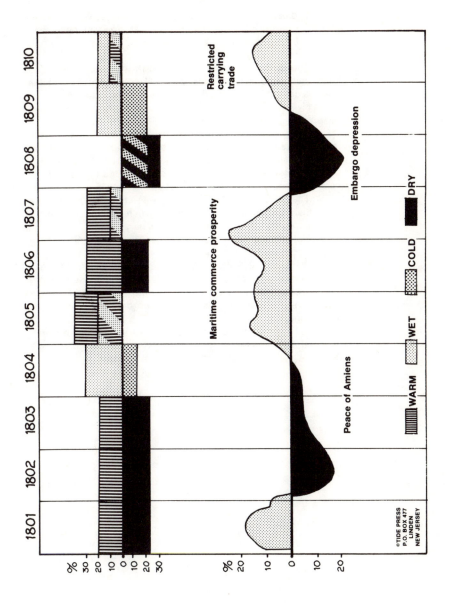

Chart 3.   American Weather and Business Trends, 1811-1820

Ordinarily wars do not start during dry years, as did the War of 1812. The spirit that precipitated the war, however, developed with the emergence of the War Party during wet 1809, 1810, and 1811.

The cold wave from 1814 to 1818 was world-wide, and historically famous. Rebellions against Napoleon broke out at this time, as did the revolutions that eventually freed Latin America. It was a civil war period the world over, as cold periods have always been.

There is little doubt that, had the War of 1812 not occurred, there nevertheless would have been a depression at this dry time.

Again business revived during wet 1814. Dry 1816 and 1817 did not produce much of a depression, but there was a sharp decline in business volume from the levels of 1815.

The so-called postwar recovery was a function of wet years more than the consequence of peace. There would have been a boom here regardless of the previous war.

Note how a single wet year, 1818, was accompanied by a single boom year.

Warm-dry 1819 and 1820 were depression years. There has been a tendency throughout history for depressions to be more severe during warm-dry than cold-dry times — about 50% worse since 1794 — evidently because warm-dry times are more debilitating.

In this chart, the principle of wet year booms and dry year depressions works for 9 out of 10 years while cold-dry 1816 saw a rapid deceleration of the boom then in progress.

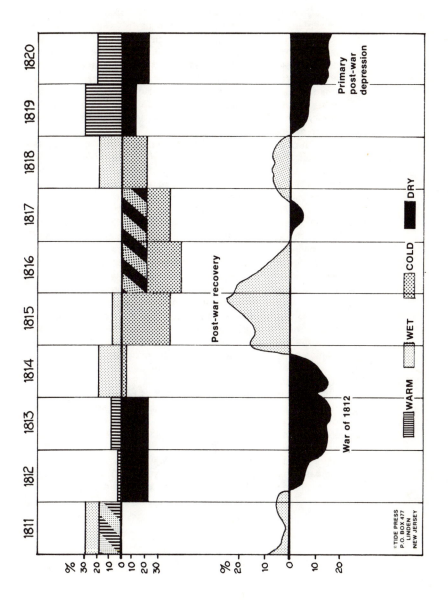

Chart 4. American Weather and Business Trends, 1821-1830

Compare this chart with Chart 15, the 1930s. The warm-dry phase of the 100-year cycle occurred in the 1820s and again in the 1930s, 110 years later. These charts disprove the claim so often made that nothing like the warm-dry wave of the 1930s ever happened before. The warm-dry rhythm is traceable back to ancient times. Look ahead to Chart 5 and notice that it suddenly turned cold after 1830. The warm-dry phase always terminates the warm part of the 100-year cycle. It did so again in the twentieth century. The cold-wet phase of the 100-year cycle is in the process of forming again in 1950-1951.

Throughout history, warm-dry phases of the 100-year cycle have been associated with climaxes of despotism, absolutism, fascism, socialism, and communism. The 1820s climaxed the famous Metternich epoch in European history, even as the 1930s saw the rise of Hitler and Stalin. They have also been associated with economic decline throughout history. The health and vitality of civilization, including the birth rate have declined during these periods. It is not true that there were no business booms and depressions prior to the industrial revolution as certain economists have asserted. On the contrary, there have been many industrial revolutions in the course of history, not a few of which have had as far-reaching effects as did the industrial revolution of 1800.

In this chart the principle of wet-year booms and dry-year depressions is working in better than 7 years out of 10, but that is not the conspicuous feature of the chart. Note the overall preponderance of dry years and of depression years. When the weather trends vary, business trends vary in a corresponding manner. More dry years produce more depression; more wet years produce more prosperity.

The great crash at the end of 1929 began just as a great drought began, and lasted as long as the drought lasted. Observe how, in this chart, wet 1821 was associated with a business recovery which lasted for a short time into 1822. As rainfall improved in 1824 and 1825, so did business; and wet 1830, the beginning of a succession of wet years, initiated a 4 year boom. Compare Chart 15, where a single wet year, 1937, was associated with a single year of recovery from the Great Depression.

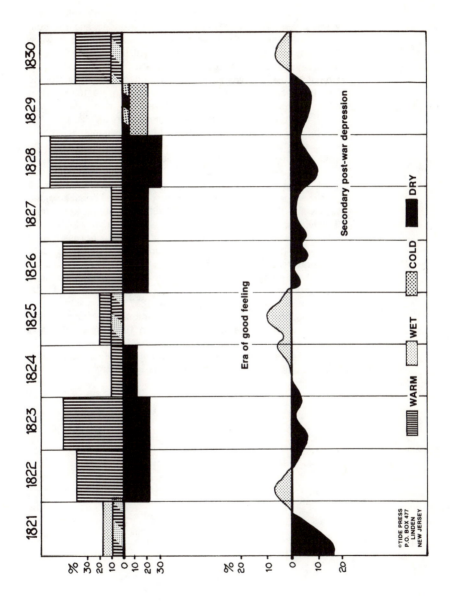

Era of good feeling

Secondary post-war depression

WARM   WET   COLD   DRY

Chart 5.   American Weather and Business Trends, 1831–1840

Notice the absence of warm-years in this chart signifying the warm phases of this 100-year cycle have ended and the cold phases have begun. Cold-wet 1831 and 1833 intervened between the warm-dry and the cold-dry phases of the long cycle, as is generally the case. The cold-wet phase was broken by warm 1832. One of the reasons why the world has been getting warmer for the last 100 years is that climate grew so cold in the 1830s that it reached what was presumably a 100 year low at that time.

The boom of 1830-1833 and the recovery at 1835 and 1836 belong to the same phase of the weather and economic cycle to which our 1950 boom belongs. It is the boom associated with the cold-wet phase of the 100-year cycle.

Climate turned dry suddenly and a depression developed in 1834. However, this time the economic recovery led the rainfall recovery. On the other hand, the main part of the boom coincided with wet 1836. It is quite possible that 1835 was actually wetter than is indicated.

Note that the dry times in the cold phases are not associated with as long depressions as occur during warm-dry times. Cool temperatures are more energizing than are warm temperatures, and tend to compensate in some measure for loss of vitality due to dry conditions.

Once more, as it turned dry, in 1837 a depression began. This time, however, economic or other factors were strong enough to cut across the weather factors and, in 1839, the weather and business trends ran counter to one another.

The principle of wet with booms and dry years with depressions works for 7 out of 10 years in this chart.

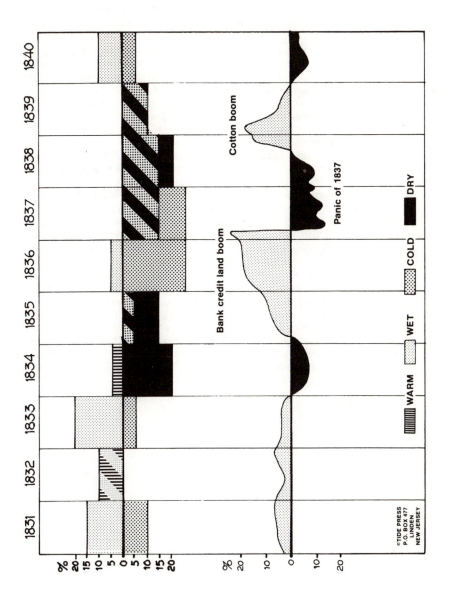

Cotton boom

Bank credit land boom

Panic of 1837

WARM   WET   COLD   DRY

1831 1832 1833 1834 1835 1836 1837 1838 1839 1840

% 20 15 10 5 0 5 10 15 20

% 20   10   0   10   20

©TIDE PRESS
P.O. BOX 477
LINDEN
NEW JERSEY

Chart 6. American Weather and Business Trends, 1841-1850

In a continuation of the cold-dry phase of the 100-year cycle, 8 years in this decade were either cold and / or dry. The cold periods of history are times of democratic reform, rebellion, revolution, civil war, and emancipation. The 1830s and 1840s are known for their reforms, as are the 1860s, 1880s, and 1890s which were also cold. Note the temporary rise in temperature in 1845 and 1846. Rises in temperature tend to produce international war and imperialism. The Mexican War occurred on this particular temperature rise.

Wet 1843 was associated with a rapid recovery from the bottom of a depression. Not infrequently a sudden change in temperature acts as a stimulant and overrides the effect of low rainfall as it seemed to do in 1845. Even with this variation or "exception", the peak of the boom in 1847 coincided with a peak in rainfall. The chances are almost certain that, even without the Mexican War there would have been a period of prosperity at this time, because rainfall and storminess produce that aggressiveness which in turn predisposes men to find, or create, economic incentives. Note again the association between dry and depression in 1848 and 1849. 1848 was cold world-wide and a year of revolutions.

The principle of wet booms and dry depressions works in 8 out of 10 years during the 1840s. Only one of the first 5 years of the decade was wet, and practically the entire half decade was occupied by a depression. During the 18 years from 1827 to 1845, 14 involved depressions. (When the originals of these charts were first prepared in 1951, we were approaching a similar era when Wheeler thought at least 2 out of 3 years would be spent in depressions.)

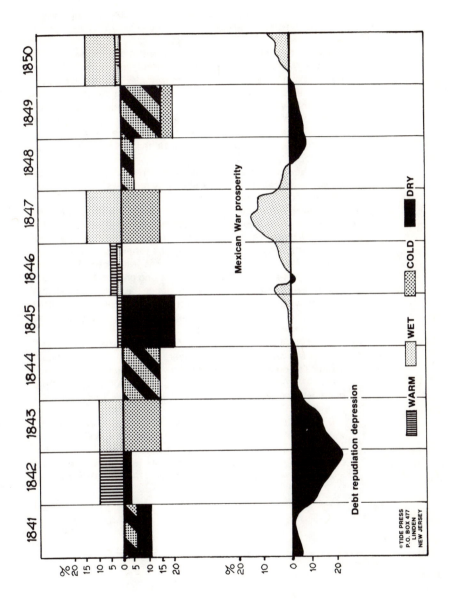

Debt repudiation depression

Mexican War prosperity

| WARM | WET | COLD | DRY |

© TIDE PRESS
P.O. BOX 477
LINDEN
NEW JERSEY

1841 1842 1843 1844 1845 1846 1847 1848 1849 1850

% 20 15 10 5 0 5 10 15 20

% 20 10 0 10 20

Chart 7. American Weather and Business Trends, 1851-1860

A secondary cycle appeared in the 1850s, creating a warm interruption of the cold phases of the 100-year cycle. On every rise of temperature of this sort throughout history, there has been a tendency for imperialism to break out. It did so this time. The Crimean War was a symptom of this trend, as was the American demand that Japan open her doors to trade. Notice that dryness increased as this warm period continued, so that a short warm-dry period followed the warm-wet one, which is usual regardless of the length of the cycle. During the latter part of the decade, governments became reactionary the world over, as they always do during warm-dry periods. In the United States the proslavery Dred Scott decision was a typical warm-dry event.

The California Gold Rush was a typical symptom of the dynamic, aggressive drive exhibited by societies everywhere on the climatic transition from cold-dry to warm-wet. The aggressiveness of the Prussians under Frederick the Great in the 1740s and 1750s, and the quarrels between France and England in which the United States participated, illustrate the same type of era brought about by weather trends on the shorter cycles. The "drive" characteristic of societies at this time is evidenced in the long boom from 1850 to 1857, which was strong enough to counteract the force of the weather moves. Yet, notice the interesting fact that each dry year caused a drop in business volume and precipitated incipient depressions — 1851, 1854, and finally a panic in 1857. The end of the boom started with dry 1856.

It is not surprising that in a young, growing nation, a "boost" such as was provided by the discovery of gold in California should produce a boom so vigorous that dry years had less than the usual effect. Nevertheless, that dry years are a powerful influence is demonstrated as effectively as if the depressions had fully matured.

Wet 1859 brought a recovery from the panic, and dry 1860 was associated with a drop again to the depression side.

In this chart, on a relative but not absolute basis, the principle of wet-year booms and dry-year depressions worked for 9 out of 10 years; on an absolute basis, 6 or 7 out of 10 years.

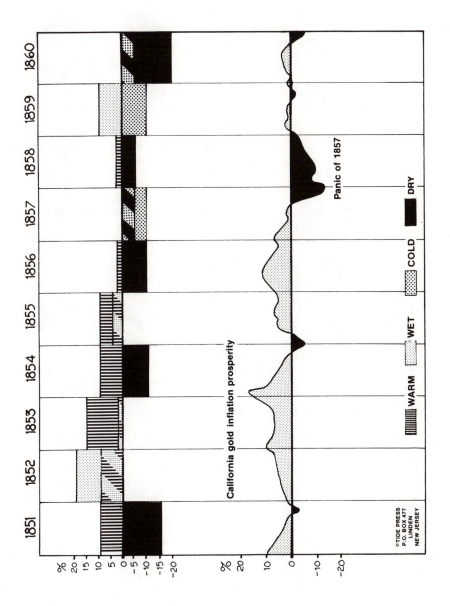

California gold inflation prosperity

Panic of 1857

WARM WET COLD DRY

©TIDE PRESS
P.O. BOX 477
LINDEN
NEW JERSEY

Chart 8. American Weather and Business Trends, 1861-1870

The warm-wet, then warm-dry phases of the short cycle as shown in Chart 7 were world-wide, as was the drop in temperature during the 1860s. However, Europe remained warmer than the rest of the world. The decline in temperature brought with it civil wars the world over, including the United States. There can be little question but that cold 1859 and 1860 paved the way for the precipitation of the war by intensifying the spirit of rebellion. The revival of rainfall in the second half of the 1860s was world-wide, as was the drop in temperature.

Again, when there are fewer dry years, there are fewer depression years. The drop in business activity in 1861 began the previous year and was associated with the onset of dryness. The outbreak of the war undoubtedly prevented a recovery in 1861, when it was wet although wars produce a certain kind of prosperity at any time. The rise in business volume through 1862 was presumably a result of the war. In 1864 and again 1916 to 1918, war maintained a boom against the influence of dry years. At the end of the war, there was the inevitable decline in business arising out of problems of conversion to a peacetime economy. The same thing happened on a mild scale in wet 1919 and in wet 1946.

The continuation of wet years was associated with mild prosperity most of the time in the latter half of the decade.

Notice, that the sudden drop in rainfall in 1867 was associated with a tendency toward a depression, even though rainfall still averaged wet. Then, dry 1870 produced a mild depression that probably would have continued but for the fact that 1871 turned wet again.

The rise in temperature at 1870 produced another tendency toward imperialism, as it had in 1846. This time in the form of the Franco-Prussian War. Under such circumstances, a minor war is almost sure to break out somewhere.

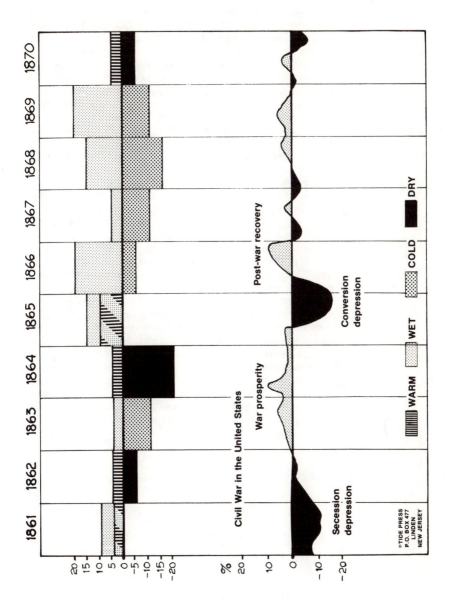

Chart 9. American Weather and Business Trends, 1871-1880

Cold-wet years in the early 1870s were again world-wide, as were the rise in temperature and the revival of rainfall in the second half of the decade. The year 1878 was famous for its excessive heat and rainfall on all five continents, including the tropics.

The main part of the warm-wet period in this second short cycle was followed by a conspicuous warm-dry year — again, the normal sequence but in miniature time intervals. The normal sequence after that is cold-wet, then cold-dry, and these developments can be seen as the trend in Chart 10.

The depression that began in the year 1870, associated with a return to dry times, did not last because climate turned wet again. While there were signs of instability during dry 1872, the fact that it was cold possibly helped to maintain the boom. Again, the climax of the boom was reached during a wet year, 1873.

In late 1873 economic factors overpowered the weather factors and produced a depression while it was still wet. For 10 years prosperity had prevailed and, as a consequence, serious overexpansion and inflation had occurred. Had 1874 been wet, there might have been an immediate rebound, but it was dry.

It is quite evident that the depression of the 1870s was intensified and prolonged by dryness and possible excessive heat as well. The boom of 1871 to 1873 was very vigorous and, because it was extreme, it called for a vigorous reaction on purely economic grounds. Mildly wet 1875 was evidently not strong enough to produce a recovery. Rainfall hit bottom in 1876, when the depression also hit bottom. Then, as rainfall revived the depression lessened. Perhaps the "boost" from the rainfall of 1878 cut across the effects of the heat and gave the recovery sufficient momentum to continue through dry 1879. At the same time, lowered production gave rise to a slowly accumulating demand for goods as needs accumulated. The overall picture is one of a nice balancing of climatic and economic causation. The recovery was stabilized by wet 1880.

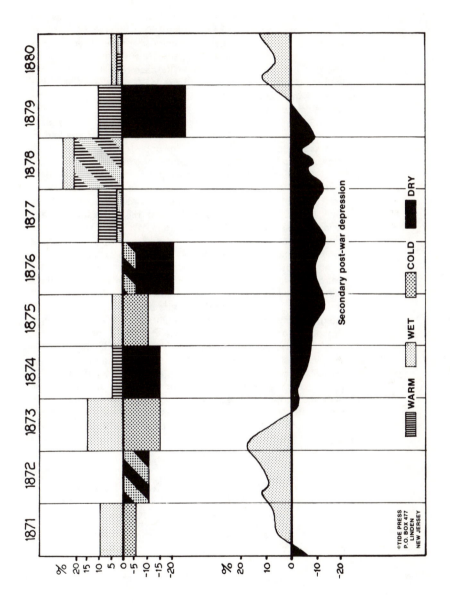

Secondary post-war depression

WARM · WET · COLD · DRY

© TIDE PRESS
P.O. BOX 477
LINDEN
NEW JERSEY

Chart 10. American Weather and Business Trends, 1881-1890

Once the warm wave was over, which was only an interruption of the cold phases of the 100-year cycle, the weather trends turned back to the major cold-dry phase. Then, on the sunspot cycle, climate warmed again as a sunspot minimum was approached in 1889. As is very often the case, rainfall revived along with temperature, for in the long run the two variables fluctuate together in a parallel fashion (except when it is temporarily warm-dry or cold-wet).

This decade was characterized by world-wide social, economic, and political reforms, all of the kind that resulted in increased liberty for the masses. The cold-dry period was world-wide, as was the warming at the end of the decade.

Recall that a period of prosperity matured during wet 1880. This period lasted until well into 1883. Unsteadiness developed in dry 1881, but during that year rainfall was nearly normal. Another peak in the boom occurred during wet 1882. The decline that followed was associated with dry 1883. While it is true that the depression of the middle 1880s centered in a dry period, as the overall results of this study would lead one to expect, wet 1884 failed to show any effect; the depression grew worse. Perhaps this was because the economically important eastern part of the United States, including New York, was actually dry in 1884. Generally speaking, however, prosperity and its opposite, depression, are integral, holistic conditions pertaining to the entire country. Prosperity does not appear to be generated or caused by conditions in any one isolated part. The recovery in 1886, when it was dry, was an unusual event and proves that at times economic and other nonmeteorological factors are more powerful than are the weather trends. Moreover, the brief and mild decline in 1888 occurred during a wet year. In short, for a time the business trends ran counter to the weather trends. In this decade only 4 out of 10 years strictly followed the general principle of wet boom years and dry depression years.

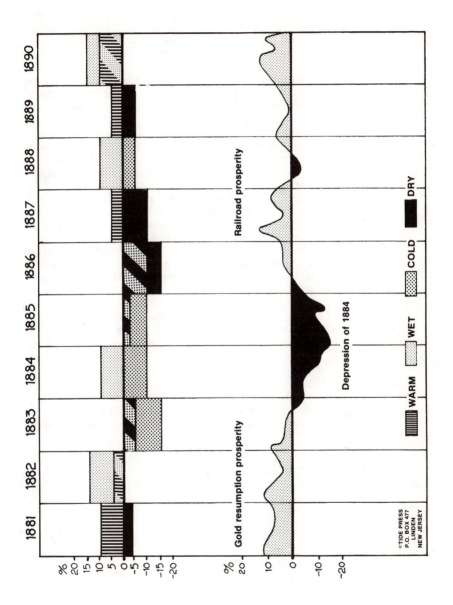

Chart 11.　American Weather and Business Trends.1891-1900

The last part of the long cold-dry phase of the 100-year cycle came during the 1890s. The bottom was reached in 1895. Already, in 1894, there had occurred a mild foretaste of what was to come; namely, the shift from the cold to the warm phases of the long cycle.

The drop in temperature in the early 1890s was world-wide, as was the tendency toward higher temperatures in the middle of the decade. Warmer temperatures on the approach to the twentieth century were also world-wide. If the weather trends had been measured in terms of averages, rather than the median, more years would show warm between 1895 and 1920; several borderline years that show cold in terms of the median show warm in terms of the average. However, 1898 was wet world-wide, 1899 was cold and 1900 was warm.

Although the year-by-year correlation between business and weather trends through the 1880s was poor, nevertheless the general trend of business paralleled the general trend of weather throughout the decade. The depression of 1884 and 1885 occurred in the center of the years 1883 to 1887 which averaged dry, and the periods of prosperity occurred at both ends of the decade when the weather trends averaged wet. During the 1890s the year-by-year correlation was much higher. The rule worked in practically 8 out of 10 years. A severe depression was associated with a 5 year drought period, the depression lasting exactly as long as the dry years lasted. The boom begun in the late 1880s continued as long as it remained wet and ended in a dry year. The temporary recovery in 1895 was mostly conditioned by economic as opposed to weather factors. The recovery associated with wet 1898 continued during dry 1899 due to the Spanish American War. Perhaps the drop in 1900 was a reaction to the end of the war. Notice again the tendency for depressions to be worse during warm-dry and cold-dry years. The long trend correspondence remains valid in the face of exceptions in the form of individual years.

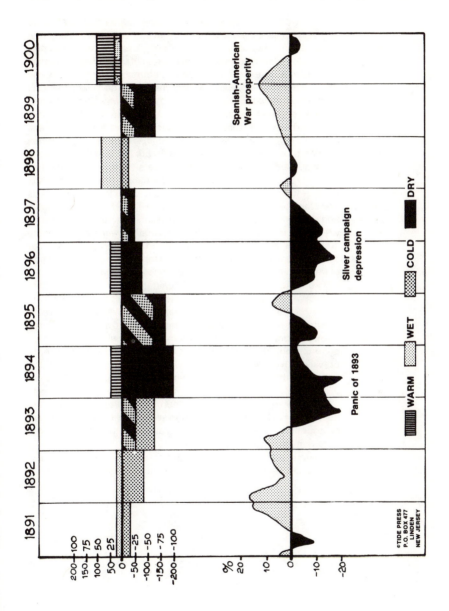

Panic of 1893

Silver campaign depression

Spanish-American War prosperity

WARM | WET | COLD | DRY

©TIDE PRESS
P.O. BOX 477
LINDEN
NEW JERSEY

Chart 12.   American Weather and Business Trends, 1901-1910

It would seem legitimate to say that the warm phases of the 100-year cycle really began in 1900, but this fact is not evident from the chart. Two factors prevent the warm phase from showing this. First, the median throws a certain number of slightly warm years to the cold side. The present standard of comparison includes as one of its sources the very warm years of the 1920s and 1930s. This long succession of warm years pulls the median away from its former position into higher temperatures, causing one to define as cold years those which were once defined as warm. To illustrate the same principle with the average, in 1920 the average annual temperature in New York was 51.8°F, but in 1950 it is 55°. As a consequence of this difference, years having temperatures between 51.8° and 55° that would have been called warm in 1920, were now called cold in 1950. According to the standards prevailing before the long 1930s heat wave, 1897, 1898, 1901, 1910, and 1918 would probably turn out warm over the country as a whole. In other words, one would say that the warm phases of the 100-year cycle really began just prior to 1900 but do not register this way because of the idiosyncracies inherent in the construction of the mathematical data. This warm phase was interrupted in 1902 before it proceeded very far and again in 1913.

We have gone into this matter because the evidence from history points to long eras of prosperity on the transition from cold to warm phases as long as rainfall remains good and temperatures average cool to moderately warm. This is what happened in general from 1898 to 1929 — 31 years during which prosperity prevailed over depressions. This is a time of golden ages and nation building, but also a time for world wars. Out of the 31 years, 23 were prosperous and 18 out of the 31 were wet, about a ratio of 3:2 in favor of prosperity. The depressions were short and the booms long. Three dry years during World War I were boom years on account of the war. The point to all this is that the long era of prosperity was predictable.

In this chart the principle of wet-year booms and dry-year depressions holds for 7 out of 10 years.

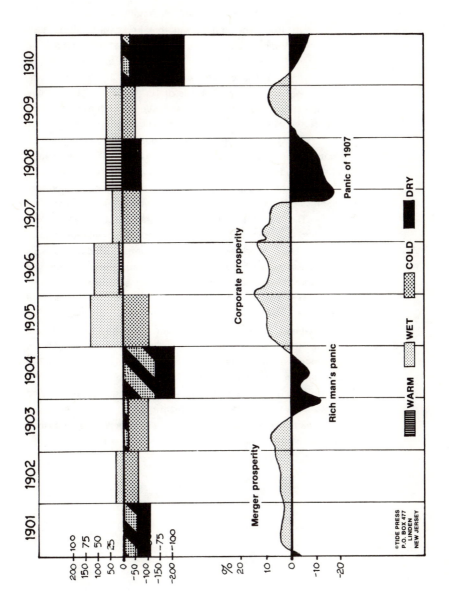

Merger prosperity

Corporate prosperity

Rich man's panic

Panic of 1907

WARM WET COLD DRY

Chart 13. American Weather and Business Trends, 1911-1920

The United States weather trend briefly became warmer and wetter in 1913. The imperialism that broke out around 1900 (Spanish-American War and Russo—Japanese War), on the rising and falling sides of a low warm-wet peak, now broke out again on the rising side of this warm-wet peak. This time the result was World War I. Because 1914 was dry in the United States, there presumably would have been a recession that year even without a war scare. War production maintained high volume through 3 dry years during which there is very little doubt but that a depression would have occurred had there not been a war at the time. Even as it was, production declined across the dry years and picked up when rainfall picked up. The rule of wet booms and dry depressions holds through 7 of the 10 years of this decade.

The cold years in the middle and early parts of the 1900s and the cold years in the second half of this decade both brought with them many outstanding democratic reforms, including women's suffrage at the federal level in the United States and several other of the more civilized nations of the world. Some 20 new democracies were formed at the end of World War I. There is little question but that the sharp drop in temperature either spurred on, or precipitated, the Russian Revolution, and the continued cold helped to bring on the revolution in Germany. But none of these democratic revolutions resulted in permanent democracies. The reason is to be seen in Chart 14. Climate turned warm-wet, then warm-dry. Such a sequence of weather trends has never failed historically to produce totalitarianism in some form or other. With a long warm period ahead, democracy in these new nations had little or no chance to take root.

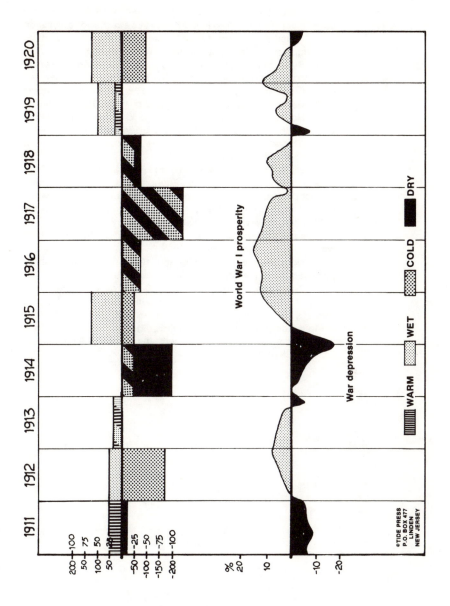

Chart 14. American Weather and Business Trends, 1921-1930

Notice the very sharp depression associated with extremely hot and dry 1921. For the United States this was the hottest year on record. Then came the so-called Coolidge era of prosperity, which Coolidge actually had nothing to do with. Out of 8 consecutive years, 6 were wet. No such sequence since 1794 — and we are safe in saying that no such sequence at any time in history — had failed to produce an era of prosperity. This was the last and the strongest warm-wet trend of the warm-wet phase of the 100-year cycle.

Now look at what happened in 1930 which was the driest year over the country, as a whole, of the 154 years covered in this study. This was also the year of the great crash, the most severe in the history of the country.

In this chart practically 9 of the 10 years follow the rule of wet booms and dry depressions. Economic factors were strong enough, apparently, to bring about a revival during dry 1924 when it was cold, and the momentum of the revival carried through dry 1925. Note, however, a fairly strong tendency for the volume of business to dip during that year. Evidently the dip at the end of 1927 was wholly economic in character.

Note that in 1923, 1926, and 1929, all wet years, there occurred the highest and broadest peaks in the boom.

The warm-wet phase of the 100-year cycle is now in full swing. While it suffers interruptions, they are not so long as formerly. Beginning with 1930 there were 10 consecutive years without a drop of temperature to the cold side. Contrast the 6 wet and 6 boom years on this chart with the 8 dry and 9 depression years in Chart 15.

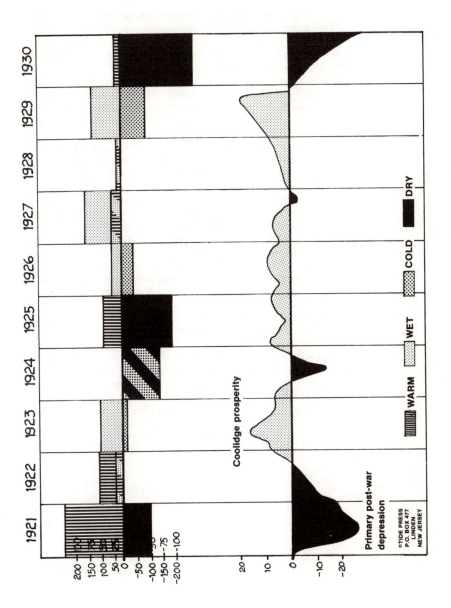

Primary post-war depression

Coolidge prosperity

WARM WET COLD DRY

©TIDE PRESS
P.O. BOX 477
LINDEN
NEW JERSEY

1921 1922 1923 1924 1925 1926 1927 1928 1929 1930

200 150 100 50 0 -50 -100 -150 -200
100 75 50 0 -50 -75 -100

20 10 0 -10 -20

Chart 15. American Weather and Business Trends, 1931-1940

A high official of the United States Weather Bureau once stated that nothing like the great heat and drought of the 1930s had ever happened before — according to the records possessed by the Weather Bureau — and hence, meteorologists had abandoned the hope of ever being able to make long-range forecasts by means of the cycle method. Contrary to the statement of this official, all of the rainfall and temperature records from both Europe and the United States that go back through the 1820s tell the story as it is pictured in Chart 4, and many of the records came from the publications of the United States Weather Bureau. Also, the chronicles of those times, abound in reports of excessive heat and dryness, and trees across America recorded dry years by forming narrow annual rings. Masses of miscellaneous information, together with tree rings, demonstrate recurrences of these warm-drought phases of the 100-year cycle back to ancient times.

The intervals between the major warm-dry phases of history are by no means constant, but they average 102.5 years from the fifth century A.D. to the present time. The main warm-dry periods centered on the following dates: 547 A.D., 613, 710, 817, 920, 1025, 1130, 1270, 1365, 1455, 1530, 1630, 1690, 1825, and 1935. Each of these phases prior to this last one, was followed shortly by a shift from the warm to the cold side of the 100-year cycle. Each was followed by an era of very evident commercial and business stagnation after a temporary period of prosperity had intervened during the cold-wet phase of the cycle. Each warm-dry phase was evidently associated with a major economic breakdown marked by unemployment, suffering, low production, and often state charity of some kind. Each warm-dry phase has also been associated, without exception, with a climax of despotism, dictators, New Deals, or a wave of socialism and communism. Hitler, Mussolini, and Stalin are typical hot-drought specimens along with Cambyses, Philip of Macedon, Domitian, Diocletian, Cnute the Mighty, William the Red, Tamerlane, and Peter the Cruel.

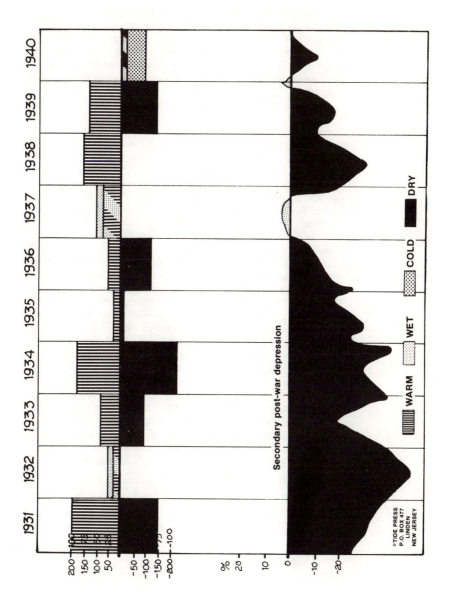

Secondary post-war depression

WARM | WET | COLD | DRY

200 150 100 75 50 25 -50 -100 -150 -200 -100

% 20 10 0 -10 -20

1931 1932 1933 1934 1935 1936 1937 1938 1939 1940

Chart 16. American Weather and Business Trends, 1941-1950

Turn back to Chart 15 and note that during cooler and wetter 1932 there was a tendency for the decline in business volume to reverse and start up. The reversal had gathered enough momentum to carry it part way through dry 1933. Then decline set in again. After 1934 the trend in rainfall was upward, and so also was the business trend, the mild recovery culminating in a lone wet year, 1937.

Obviously the war situation itself would have been sufficient to produce a boom through the wet 1940s. Under ordinary circumstances there probably would not have been a revival to the boom side in 1941, but recovery would have waited until 1942. The war not only lifted business to the boom side in 1941; it probably prevented a decline during dry 1943. The drop in 1946, of course, was due to conversion to a peace time economy. The principle of wet-year booms and dry-year depressions worked in this chart for 6 out of 9 years on which complete United States weather data are available.

Notice that 3 out of the 9 years were cold. This is the first showing of the downward trend that will eventually take the country, and the world as a whole, over to the cold side for a prolonged period of time. In order to obtain a glimpse of the pattern of weather trends that lies ahead, turn back to Charts 5 and 6, to the 1830s and 1840s. The years 1831 to 1836 correspond to 1941 to 1950. For a glimpse of what presumably lies ahead in the way of business trends, look at the years 1837 to 1845!

Most of the "experts" have been saying right along that we will continue to enjoy prosperity for an indefinite period, that there is no real depression in sight in the foreseeable future. Some tell us that our improved means of production and the rise in population will keep us in a perpetual boom. This sounds very much like the misguided optimism of the late 1920s. Such pronouncements are dangerous in the extreme. The weather patterns that will bring the country into a long depression era during which 2 out of 3 years will be depression years, have repeated themselves 26 times since the days of Ancient Greece. They are not likely to stop now.

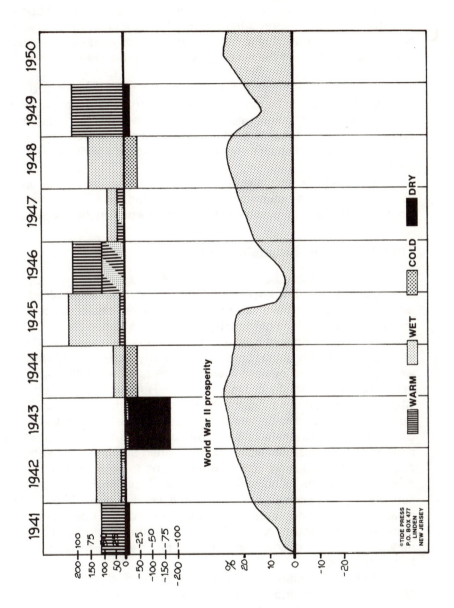

World War II prosperity

200—100
150—75
100—50
50—25
0
-50—-25
-100—-50
-150—-75
-200—-100

%
20
10
0
-10
-20

1941 1942 1943 1944 1945 1946 1947 1948 1949 1950

WARM   WET   COLD   DRY

©TIDE PRESS
P.O. BOX 477
LINDEN
NEW JERSEY

In terms of direction of change the correspondance between cold-dry years and depressions was 66%. When trends or "periods" are considered, the correspondance between wet years and booms and dry years and depressions was 84%. That is, when the criterion was taken that, for the rule to hold, the majority of years occupied by a boom must be wet and the majority occupied by a depression must be dry.

Because cold temperatures in themselves tend to be invigorating, it was to be expected that the correspondance between cold-dry and depression years would be the lowest of the four combinations. In other words, it was to be expected that cool temperatures would offset the lack of storminess as a factor in creating depressions.

When entire eras are considered, correspondance has been 100% since 1794 as determined by positions on the climatic cycle — booms during wet transitions and depressions during the dry phases.

Theories of the Business Cycle

Meteorological business cycle theories go back to British economist, W. Stanley Jevons, who concluded in 1875 that variations in the sun's atmosphere, associated with sunspots, produced the rhythmical fluctuations of industry. Later, in the United States, Henry L. Moore concluded that business fluctuations were associated with fluctuations in agricultural crops. In his theory, however, the effect of weather trends on business was indirect, exerted through the influence of rainfall on crops. Ellsworth Huntington believed that vitality or variations in health were important factors in creating fluctuations in business trends. Carlos Garcia-Mata and Felix I. Shaffner demonstrated a close correspondance between nonagricultural business activity in the United States and the sunspot cycle. Their conclusion was that variations in solar radiation may produce variations in human vitality. This is probably true, but the sunspot cycle is both an electrical and a weather cycle, and it is not clear whether its effects on man's behavior are due to the electrical or meteorological factors or both. Edgar L. Smith concluded that both meteorological and solar factors are important in producing the business cycle.

Most economists consider meteorological theories to be fanciful, quackish, and unproved. The obvious explanation is that economists have never bothered to check the facts for themselves. However, in light of Charts 1 to 16, as well as the other historical studies summarized in this volume, it hardly seems necessary to further comment on the prevailing skepticism toward the meteorological approach. There is always a weather factor affecting human vitality, which, we believe, predisposes the business world to find economic excuses or reasons for their judgements and policies. The immediate causes are economic in the sense that economic processes are the instruments of booms and depressions, but how the essential instruments will function at a certain time depends largely on the effect of weather trends on man's vitality and moods. The economic processes are therefore the results of man's own choosing. The facts simply defy any interpretation of random correlations between business and weather trends. The probability of only a coincidental relationship between the two series of events is fantastically low.

Obviously, business trends cannot time weather trends. But the two events are consistent in relation to one another, and have been throughout history, generally with little or no leading or lagging. It is the timing of the economic changes or shifts in trends that no economic theory seems able to explain. Either weather trends time the business trends and condition the energy basic to business fluctuations, or else both weather and business trends are timed by a third, still more fundamental factor common to both and as yet unknown — such as an electronic or electromagnetic factor.

Production, in the last analysis, can be seen as a matter of man's choice; a matter of judgement. This view holds that man is the instrument of production and the economic world is largely a world of his creation. He may decide the time is ripe for production and expansion, or that conditions require contraction. But, along with the majority of his associates, why should he decide at a certain time that it is safe to produce or invest? Why are these decisions made independently at the same time all over the world? And why are decisions to cut production or refrain from investing also made independently at the same time on a world-wide basis?

Some theorists hold that booms and depressions get underway without any significant amount of conscious deciding. The business world simply expands or contracts, finding the incentives to do so without much, if any, deliberation. The mood simply changes.

Another approach stresses there is no doubt that certain types of social and political events, wars, and scientific inventions profoundly affect business trends. A world war, for example, creates a huge volume of production. But booms also occur in the absence of any known economic cause. This would seem to be good reason for believing that there is none; for if there were, the economists ought to have been smart enough to have found it by now.

Still other theories proclaim that new inventions, new commodities, and new markets based on the availability of new credit help produce booms and rising prices. However, why should not the innovations, industrial revolutions, new commodities, and new markets also be subordinate to weather trends? These phenomena emerge regularly on wet climatic transitions, and at no other time. What determines the strength and duration of these innovations and, hence, times the turning points? The new markets theory assumes these processes are cyclic, but why should they be, and what determines the lengths of the periods? Again, it seems, we must fall back on weather trends for the ultimate answer.

Certain theories stress that investment spending by promoters and producers, when not accompanied by a corresponding saving by the community, will create a boom. On the other hand, saving in the absence of capital investment tends to produce a depression. Regardless of the economic merits or demerits of this kind of theory, why should people prefer to save at certain times and spend at others? Saving or spending is a matter of mood or attitude. What produces the mood and what causes it to change? No economic theory to date has supplied the answers, whereas weather trends do offer an answer.

We are also told that a given level of consumption depends on the amount of current investment; but this depends on some kind of inducement to invest. In turn, the inducement to invest depends on the marginal efficiency of capital, which depends on the entrepreneurs' expectations. Hence, their expectations are raised or lowered by their projections of the future. And so we go around and around without hitting on anything basic or fundamental until we return to the producers' moods. But again, what causes the high spirits that create booms and the low spirits that produce depressions?

Once a boom is underway, we are told, conventional habits of consumption cause the community to spend a diminishing proportion of an increasing income, which, in turn, supposedly causes a reversal of the expansion process. But here again the economic theorists are in trouble offering no explanation of why conventional habits of consumption should cause a reversal at times within a year of the onset of a boom, at other times in 3 or even 10 years. What alters mankind's conventional habits in this manner? The answer would seem to be that people spend more when they have vitality and less when they are lethargic. Again, we must return to weather trends, this time with the assumption that reversals in weather trends will reverse spending patterns by changing people's vitality levels.

Economists are generally the first to admit they, as yet, have no satisfactory theory of business cycles. They are also the first to admit that the turning points are the most difficult features of business trends to explain. What changes the direction of a trend? In this connection the existance of a universal timing factor seems to be vital. Various economic factors may indeed contribute to trend reversals as well as to the trends themselves. Different factors will contribute at different times, but all must have something in common to produce the same kind of result. What is that something in common? Most economic theories rely on some kind of starter or primer but there is little or no agreement as to what that starter is. The facts favor weather trends. They appear to be the common denominator that gives various economic processes, whatever they may be, the variable energy factor that, regardless of the specific economic facts, determines the fact and timing of the reversal, and the duration of the boom or depression.

Regardless, then, of the economic factors involved, something fundamental is obviously missing in all purely economic business cycle theories. It is not the monetary factor, nor bank credit, nor the levels of production, spending, or saving, nor a fading or a waxing of expectations, nor the level of interest rates or wages, nor inventory levels of consumers' goods, nor innovation, nor is it the fault of the producer, broker, farmer, political leader, or any one class of people. All these, when relevant, are secondary factors at best. The one basic common factor is an energy factor that is conditioned by the weather trends.

An Important Qualification

These conclusions in no way attempt to supplant or deny those features of the various economic theories of business cycles based on obvious facts. There is not the slightest doubt but that numerous economic factors are essential to business cycles. But doubt legitimately enters the picture when it is assumed that economic factors alone, either singly or collectively, can adequately explain business cycles.

The theory of climatically conditioned business cycles, as advanced in this chapter, is offered not only as a supplement to the economic factors, but as a supplement without which no economic theory is complete. This writer believes the reason why no purely economic theory has ever been satisfactory is that no purely economic cause of business cycles exists. On the other hand, neither the letter nor the spirit of this study would be interpreted correctly by assuming the denial of economic causation as a partial explanation of business cycles. Surely the day has passed when a scientist would attempt to explain an event in terms of a single cause. Causes always function in integrated patterns and configurations. They come from the whole of which the event is a part. The sooner science agrees that economic events are not just due to economic causes, but also to causes from a larger whole, and the sooner it stresses the noneconomic causes as being as important as the economic — in some respects even more important — the sooner will business cycles be understood and their occurrance successfully predicted.

Supporting Evidence for the Meteorological Theory of Business Cycles

The following evidence supports the conclusion that the basic underlying factors in business cycles are the stimulating and debilitating effects of weather trends; not through their effects on agricultural products, but through direct effects on man's own constitution and mentality. Many of these points have been presented at length in the literature of human ecology but have never before been integrated into a unified theory.

1. The most advanced civilizations are found in cool, moist climates. That this combin ation of climatic factors produces more advanced peoples is a fact that has been recognized since ancient times
2. The physiologically largest people are found in this same cool, moist belt, which is also where the greatest crop yields per acre are found.
3. Species by species, the largest varieties of wild animals are found in cool as opposed to warm regions. However, temperatures can become too cold for animals just as it can be too cold for most plant life.
4. Other things being equal, storminess is known to enhance human vitality, activity and alertness.
5. Optimum temperatures are known to exist for animal and human vitality, efficiency, health, and fertility.

6. People the world over are known to vary in health, vitality, and fertility, depending on the climate of the region in which they live.
7. People the world over are known to vary in health, vitality, and fertility with the seasons of the year.
8. Longer term climatic cycles reveal the same patterns as do the annual seasons of the year — warm-wet (spring), warm-dry (summer), cold-wet (autumn), and cold-dry (winter).
9. People the world over are known to be more active during the more moderate, cooler, and wetter phases of climatic cycles than in the warmest and driest phases. It is wettest when temperatures are moderate to cool on transitions in the climatic cycle, especially during the 100-year cycle. These are times when cultural achievement is highest and when the best leadership is evident. These are the only regular times of prosperity.
10. People the world over are known to be less healthy, less active, less fertile, and less stable behaviorally under tempera ture extremes, as during the warm-dry, and to a considerable but lesser extent, the cold-dry phases of the 100-year cycle. These are the only regular times of economic depression.
11. Since 1794, eras of prosperity in the United States have coincided with eras of maximum vitality, as measured by cultural achievement, wars, and many other forms of human activity. These dynamic, prosperous periods occur regularly on the climatic transitions when it is wet and temperatures are moderate, and do not occur at any other time.
12. Conversely, since 1794, eras of depression have coincided with eras of limited cultural achievement and often shabby

human behavior such as despotism, socialism, and communism on the one hand and anarchism on the other. These are, respectively, the warm-dry and cold-dry phases of the climatic cycle. Eras of depression do not occur at any other time.

13. Eras of prosperity, which are climatically wet, coincide with eras of high birth rates in both domestic and wild animals and in humans, thus suggesting a vitality factor. Economics cannot explain a consistently higher birth rate in animals at these times.

14. Eras of depression, which coincide with dry periods, also coincide with eras of low birth rates both in humans and animals. Economic factors cannot explain the lowered birth rates in animals. Moreover, whole empires of animal life have died or greatly thinned out during the hot and dry phases of long climatic cycles.

15. The devitalizing effects of excessive heat are well known, as is the necessity for living more moderately and doing less work when climate is warmer.

16. Prices are consistently higher during the wet phase of the 7-year rainfall cycle, and lower during the dry phase.

17. The crest phase of the 9-year price cycle is dominated by wet years and the trough phase by dry years. The 9-year price cycle is a rainfall cycle.

18. The expanding side of the 18-year real estate cycle is wet; the contracting side is dry. The 18-year business cycle is integrated with the 18-year rainfall cycle. In other words, the 18-year business cycle is a rainfall cycle.

19. The sequence of booms and depressions in the United States since 1794, with few exceptions, has been a sequence of wet and dry periods.

20. Even single wet years are frequently associated with single years of business

revival, and single dry years with single years of depression.

21. Most of the peaks in the 680-year British wheat price curve have corresponded with wet periods in history, and most of the troughs with dry periods. (This will be illustrated and documented in a separate publication.)

22. There are many documented eras of both prosperity and depression in history. All the known prosperous eras have been wet and all the known depression eras have been dry.

23. A continuous alternation from eras of evident prosperity to eras of evident depression and back again, four times in each 100-year climatic cycle (two eras of prosperity and two of depression) can be traced back through 27 cycles to 600 B.C. Without exception the prosperous times have occurred when the evidence points to wet phases of the cycle, and the depressions when the evidence points to dry phases.

24. The same cultural data that could, if necessary, correctly identify the eras of prosperity and depression during the last 200 years, can also be used to identify and time the corresponding eras throughout history, even in the absence of economic data as such. However, the economic facts themselves leave no doubt concerning the alternating eras.

25. It is not difficult to see how weather factors work as energizers. When man has been energized by the weather, he is more active and alert; possesses a more powerful drive; has greater and higher aspirations; is more optimistic; possesses better judgement; has more imagination, self-confidence and confidence in his fellow men, the business world, and society in general. Under these conditions he will

find or create economic incentives and reasons for doing things. He will use readily available economic processes, tools and instruments which at other times would lie idle, or remain non-existent. Beyond the necessities, economic processes are secondary to one's mood, alertness, will and imagination. They exist when one creates them and not otherwise. People make the monetary system flexible when they want it to be and inflexible at other times. People are willing bankers when their energy level promotes this feeling and unwilling bankers when their energy level declines. They expect profits when they feel optimistic and losses when low levels of vitality makes them pessimistic and destroys their faith. They demand expansion when stimulated and contraction when depressed.

26. Once set in motion, economic processes behave under certain rules of their own, which cut across and interact with the weather factors. It is the same with political processes and international relations. But weather trends are basic to these other trends.

27. The weather factors are sufficiently well synchronized with economic and business events to be the main primers and timers of business cycles.

28. Since economic processes are not the only forms of collective human behavior conditioned and timed by weather trends — in fact, since everything else that is basic and that is done by man varies with the weather — it is hardly thinkable that business trends should be exempt.

The conclusion is drawn, therefore, that weather trends are essential to any business cycle theory because of the direct effects they have on human vitality and intelligence.

Summary

In this study a comparison has been made between United States weather trends since 1794 and the business cycle as measured in terms of Ayres' Index of American Industrial Activity.

a. There is, in round numbers, a 74% correspondance, on a year to year basis, between wet and boom years on the one hand and dry and depression years on the other.

b. The highest correspondance occurs between boom and cold-wet years; namely 85%.

c. The next highest correspondance is between boom and warm-wet years; namely, 78%.

d. Correspondance between warm-dry and depression years is 75%.

e. Correspondance between cold-dry and depression years is 56%.

f. The 56% correlation is not the exception to the rule it appears to be. Many studies pertaining both to humans and animals show that cool temperatures are in themselves invigorating, regardless of rainfall. A poorer correspondance between cold-dry years and depressions is therefore to be expected because the stimulant effect of cool temperatures tends to offset the depressant effects of low rainfall.

g. When, for the rule to hold, the criterian is that the majority of years occupied by a boom should be wet and the majority of years occupied by a depression should be dry, the correspondance between all wet phases and booms, and all dry phases and depressions, is 85%.

A boom era was defined as a period on a climatic transition during which boom years outnumbered depression years. Eight such eras are distinguishable in United States history since 1794. Without exception, these were the wetter periods.

a. The first boom occurred from 1790 until about 1818 on on the transition from the cold to the warm side of the 100-year cycle, and into the warm-wet phase of the cycle.

b. The second boom occurred on the reverse transition, from the warm to the cold side of the cycle in the early 1830s. This was the cold-wet phase of the 100-year cycle.

c. The third boom occurred in the late 1840s and early 1850s on a secondary cycle and transition from cold to warm as rainfall shifted to the wet side. This secondary cycle identified the emergence of a 10-year warm period through the 1850s.

d. The fourth boom occurred on the reverse transition of the short cycle in the 1860s as temperatures shifted back to the cold side and rainfall picked up again after a lull in the late 1850s.

e. The fifth boom occurred on another secondary short cycle transition as climate turned warm and rainfall picked up again in the 1870s.

f. The sixth boom was on the transition of the second short cycle back to the cold, as rainfall picked up in the 1880s.

g. The seventh boom occurred from 1898 to the 1920s on a major climatic transition from the cold to the warm side of the 100-year cycle and lasted, as such eras generally do, as long as the warm-wet phase of the 100-year cycle lasted.

h. The eighth boom in the early 1950s, like the one in the early 1830s, is occurring on the reverse side of the 100-year cycle as the warm-dry phase is changing to cold-wet. The present 1950s boom is a feature of the cold-wet phase of the 100-year cycle.

In terms of eras, therefore, there have been no exceptions since 1794 to the rule that boom eras average wet.

A depression era is defined as one in which, for any period from 5 to 20 years, the time spent in depressed economic conditions exceeds the time spent in periods of prosperity. These periods are identified by their positions at the crests and troughs of the temperature curve. There have been six such periods since 1794, four major and two minor. The major ones occurred on the main 100-year cycle, the minor ones on secondary cycles. With one exception, these eras occurred during times that averaged dry. The one exception was a minor period in the late 1870s.

    a. The first of the depression eras occurred in the 1820s during the warm-dry phase of the 100-year cycle. This was a major depression associated with a major phase of the climatic cycle.

    b. The second depression occurred in the late 1830s and early 1840s during predominantly cold-dry times. This was a major depression period, associated with a major phase of the 100-year climatic cycle.

    c. The third depression was short but is included because it was associated with the warm-dry phase of a short cycle in the second half of the 1850s. The depression was not as severe as might have been expected, probably because poor conditions were mitigated by the opening of the American West to mass settlement.

    d. The fourth was the long depression of the 1870s. In terms of the weather cycle pattern, there should have been a warm-dry phase at this time. Instead, there were three very dry and three wet years making this a minor era.

    e. The fifth depression occurred in the 1890s during the end of the 100-year cycle's cold-dry phase. The cold-wet and cold-dry phases of this cycle had been interrupted twice, once in the 1850s and again in the 1870s, by reversals to the warm side, with the invariable recoveries in rainfall and business on the transitions back and forth. This was a major era.

f. There was a tendency toward depression from 1908 to 1911, in another secondary cycle, when dryness and coolness prevailed.

g. The sixth and most recent (from the vantage point of the early 1950s) depression era, a major one repeating the pattern of the 1820s, occurred in the 1930s during the warm-dry phase of the 100-year cycle.

In terms of eras, then, there have been no exceptions since 1794 to the rule that depressions average dry.

There is a conspicuous 100-year cycle of nation-building and nation-falling that is also a climatic cycle, and has been traced back to 600 B.C. There are two places on this cycle when prosperous times can be expected with almost absolute certainty, and two places where depressions can be fully expected. The prosperous times occur on the transitions from dry to wet and continue into the respective warm-wet and cold-wet phases of the cycle. The depressions occur during the dry phases of the cycle at temperature maxima and minima respectively.

a. Since 1794 booms have occurred on all transitions from cold to warm and warm to cold and into the wet phases of the cycles and, regularly, at no other times. Depressions have occurred during most of the warm-dry and cold-dry periods since 1794 and, regularly, at no other times.

b. The two major wet and two major dry periods of the 100-year cycle were traced back to the sixth century, B.C. From the types of rulers and events prevailing in these four periods it was evident, without specific economic documents, that the major boom and depression eras can be identified throughout history. Human behavior has been similar in pattern in each of the repeating phases, and in each case the pattern resembles that of the last two cycles.

c. From this it can be concluded that prosperity and depression eras are predictable if the weather cycles continue to behave in the future as they have in the past.

d. We have said that eras of prosperity regularly occur only during wet periods. These eras are of two kinds. One is associated with nation-building, imperialism, industrial revolutions, mergers, the growth of monopoly, and a trend toward socialism; the other with nation-falling, insurrections, democratic reforms, and a trend back toward individualism. Both eras are associated with underlying waves of optimism and assertiveness. The first is optimism in regard to national destiny; the second is optimism in regard to individual destiny.

e. We have said that eras of depression occur only during dry periods and are of two types. The first, characterizing warm-phase depressions, is a break-down of the economic system at the end of a nation-building period, when centralizing trends reach a climax economically and politically. This depression is characterized by state paternalism, oppression, and socialistic or communistic trends. The second type, characterizing a cold-phase depression, is associated with the collapse of an individualistic economy during periods of inadequate government and trends toward anarchy and chaos.

f. Each of the four eras, two prosperous and two depressed have occured repetitively in the 100-year climatic cycle since 600 B. C.

It has been seen that booms and depressions are not isolated phenomena, independent of the cultural pattern prevailing at any given time in history. Economic facts and principles, like specific forms of government, specific styles in art, and specific concepts in science, are all subordinate to this cultural pattern as a whole. In each case the detail is subordinate to the pattern, the part to the whole.

The details of these vast changes including the vacillation between boom and depression, do not occur independently in an isolated manner, nor can they be explained by means of principles available only within the field or area in question. For example, principles of government will not explain the sequence of political events; what is happening in art cannot be explained by the principles of art; what is happening in business cannot be explained by business or economic principles; what is happening to costumes cannot be explained by principles of design. The explanation must come from factors that pertain to the whole of which each specified field is a part.

Specific patterns of government, specific forms of art, specific theories in science, and specific economic phenomena such as production, consumption, monetary systems, innovation, interest, credit, and so forth, are all secondary and incidental, albeit essential. Whatever phenomena exist at a given time are instruments through which forces transcendent to the phenomena are working. In the case of booms and depressions, economic phenomena and forces are the essential instruments through which man's level of energy finds expression. In this theory of the business cycle, then, monetary systems, interest, production, consumption, credit, and securities are means to ends, instruments through which man finds and creates incentives and reasons for a particular course of action. The fundamental factor, however, is the level of vitality in terms of which man either accepts or rejects the incentives. In all this the economic factors themselves play an essential but secondary and variable part.

There has never been a satisfactory economic theory of the business cycle for the basic reason that no such theory can exist; business cycles are not simply or even basically economic phenomena. This does not mean these are mutually exclusive concepts; there could no more be a business cycle without economic phenomena than there could be walking without legs, for protoplasm is basic to legs as energy is basic to economic processes.

The most fundamental of all single, known factors involved in the business cycle seems to be the fluctuating energy level produced by weather trends.

> a. This fluctuating energy level is the only factor, as far as we know, common to all booms and depressions, save under special circumstances such as war.

However, it can be demonstrated that wars are also subordinate to the weather pattern.

b. The weather factor is the only one common to all peoples and all times in history, and no factor not common to all peoples, cultures, and times in history will account for the business cycle because the business cycle is as old as history. It is a mistake to think of business cycles exclusively in terms of current phenomena such as modern banks, capitalism, stocks, and the like. These are passing and incidental, while periods of prosperity and depression have occurred regularly throughout recorded history.

c. The weather factor is the only one relating economic cycles to corresponding cycles in numerous other areas of human behavior in the manner that the existing synchronizations demand. It would be absurd to attempt a final explanation of each different cycle by different means — a political explanation for the political cycle, an aesthetic explanation for the art cycle, an economic explanation for the business cycle. This approach would disregard the most important feature about them, namely, that they are all aspects of one cycle.

d. The weather factor is the only possible means of interpreting the consistent correspondance between weather and business trends.

e. Specific economic factors are not the basic factors, not because they are unessential, but because they lack the necessary generality.

f. Economic factors frequently cut across weather factors, making the entire community more sensitive to weather trends in one area than another, or at one time as opposed to another; thus creating slight leads and lags or clear exceptions to the usual correspondance. Thus economic factors alone will reduce the correspondance, on a year by year basis, from 100% down to a lesser figure according to the yardstick used. But in the long run the rainfall curve and business volume and price curves follow one another continuously.

g. Business trends vary consistently with weather trends. Prosperity ordinarily lasts as long as rainy periods last and stops when precipitation falls. Depressions last as long as dry periods last and end when it starts raining again. Time after time, single wet years will be associated with single boom years, and single dry years with single depression years.

h. On average, depressions are 50% worse in intensity during warm-dry than during cold-dry years, evidently because during warm-dry years annual temperatures are much too high for normal human vitality. On the other hand, it can also become too cold for normal vitality. Extremes in temperatures are associated with both dry geographic areas and dry times.

i. It turns out, therefore, that instead of being a fanciful, quackish theory, the meteorological theory, assuming business and weather trends to be inseparably and causally related, is an evident prerequisite to any successful explanation of the business cycle.

The meteorological theory is important to the businessman from a practical standpoint for it opens up the possibility of long range business forecasting based on long range weather forecasting.

We have evaluated the agricultural theory of the business cycle and have found it unsatisfactory, as many economists have shown. While it is true that crops are better during times of prosperity, it is because the same weather conditions that produce vitality in people also produce vitality in crops. Huntington pointed this out when he observed the greatest yield per acre of potatoes, wheat, corn, or rice came from the same geographic areas that produced the largest, most intelligent, and most prolific people.

The agricultural theory leaves out the most important fact of all; namely, that weather trends affect people directly, and only incidentally through crops. To be sure, when people are hungry as a result of droughts, they are weakened in health and vitality. They have a much better chance to be strong when their food supply is ample. Good crops undoubtedly help, but that crop yields alone could produce booms and depressions through their effect on man's health is hardly tenable; for it is well known that during intense heat people and animals eat less and will even develop dietary deficiencies with an abundance of food in front of them.

Moreover, periods of prosperity and depression are associated with rainfall regardless of the ratio of agriculture to other kinds of production in the economic order. In short, there is no evidence that the more agricultural countries today, or the more agricultural periods of history, are any more prosperous than are any other countries or centuries. On the contrary, there is more prosperity today with a smaller percentage of the economy concerned with agriculture than in previous ages when agriculture dominated economic processes. The relationship of business to rainfall goes back into history, remaining the same regardless of the relative importance of agricultural production.

Carrying the argument further, we note that the fluctuations of business and weather occur simultaneously. There is no time lag for agriculture to affect the business structure to the extent of producing booms and depressions.

Furthermore, the short-run effects of agriculture are the opposite from those that the agricultural theory requires. Reports of good crops send prices down temporarily, and reports of bad crops send prices up, but in the long run, the relationship between crops and prices is just the opposite as will be documented in a future publication. It would appear, then, that if agriculture did have an appreciable effect on the total price structure, or on business volume, the short-term influences would cancel out the long term ones.

Economists have not been able to agree on whether agriculture is cause or effect. Does a boom produce prosperity on the farm, or does prosperity on the farm produce a boom? Moreover, farmers plant more at certain times than at others, and hence have larger crops at certain times, and these are the same times that businessmen are expanding their businesses. The one does not cause the other, except incidentally. It is all simultaneous. The main cause is common both to the farmer and the businessman; namely, greater aspiration due to higher energy levels. Both men are at the same time willing to work harder and take greater risks.

Millions of people simultaneously come to life, or as suddenly lose vitality. All start producing, or demanding work; all start consuming more at the same time. All think and talk more business. Better crops have little or nothing to do with the awakening of the farmer, or the businessman, or the laborer, or the consumer. Nobody's diet has changed, but a moderate to cool wet period has set in.

Finally, weather trends create two types of booms and two types of depressions, while agriculture remains the same from one boom or depression to the next. Warm-wet booms are not the same as cold-wet booms, and warm-dry depressions are not the same type as cold-dry depressions.

We repeat our main conclusion, therefore, that, through their direct control of expendable energy levels, weather trends condition those varying degrees of aspiration and activity that lead men either to find and create economic incentives and processes, or fail to find and create them. In one case there will be a boom and in the other a depression.

Professor Alvin H. Hansen of Harvard University believes the oscillatory nature of the business fluctuation can now be pretty well explained. This includes the turning points and presumably their timing. He believes booms are limited by a falling marginal efficiency of capital. Available investment becomes progressively more scarce the longer the boom lasts. New investment opportunities are exploited more rapidly than the normal rate of economic growth. When investment falls off, income recedes by a magnified amount. As a consequence, the boom dies a natural death. The relation of consumption to income is such that normally a certain rate of change in the relationship between them contributes to the oscillation. Thus, in a depression, as real income falls, consumption falls less than income. In this way the forces producing the contraction are lessened. Then as the rate of decline slackens, the forces contributing to the decline weaken. In the end, continued technical progress opens up new investment opportunities.

All this, of course, is of necessity an oversimplification of the economist's position; nevertheless, Professor Hansen, along with his predecessors from whom he drew his theory, begs the final question. Why do the self-limiting factors operate more slowly or rapidly in some depressions than in others? What determines the arrival of the cycle at the critical point where the reversal starts? What determines the rate of change of correspondence between consumption and investment that is supposed to time the reversal? Why should these internal processes, rates of change, multipliers, accelerators, consumption functions, slopes, and all the rest harmonize so conveniently most of the time with weather trends? If weather trends have nothing to do with all this, then a terrific and incredible cosmic conspiracy of some kind must be at the bottom of the matter!

We are told in Hansen's theory that the economic structure is so constituted that wave-like movements tend to fall between fairly well defined upper and lower limits, and that these facts and relationships are rigorously disclosed by the construction of economic diagrams and models. In other words, external factors are unnecessary. But when all is said and done, one's imagination is the final arbitor regarding how much of this or that factor is necessary, under a specific set of conditions, to explain the rate of economic recovery or decline, the extent of boom or depression, its length, and the timing of the reversals. One cannot help but wonder if the theory is the precise, complete, and satisfactory affair that Professor Hansen seems to imply.

With this theory, as with so many others, one seems always to come to an anticlimax in the end. Certain economic processes limit both the expansion and the contraction. So far, so good. But when we read that, after these internal forces have run their course, a particular turn is after all apparently due to technical progress that opens up new investment opportunities, it would seem to be an admission that the theory is not satisfactory. Outside factors always have to be dragged in to save the theory from eventual failure. Before the account is completed, one author admits dissatisfaction by shifting from endogenous to exogenous factors to bolster his theory, and another shifts from exogenous economic to exogenous noneconomic factors!

None of these refutations of economic theories of the business cycle is intended to disparage economic explanations as far as they go, or to reflect on the brilliant and admirable work of many economists, but only to point out again that, in the nature of the case, economic behavior must occur in relation to environment; and hence, economic explanations alone are not, and cannot be, sufficient.

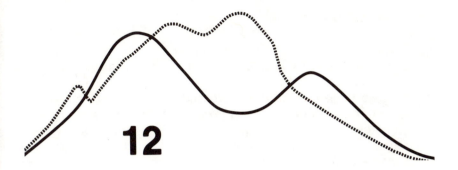

12

Pessimism Versus Optimism

Freedom Through Knowledge

The theory that has been developed so carefully on these pages leads to the conclusion that the behavior of man from the very beginning has been conditioned by the climate in which he has lived. At first glance this may seem to indicate that man is nothing but a passive victim of climatic forces, but this does not necessarily follow. Although his behavior can be shown to have always and regularly varied on these tides of climatic change, this need not lead to the conclusion that man is forever predestined to behave in definite ways at definite times. Although the environment can, and certainly does, influence and exert a strong control over man, there is no fatalism involved. Throughout history some men were able to achieve mastery over their environment. In the future, increasing numbers will do so.

There is an almost universal but mistaken notion that because man must obey natural laws, he is not free. On the contrary, obedience to the law is liberty, not only in everyday social life but also scientifically and philosophically. If man and nature together were not subject to natural laws, then indeed there would be no such thing as freedom. That man can secure freedom for himself through an understanding of these laws can be demonstrated in various ways.

The most obvious of all is the freedom with which man can now move about in his environment. Through a knowledge of the laws, he has invented engines that carry him across the land in trains and automibiles, across the seas in ships, and through the air in airplanes. Through a knowledge of the laws of electricity he has made for himself light, heat, refrigeration, sound, moving pictures, television, computers, and power. By a knowledge of sanitation and medicine he has more than doubled his average life span; he has rid himself of innumerable diseases and has increased his stature. Directly and indirectly through these and other laws which he discovered, he has vastly increased his wealth and the standards and comforts of living.*Freedom is derived through the conscious application of the laws to which man and nature are subject.*

But this is by no means the only source of his freedom. Through the proper self-analysis and understanding of his own mind, he can and does free himself from the fetters of impulse, habit, and emotion. And through an understanding of the laws of society he has progressed from lower to higher moral levels. All this, however, is a matter of learning, and man learns the hard way. He always has and he always will. The important fact, however, is that he does learn and will continue to do so.

As far as making social progress is concerned, the main difficulty lies in the fact that the lessons learned by one generation of conscious individuals are not passed on to the next. There are too many things which each generation has to learn over again. A generation passes on its literature, art, inventions, and philosophy, but it does not pass on its mistakes. We are making the same mistakes today that our 80th great-grandfathers made four hundred years before Christ, and possibly the same mistakes that their great-grandfathers made before them.

Moreover, one group of people, or one nation, cannot learn from the mistakes of another, even within the same generation. You cannot truly understand the effect of placing your finger on a hot stove until you yourself are burned. And so each generation has to get burned over again. Right now two world wars in one generation are not enough to teach Russia the disasterous lesson of armed imperialism. Hitler's defeat meant nothing to Stalin; the Kaiser's defeat meant nothing to Hitler; Napolean's defeat meant nothing to the Kaiser; Louis XIV's defeat meant nothing to Napolean; and so it has gone all through history.

When one is forced to contemplate how slow and painful progress is, it is always possible to derive comfort from the fact that we do not want to reach Utopia too soon. The question, "What will there be to do after that?" is quite pertinent. The answer, of course, is that Utopia will never be reached in this world, although it can and should be approached.

The theory of climatic conditioning for human behavior, as set forth in this work and its companion volumes, raises some old questions. Does history mean anything? Are we going anyplace, heading anywhere? Is there or isn't there such a thing as social progress or evolution? Is there a "goal" and, if so, do we know what it is? Can we do anything about bringing it nearer? Is life worth while? In these days of world wars, confusion, communism, class struggle and atom bombs, is it possible to look ahead with any assurance?

First, let us remember that ours is neither the first nor the last generation to face these and similar problems. Every generation has faced them since the dawn of civilization. You can read comments written today that sound almost word for word like comments written 200 or 2,000 years ago. Does this prove we are making no progress? Certainly not.

There are many theories of history and of human progress. For some, including contemporary scholars like Bertrand Russell, history is an accidental venture of mankind with no meaning. Man is but a stupid machine, subject to blind, mechanical laws, and living for no purpose. Basically there is nothing to life but the seeking of pleasure and the avoidance of pain. Because it is Epicureanism in its worst form and offers no hope for mankind, people who accept such views probably do not consider it important to make the world a better place to live. Fortunately only a few individuals hold this view and usually their pessimism can be traced to early incidents in their individual lives. It is not a view accepted by a majority of the world's best minds either past or present, and its greatest popularity has been during materialistic and mechanistic times in history.

Next is the theory best illustrated by Karl Marx that economic factors determine historical development. Under this theory, history is a record of the economic conflict between the "haves" and the "have nots." Beginning with a system of primitive communism, mankind has progressed through a slave system of production; feudalism; capitalism; then a transition stage during which the proletariat will first replace the capitalists with a temporary dictatorship before moving into a state of Utopian communism. At this point conflicts and class exploitation will cease, and all people will find security, freedom, peace, equality, and abundance. All this is nonsense and Russia today is a living contradiction of the Marxian theory with a stratified society far more rigid and exploitive than capitalism ever produced. All known facts of biology and psychology point to the impossibility of a classless society. The repeated warm-wet times of history vividly illustrate that the richer the environment, the greater is the opportunity for stimulation and incentive, causing individuals to deviate widely from one another in intelligence, personality, accomplishments, and aggressiveness.

For Oswald Spengler, civilizations were born to pass through childhood, adulthood, old age, and death after the fashion of individuals. Living in Germany at a time when governments were centralizing and the great powers were engaged in the armaments race leading to World War I, he correctly foresaw the chaos and insecurity confronting the world at that moment. However, like many others, he tried to explain everything in terms of the trend which if extended to its logical conclusion suggested that western culture was on the decline and about to die. What he failed to consider was the cycle which, when carefully inspected without preconception or bias leads to a more optimistic conclusion. True, we were in a period of decline, but this decline was of two kinds: the kind that recurs every one hundred years during the period of maximum temperature and minimum rainfall in the 100-year cycle and the kind that recurs every 500 years during a similar but more extreme temperature and rainfall climax. These climatic facts by no means completely explain the decline but they certainly help explain it, and seem clearly to be the main causes *timing* the declines.

For Albert Schweitzer, progress is only possible when civilizations are morally healthy. He makes the extremely important point that progress is not automatic, as Herbert Spencer seemed to imply, but is man made and achieved only by the most sincere and persistent of efforts. It is easy to agree with most of Dr. Schweitzer's thesis. It is unquestionably true that only those civilizations will survive that place an adequate evaluation on individual human life, which evaluation is generally lost under dictatorships or socialistic trends. One can agree that civilization is doomed when its moral tone declines and its moral purpose is lost. But it is impossible to agree with Dr. Schweitzer and others that machinery, science, technology, and wealth have caused the decline. While true that too much wealth tends to produce moral decay, there are many examples of individuals who have achieved great wealth and were living models of cultural refinement and moral virtue. Further, history reveals indisputably that wealth has accumulated fastest during prosperous times when the moral tone of the society along with its science, art, and literature were at their best. These were the golden ages of history. Therefore, while it is a definite moral hazard, it would seriously oversimplify the picture to say that wealth is the main cause of social decline. There is no single cause but a vast complex matrix of interrelated factors.

P.A. Sorokin similarly argued that materialism corrupted civilizations. Our present trouble, he avers, lies in the failure of the Sensate culture on which we have based our current civilization to generate an adequate moral system and adequate spiritual objectives. In this respect Sorokin and Schweitzer stress the same problem in different ways. He thinks we need to change to an ideational culture based on religion, substituting duty, love, sacrifice, and God for material values. While we can agree on the need for acquiring a fresh moral outlook, contrary to Sorokin's analysis, societies do return to God during those times he describes as Sensate and we call mechanistic. It is during these periods that a revival of religion and a reconstruction of society takes place on the basis of rediscovered moral principles. The Godless times occur when Sorokin's Ideational culture, based on religion and asceticism, becomes stereotyped and empty and when allegiance shifts from the God of the Church to the God of the State. The most morally corrupt times in history are not during periods of empiricism and materialism but during periods of rationalism and dictatorship.

Finally Arnold Toynbee championed the idea that constant challenge is the only source of social and cultural integrity and the foundation of all civilized progress. One of the chief causes of cultural decline, according to Toynbee, is militarism, and we must be careful not to ruin ourselves by becoming too militaristic. In any event, past civilizations have collapsed through their own acts, including resting on their oars, and modern civilization is in the process of doing the same. The key to Toynbee's position is that societies must face hardship to remain healthy. Challenge is the source of social and cultural integrity. Among the challenges is climate, which Toynbee misses altogether.

While some elements of these various theories allow profound insights into the nature of civilization and human progress, others suffer from logical inconsistencies and still others amount to little more than unadulterated nonsense.

A Theory of Progress

It would seem to this writer that the major causes of progress — and the main factors in the causation of history — can be boiled down into six categories. These are: free will; the concept of a "unified energy field"; human heredity; geographical and climatic environment; economic stability; and the all important cultural factor.

Human Free Will

The first consideration must be man's indomitable will. There can be no progress unless man desires it and proceeds to set the proper goals. There is no question that in the long run these goals must be spiritual and not material, moral as opposed to ammoral, and ideal as well as practical. The goals must not only bring mankind freedom from oppression, insecurity, suffering, and fear, but positive inspiration and incentive. The goals must be those of humanitarianism and peace, not cruelty and war. The comforts, leisures, and securities of life must be subordinated to willingness to share, to unselfishness, tolerance, compassion, and sacrifice. The Golden Rule must be the rule of life.

Associated with the will to self-discipline for the sake of progress must be the will to work. The most important thing about social progress is, as Schweitzer has said, the fact that it is man made. Harmony within a given society is man-made. Often progress is achieved only at the price of "blood, sweat, and tears." The strength of a civilization is measured by its willingness to endure hardship and its unwillingness to compromise its honor. And so the will to labor involves the will to fight, if necessary. That culture or nation unwilling to fight for its survival is a vanishing culture, a vanishing nation.

A Unified Energy Field

The second cause of progress will take a little time to explain, but it is important. In general there is one condition under which action in its various forms occurs in nature. By action is meant any activity whether in the outside world or in ourselves — physical, chemical, biological, psychological, social, political, animate, or inanimate. It includes all motion, all flowing, all processing, whether of falling bodies, winds, electrical currents, chemical reactions, or human achievement. It includes the mental and the physical, the material and the immaterial.

This one condition for action is the existence of a "unified energy field" of some kind capable of being disturbed, that is, of being put in a state of imbalance. This state of imbalance implies the existence of two kinds of energy — potential and kinetic — the energy of position and the energy of motion. The term "potential" has a relative meaning. It is relative first to kinetic, but also relative in the sense that a potential is meaningful only when defined as higher or lower than another potential. Consider two flatirons placed side by side, one hot and the other cold. The hot flatiron is for the moment at a high heat potential, the cold one at a low heat potential. In this state of imbalance of temperatures, heat will flow from the higher to the lower until the two are equal. The heat will also flow out into the environment if the temperature of the environment is lower than that of the irons. Consider a high pressure area in one part of the earth's atmospheric envelope and a low pressure area in another. Air will flow from one to the other in an "effort" to equalize the pressures. Nature abhors imbalance just as she abhors a vacuum.

Electric currents, to cite another example, flow from their source in the generator, where there is high potential, over conductors toward points of lower electrical potential. Rivers flow from higher altitudes or positions of higher gravitational potential to the ocean level, where the waters of the earth find temporary equilibrium because the ocean floor prevents water from reaching the point in the system of lowest gravitational potential, the center of the earth.

People are capable of physical movement because they have centers of high energy potential in certain places within them and centers of low potential in other places, thus making muscular contraction possible. In a similar way, the human will is a product of imbalance within the individual. Without that imbalance he would have no will. The psychiatrists who would have us eliminate all internal conflict, all tension and frustration for the sake of normality, are in reality leading us down the path of soft pedagogy to ultimate stagnation and oblivian. We can truly say with Toynbee that adversity is the mother of progress not only in the collective but in the individual life. The less the growing child is disciplined the more unhappy he is going to be. The less a growing society is disciplined (not by a king or dictator but voluntarily, by its individuals) the more unruly it will be.

There is no action without imbalance. If the imbalance does not now exist, it must have existed at one time. Kinetic energy by definition comes from no other source. Biological evolution is a series of connected actions involving successive generations of organisms. Social evolution is a continuous human act, a stream or flow of complex human activities. It is unthinkable that biological evolution could occur without a high evolutionary potential behind it and a low evolutionary potential ahead of it in the "unified field" in which evolution takes place, namely the cosmic whole.

Before this discussion goes any further, consider for a moment the logical implication underlying the derivation of action from imbalance. The position of low potential with respect to the position of high potential gives direction to the action that is occurring. Because two potentials of different degree are necessary for the action, and because low potential is that which gives direction to the action, it follows that the low is the goal of the action. In short, in a logical sense nothing can happen in this world unless it has a goal! All action is, in this sense, goal directed, and is not unlike purposeful behavior in human life. Stated differently, purposeful behavior in human life is no different in principle than is action anywhere else in the realm of nature, for all action is goal-oriented and is in that sense purposive. Our modern literature, both in science and philosophy, is full of such implications, even in chemistry and physics. All this will be explained in a future volume to be titled, *The Principle of Unity - A Guide to Understanding the Process of Change.*

From this it follows that evolution in the biological kingdom is heading somewhere. We are not interested for the moment in asking where. We are only interested in the principle. And so, social evolution — the evolution of civilization — is heading somewhere under the laws of nature. It has a goal. There are scientific and rigorously logical reasons, as well as moral reasons, for assuming that this goal is universal peace and harmony among the peoples of the world. This is just as plausible as a scientific concept as is the principle that the goal of all physical action in the universe, under the Second Law of Thermodynamics, is a state of heat equilibrium. Equilibrium of some kind lies at the end of every series of acts. Further, aesthetic harmony is the goal of every painter, sculptor, and architect. There would be no art without such a goal. And so it turns out that equilibrium, harmony, and peace are three varieties of the same thing, and they are all reached by the same method, namely, action of some kind

Well, you say, if that is the case, then why worry? Social progress is inevitably and immutably carrying us on to the goal. There is nothing we need do. No! That does not follow.

We are told by an outstanding authority in physical science that there is no predetermined path that compels a beam of light to travel from its source to its destination over a certain route. There is no groove down which it must travel, no channel mapped out for it in advance. While it must obey a certain law in its passage through space, making the path predictable, the light "applies" the law anew, figuratively speaking, each step of the way as it goes along. In principle, if not in fact, it "explores" its way through space. It must "find" its own way under the law.

This principle is easier to understand by using the example of a river. Suppose so much water was suddenly released on the top of a mountain that it could not all be absorbed by the land over which it would flow on its way to the ocean. To be sure the contours of the land are already there for the resulting river to follow, even to the ocean. Nevertheless, over each inch of space the river "explores" its way. It demonstrates the law of "taking the steepest slant" each time the contour changes, thus changing the water's rate of flow. In short, it means nothing to say that the flowing is a mechanical process; such an idea is actually a philosophy, and a poor one at that, imposed upon the facts. The river "finds" where the steepest slant is at each point of the way when it reaches that point, not before.

Similarly, life is explorative. Consciousness is explorative. Evolution, whether biological or social, is explorative. These are all goal-seeking processes. The principle we have just been explaining, when applied to man, means that while man of necessity must follow definite laws of nature in all his behavior, there is nothing predetermined or fatalistic about life situations. The laws have existed, to be sure, since the beginning of time, but each event in nature "applies" the law in its own way. The various forces and objects of the universe all follow the law in terms of their own inner constitutions.

When the principle is applied to man it turns out, therefore, that following the law means work, not automatically predestined work, but voluntary self-exertion. In other words, progress is truly man-made. In order to make progress, man must follow the laws of nature, but he must do the work himself by applying the laws each step of the way.

There is nothing about a scientific or natural law that compels a person to do whatever he is doing. There is no law under heaven that specifies that you cannot continue sitting where you are as long as you want. As far as all the laws of the universe are concerned you can sit there forever if you so choose. No law will compel you to get up. There is no scientific or natural law that compels you even to live. You can blow your brains out if you want to. Some people do.

Similarly, there is no law that guarantees that man will continue to advance from this moment on, no law compels him to progress. Collectively he can commit suicide if he wants to. Nations have done that very thing. France came dangerously close under Napoleon. Germany almost did and Russia is on its way. Civilization could very readily wipe itself off the surface of the earth if it chose to. It won't, but it can. It will squeak through the present crisis by a very slim margin as is often the case. Progress is not automatic. It is explorative. It is voluntary. It involves toil and sweat and sacrifice. It necessitates difficult choices and hard work. But it is neither automatic nor necessary.

There is, however, one thing that is necessary. Returning to our absurd example, if you want to sit in your chair for the next ten years, you *must accept the consequences.* If man is unwilling to do the work necessary to insure progress, then he must pay the price which will be anguish and death; there is no doubt about that. It is just as inevitable as developing sores by sitting too long in your chair.

Thus, in advancing toward the goal of social equilibrium, which is peace among humanity, there is a high potential from the model civilization and a low one ahead in the cosmic system of which humanity is a part. Otherwise, it would not be moving onward at all, nor even moving. (Moving and moving onward are the same thing. There is no motion without an onward direction toward a goal.)

The cause of this great differential in potentials in the cosmic scheme of things that gives man his drive toward future goals has been called God. There is no better name for it. The differential can be measured in terms of the ignorance, superstition, primitiveness, lack of understanding, and tolerance of savage societies as opposed to the knowledge of today, the relative painlessness of life, its greater longevity, the greater effort now being made to understand one another and to get along peaceably, technological advancement, and so on.

The second general cause of history, then, may be defined as an evolutionary potential working through conscious, thinking man, but at the same time requiring work on his part. Hegel and other philosophers have called it the Infinite or the Absolute, seeking self-expression; whatever it is, it is a logical requirement for the understanding of progress.

The acceptance of such causations, of course, would be a matter of belief or faith and not a matter of science. But from a scientific standpoint, history would be meaningless without an evolutionary potential behind it, and just as unintelligible as the current flowing into an electric light would be without the voltage generated by the dynamo.

Human Heredity

The third cause of progress is heredity. Huntington treated this concept at length in *Mainsprings of Civilization;* consequently it need not be elaborated here. Suffice it that those races or groups that inherit the highest levels of intelligence and the greatest amount of vitality have an advantage over other groups. Members of certain races, for example, who come to the United States to complete their education find it very difficult and usually impossible to pass our doctorate examinations, although they were reared in an environment supplied by American built schools staffed partly by Americans. It is impossible for them to overcome their biological disadvantage. In this connection it is fantastic to assume, as some have done, that given the same economic advantages, the same amount of incentive and stimulation, the same education, the same diet, and the like, all the races on earth would suddenly develop the same average intelligent quotients. It is not fantastic, however, to assume that there is no race on earth not already doomed by biological factors that, given time and the right environment, could not evolve to levels of intelligence equalling those of western Europe or the Western Hemisphere. Moreover, there is good reason to assume there are different kinds of intelligence and that one race is superior along certain lines while another is superior along other lines. In any event, the question of intelligence has nothing to do with the question of human importance or worth. The race that, for any reason, considers itself superior is not only unreasonable but stupid.

Geographic and Climatic Environment

The fourth cause of progress is environment, which includes both geography and climate. Because this entire volume is dedicated to this category of causation, it will not be elaborated here. Suffice it that no one with a sufficiently broad outlook would consider history, or social progress, to be caused by a single factor. It is unscientific to talk about the geographic or climatic determination of history, the economic determination, or the cultural determination. Each specialist is prone to evaluate causation through his own narrow range of knowledge and to explain history in terms of a single cause. It is more scientific to speak of the biological factor in history, not the biological cause; the cultural factor, not the cultural cause; or the climatic factor, not the climatic cause; for there are many factors, and therefore many causes of history. Because history would not occur in the absence of any of these factors, each is essential. It is irrelevant to argue which is more important; if they are all essential, they are all equally important in the overall picture, although some factors are more important in understanding certain problems.

In this latter respect, there is much to be said for the climatic factor when it comes to the timing of historical events, and to explaining why the cultural pattern changes on a world-wide basis at definite times, and then back again. This means that, in the scientific realm of prediction, the climatic factor is the most important single influence. But this certainly does not mean that all history or human behavior can be accounted for in terms of the climatic factor.

The present study does not take into consideration geographic location other than in relation to the climate of the region. Yet location is important. A culture like that of the Tibetans is primitive partly because of its isolation. Peoples that in earlier centuries happened to live along the shores of the Mediterranean had the advantages of trade and commerce, cultural borrowings, mutual stimulation and challenge, and numerically limited populations. Hence they advanced faster than people anywhere else in the world. Western Europe had similar advantages over the Balkans. Needless to say, the arability of the land as well as mineral and other resources have had much to do with the progress of specific civilizations.

Economic Stability

The fifth main cause of history is the economic factor. It stands to reason that those people who settled down to a stable pattern of living based on agriculture or some kind of manufacturing, and whose health and standard of living were thereby improved, possessed an important advantage over their less fortunate neighbors. Permanent cities and homes were not the only consequences of a stable economy. Schools, libraries, education, literature, artistic expression, and perhaps most important of all, science and technology, were all products of a stable society and economic wealth, both of which permitted the leisure necessary for research and reflection.

Economic opportunity and gain have always been incentives to hard work. They have stimulated productivity and invention, although much creative work has been done without thought of monetary reward. Throughout history cultural progress has reached its peaks along with periods of economic prosperity, and cultural decline has been associated with economic depression and stagnation. Thus the economic factor has always been an important catalytic agent in the onward march of civilization.

The Cultural Factor

Sixth and last is the cultural factor. There are those who believe the cultural factor is the all-important cause of history. The cultural determinist minimizes the importance of the physical world and environment. He believes that while climate may be in the picture, it is unimportant because the cultural factor determines whatever is acted on by the climatic factor.

Consider the example of the American Civil War. How could weather have caused the war, the cultural determinist would say, when, as everyone knows, the cause was a dispute over the cultural factors of states' rights and the right of one of the regions to pursue its economic pattern of living? The culturist, however, does not look far enough, because all through history slave economies have tended to fluorish in the warm countries when they have not done so in cooler countries. Why? The warm-climate individual cannot exert himself physically to the extent that the cool-climate individual can, for well-known physiological reasons, as explained in Chapter 4. Accordingly, more people are required to carry a warm country economy than that of a cool country. Without the aid of machinery, warm-climate civilizations could not have progressed in the absence of slave labor, for they did not have the manpower to keep the economy going. Production was not sufficient with the methods at hand to permit an economy based on wages. The South developed a slave economy basically because under the circumstances it was normal and natural for it to do so. The same phenomenon holds all around the world between peoples of northern and southern latitudes. Thus it is that climate had a lot to do with causing the American civil war, because the climate produced two types of economy, two types of culture, two philosophies of life. These differences of temperament and attitude still exist, and will remain as long as the climate of the United States stays as it is. (Right now, as annual temperatures are slowly dropping in the South, the South is waking up. It is rapidly industrializing and will continue to do so. The migration of the textile industry southward to be nearer the source of cotton and to take advantage of lower wages is only incidental compared with the effect that weather trends are having and will continue to have on the activities and thoughts of the South.)

These remarks are not intended to minimize cultural and economic factors. They are merely an attempt to show that the culturalist would err just as seriously if he assumed the cultural factor to be the exclusive cause of history as would the climatologist who considered weather trends the only important cause. It is very difficult for the specialist to understand how any cause outside his own field could be important. This is the universal bias of the specialist.

Consider one or two more examples. A friend of the author said recently, "World War II could have occurred only in the twentieth century." In the sense that twentieth century inventions and fighting techniques were involved, yes; just as twentieth century, not fifteenth century people, were involved. All that is self-evident. It is self-evident, too, that the alignment of political and economic forces in the twentieth century was unlike the alignment at any time in past history. But this ceases to be of basic importance when it is recalled that World War II was a nation-falling war, reflecting the decadence of world society just as other nation-falling wars in the past have done — for example, the conquests of Tamerlane and Alexander the Great. History both repeats itself and does not, without contradiction. *Types of events* repeat themselves, but each time on a higher level and with new sets of phenomena. In principle, there have been 27 sets of World War II's since 600 B.C. The general characteristics of all these nation-falling wars have been similar, and those who fought in them have all been conditioned by the weather trends.

Subsequently, this same friend mentioned that the depression of the 1930s would have been impossible in the thirteenth century. In the sense that the London and New York Stock Exchanges were not then in existence, yes. The industry that exists now certainly did not exist then. But the same type of economic decline did occur in the thirteenth century, during the 1250s and 1260s. Indeed, the same type of collapse, relative to hard times occurring because the economic machinery of the period ceased to function properly, has occurred regularly in all 27 of the 100-year cycles examined and always under similar climatic conditions.

The Case for Optimism

Let us now develop a logical argument with which to dispute the pessimism of most contemporary social critics and philosophers. First of all, pessimism is a product of warm times such as have just occurred. This relationship is evident throughout history. Pessimism is associated with the preoccupation of warm-climate and warm-phase cultures with tragedy and fate. In recent centuries, warm-phase cultures have harked back to the pessimism and fatalistic resignation of warm-phase classical Greeks to the predestined "will of the gods." The last 50 years of our own history have been no exception.

And so, an optimistic view of the future is proposed. It is unquestionably true that modern civilization is in a sad state of decline. But there is nothing new about that. The ancient civilizations were all in a corresponding state of decline in the fourth and fifth centuries. Historians have recognized this fact by ending ancient history in the fifth century. True, the change from the ancient to the medieval world was gradual, but in the fifth century the new building up processes began outnumbering the tearing down processes. Progress was painfully slow, to be sure. We speak of the next 500 years as the Dark Ages. Yet progress was being made throughout it all. There was a gradual economic and cultural recovery. Scholarship increased with painstaking slowness, but it did increase. The course of progress was not even but then it never is even. Yet all through the Dark Ages the Byzantine Empire, western Europe, and England were all growing. Feudalism was establishing itself as the new world economic and political order, to burst into full bloom during the next 500 year period.

Take a look at the accompanying diagram:

Notice that when an upward movement takes place, although its main direction is upward, it is also *forward*. When the midline is reached again, distance to the right has been gained. Let's assume that distance to the right means progress. Likewise, when downward movement is made, distance forward is gained at the same time. Thus progress is both even and uneven at the same time. Although civilization may be heading into an epidemic of dictatorships and tyranny, as it does when it moves toward a warm climax in the curve, still it is moving forward. In Russia some permanent gain was undoubtedly made under Stalin; there are certain securities, cultural and economic opportunities now open to the people that were not open to them under the Czars. But what an appalling price the people are paying for their limited opportunities! Similarly, civilization also moves the other way, toward a cold climax of civil war and anarchy. England, for example, suffered terrific losses and in some ways a serious retardation as a consequence of the Wars of the Roses in the fifteenth century. Nevertheless, during that time England was giving up its medieval feudalism and paving the way for the modern political state. Progress was made, but it was made the hard way. It is a universal human failing to progress the hard way.

However, there are more tangible reasons for being optimistic. Whereas we are now in a state of decline like those of the fifth and fifteenth centuries, so far in over 5,000 years of recorded history, every period of decline has been followed by a renaissance, and many of the awakenings far transcended anything previously recorded. There was nothing in history like the awakening of the Greeks in the sixth century

B.C., after all the ancient world civilizations prior to that time had decayed, many vanishing altogether. Later, there was nothing in recorded history like the pinnacle reached by the Roman Empire in its golden age. And nothing had ever happened to compare with the European Renaissance of the sixteenth century. Again, nothing previous could compare with the scientific and economic progress in the colonial golden age of 1790 to 1820. The Industrial Revolution was accompanied by a scientific revolution during which physiology, chemistry, geology, non-Euclidian geometry and many other branches of mathematics, embryology, comparative anatomy, and paleontology were all virtually founded, not to speak of the literary Renaissance led by Goethe and Wordsworth, the musical achievements of Mozart and Beethoven, and the paintings of Goya, Ingres, Turner, and many others.

But we are not through. The first 30 years of the twentieth century constituted another amazing period in history. Nothing that has ever happened could compare with the automobile, the airplane, radio, television, the assembly line, relativity, and the atom bomb. At no time in history have so many people enjoyed so high a standard of living. At no time has the wealth of the world been so great.

The most important thing about the world today is not its state of decline, which is deplorable enough. It is not the uncertainty, which is senseless enough. It is not the materialism and sensuousness, both of which are serious problems. It is the fact that *world civilization is in the throes of one of the greatest revolutions of all time, comparable to the revolutions of the fourteenth and fifteenth centuries that paved the way for the modern world.* The most important fact is that *a new world is being born while an old one is dying.*

The important things happening today are the freeing of hundreds of millions of people in the formerly backward countries of the world. At no time in the history of the world have so many people been freed in so short a time. Another important thing is the gains of the worker toward economic self-determinism — in other words, the movement toward sharing control of industry by management and labor working together cooperatively. This is the extension of the democratic principle to the economic realm. It is inevitable, but it is not socialism. Democracy is not complete without economic as well as political and religious self-determinism on the part of everybody. Business will gain, not lose, by this great achievement, which is no more socialism than was public education or woman's suffrage.

Another important thing happening today is the revival of the family. The younger generation fooled population experts with a revived interest in the home, and by increasing the birth rate beyond all predictions. This means the social framework is turning back toward stability again. It represents a more spiritual, less materialistic outlook on life.

This trend is accompanied by another, even more important one, that has already begun to manifest itself over the world. It is a revival of religion. Billy Graham is but a symptom of the times. The Moslem world is feeling the impact of a similar revival, as are India, Indonesia, and China. This is an excellent and hopeful sign for it is one of several ways in which the masses are expressing their demand for new freedoms. The revival of religion represents the rebirth of spiritual power among the peoples of the world; this spells doom for communism. The movement is the symptom of a democratic, not an autocratic age. But remember that during the onset of a new democratic age, chaos and confusion are to be expected and so progress in these areas may be expected to falter from time to time.

Because we are finishing a 500-year cycle, the uncertainties and confusions of the day mean the way is being paved for a great recovery. There is no reason to suppose that suddenly the processes of history are about to change their habits. There is every reason to believe that history will repeat itself as it has done so many times in the past. As this study has pointed out, great awakenings have consistently occurred at 500-year intervals. Everything indicates the next awakening will occur on time. The fact that predictions can be made does not mean that the awakening will be automatic. It means that, on the basis of the past, people have a right to keep their faith in human nature and expect man to do the work necessary for rebuilding civilization once more.

The next golden age will be in its prime beginning around the year 2000. It will be an age comparable in many respects to 1500 A.D. It will mark the beginning of a super-modern world, as much better than our present world as our present world is better than the Middle Ages. There will be a great spiritual awakening. Civilization will once again set up for itself a moral purpose. That moral purpose will reflect itself in a degree of racial tolerance never before known, a degree of class tolerance never before achieved, a degree of religious tolerance never before heard of, and a degree of political unity never before realized. The new world will be far from perfect. There may be bloodshed, but there will not be annihilation. The majority of societies are no more anxious to commit suicide than are individual people.

Not everyone alive today will like the democratic world of tomorrow because the word "progress" is not in their vocabulary.

There never was a move forward that pleased either the reactionary elements of society, or those whose thought patterns were incapable of change because for them change means insecurity and society appears doomed. The new democracy will not be like the old one any more the current form of democracy is like seventeenth century democracy. Like all things, democracy is constantly evolving. Communism is dying, not growing. Totalitarianism will remain subdued for the most part until it becomes hot once more around the 2030s. In fact, communism has been dying and democracy growing since the days of primitive societies. Anyone who fears that communism will ruin civilization is misguided; communism has ruined local states, nations and passing cultures, but it has never ruined civilization and will not do so now.

Democracy built the Greek city states. Socialism destroyed them. It built Rome. Statism destroyed it. Democracy built England but socialism will destroy her if she clings to it. Democracy built the United States but socialism in the form of the welfare state will destroy it if given an opportunity. If socialism had been a continuous force in the world, there never would have been any civilization. Time after time democracy has salvaged civilizations ruined by despots, dictators, and socialism, and by means of private enterprise has rebuilt the social structure. This is precisely what will happen again. But expect it to take through the end of this century.

Summary

In this chapter, we have examined and discarded the idea that man is not free because he must obey natural laws. History teaches us instead that true freedom comes by consciously understanding and applying the natural laws to which all things are subject. Moreover, through a proper self-analysis of his mind, man is capable of freeing himself from the impulses, habits, and emotions that are most detrimental to human progress and prosperity.

A theory of progress was developed wherein six equally essential factors of historical progress were delineated. These were: (1) free will, (2) the concept of a unified energy field, (3) heredity, (4) environment, (5) economic stability, and (6) cultural inclinations.

Finally, we discounted the pessimism prevailing in many intellectual circles today, recognizing it for what it really is — an often repeated societal symptom of the termination of a warm climatic phase, with all its attendant confusion and uncertainties. The "modern world" as we know it is dying, true. But what emerges from the chaos will be a new modern world cleansed of confusion, zealous for democracy and private enterprise, possibly even less warlike than any previous period in human history — a golden age of world culture surpassing the European Renaissance, and born at the termination of the 500-year climatic cycle.

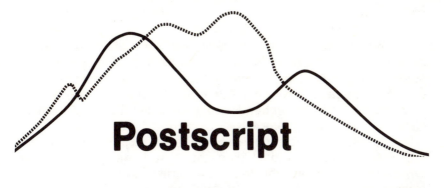

Postscript

— by Michael Zahorchak

In addition to his commentary on weather and business trends in Chapter 11, Dr. Wheeler prepared two charts forecasting climate and business conditions through the year 2000. These two charts are included here as Charts 17 and 18 to properly close the volume and to illustrate the practical value of Wheeler's work.

Wheeler's Forecast of World Climate Through 2050 A.D.

After he assembled the actual United States temperature and rainfall data from 1781 to 1950, Wheeler combined several different cycles with which he constructed synthetic curves which he compared to curves prepared using actual rainfall and temperature data. (An example of the match between the two is shown in Figure 11.)

His initial results encouraged him to proceed further. In terms of 10-year periods, his actual and theoretical curves agreed over 95% of the time. For 5-year intervals the agreement was 85% to 90%, while for individual years it was between 65% and 70%. This makes his forecast to the year 2050 extremely valuable in identifying general trends of long duration, while it is still somewhat useful in attempting to predict year-to-year conditions. It also justifies the serious attention of forecasters whose work requires them to prepare reasonably accurate long-range planning scenarios because, since 1871, climate has been drier in decades when his theoretical curves predicted drier weather ahead, wetter when they predicted wetter, colder when they predicted colder, and warmer when they predicted warmer.

219

In addition to the two charts, Wheeler projected United States climate through the year 2050. This projection, while summarized here, is not included in its entirety as it was not accompanied by a business forecast. Because weather trends in the United States correlate to world weather trends about 80% of the time, this forecast is also useful as a world forecast.

This climatic projection was prepared in response to published articles in the late 1940s concluding that the world was getting warmer. Wheeler's work showed this to be only partially true. Although world climate was then in the hot-drought phase of a 1,000-year cycle, he anticipated several cold breaks on the way to a peak. As every investor and businessman knows, all bull markets and prosperous times are punctuated by reactions that seem to herald a new bear market or depression. The same is true of climate, as Wheeler's research has already demonstrated. Thus, before the 1,000-year cycle reaches its hot-dry climax, it is likely to be interrupted by at least one period of colder than normal weather.

Contemporary articles of his day were encouraging people to migrate to northern Canada, Iceland, and Greenland. These were premature, Wheeler asserted. They were also dangerous because they made people complacent about focusing on problems associated with the low temperatures he foresaw later in the century such as the need to develop foodstuffs that would not only grow quickly and abundantly during short, cold growing seasons, but would also be drought-resistant.

As the forecast begins, Wheeler calculated the world had moved out of the hot drought period of the 1930s and was in an all-but-completed cold-wet phase, on its way into a long cold-dry phase. He calculated that temperatures should begin falling in the 1940s and forecast that 1945 would be the center of the cold-wet phase. Temperatures were actually average rather than cold during most of the 1940s, as shown on Chart 16. This can be attributed to the approach of a sunspot minimum, which historically coincides with warmer temperatures. As soon as the sunspot cycle reversed, the forecasting curves suggested that climate would become colder and drier until about 1995, with more cold than warm years and with severe droughts during much of the period.

More specifically, Wheeler expected temperatures to rise until about 1952, the time of the next sunspot minimum, then turn colder. At the same time it would become increasingly dry. Drought conditions would moderate briefly about 1952, 1959, and 1965. Then, after dropping to a low in 1970, rainfall would recover but still remain below average until 1973.

The cold-dry phase was projected to climax around 1968, after which temperatures would rise modestly in the 1970s. Thereafter, although temperatures would remain generally cool, they would not again reach the extreme cold levels of 1968 until the early 1990s when another period of extreme cold was forecast. Although drought conditions were expected to prevail throughout the 1970s, its potential severity was likely to diminish because a slightly higher level of rainfall was projected than during the previous two decades. However, most of this rain would be concentrated near the end of the decade.

The 1980s were expected to be slightly colder but wetter than the 1970s. After a cold-wet trough around 1980, temperatures were forecast to rise slightly until 1984 or 1985, drop for about 2 years, and then peak in 1987 or 1988. Rainfall levels would peak in 1980, drop until 1984, rise into 1987, and then gradually decline to a trough about 1992. Compared to the dry periods forecast for 1956 and 1970, those projected for 1984 and 1992 appear on Chart 18 to be relatively mild. As this manuscript was being typeset, this part of the forecast appeared to be on target in that late in 1982 and early 1983, New York City and many of its suburbs had been placed on a drought alert because its reservoirs had not been replenished to capacity during the intervening wet period. Theoretically, with two more years to go (as this postscript is being written) until the intensity of the drought was scheduled to climax, this particular area may yet see conditions as severe as in the previous two decades. However, even as New York was placed on a drought alert, the rest of the nation began to experience excessive levels of precipitation. Eventually this precipitation reached the Northeast causing March, 1983 to be the wettest March in recorded history and causing severe flooding in areas just recently plagued by droughts.

A brief warm-dry period late in the 1980s would then give way to about 5 cold-wet years early in the 1990s as a rising trend of moisture, then temperature, ushers in the major warm-wet phase of the next 100-year cycle scheduled to be underway by the year 2000 and extending into the early years of the twenty-first century. This rainfall could at times be so extensive as to cause serious flooding in many places.

Summarizing, the forecast for the 50 years beginning 1950 indicated more cold than warm years, with the quarter century from 1950 to 1975 also containing a preponderance of dry years. The cold-wet phase of the 100-year cycle was estimated to have centered on 1945, but its timing coincided with a sunspot minimum generating warmer than normal temperatures. For the period 1975 through 1997, Wheeler forecasted a lengthy transition into the next 100-year cycle. Through 1992 climate was expected to stay mostly dry with short,

Chart 17. Wheeler's Forecast of Weather and Business Trends, 1950-1975

What follows is a trend forecast, not a year-by-year forecast. As with Charts #1 to #16, the estimated degree of hot and wet are shown above the horizontal median line while cold and dry are shown below the line.

Note that it is expected to become cold around 1954 and continue cold through 1975 except for brief warm periods around 1963 and again from 1971 through 1973. On a percentage basis, about 83% of this 21 year period (beginning in 1954) is forecast colder than normal.

Note too, that only about one year in six will be wet. The entire 25 years from 1950 through 1975 are forecast drier than normal except for brief periods around 1952, 1959, 1965, and 1973.

This business forecast is included for the sake of completeness. It was prepared by isolating the cycles found in the Ayres Index of Business Activity data and projecting them forward. Note that a depression is expected to begin in 1952. After a recovery from the late 1950s until around 1964 or 1965, a serious depression era is expected through the mid-1980s to be relieved by only short intervals of prosperity. This depression era will correspond to those of the 1830s, 1840s, and 1860s. This 25-year period will occur during the cold-dry phase of the 100-year cycle, as were the 1830s and 1840s. Because this type of depression era has repeated itself twenty-six times without a failure since the sixth century B.C., it is not expected to miss the next time.

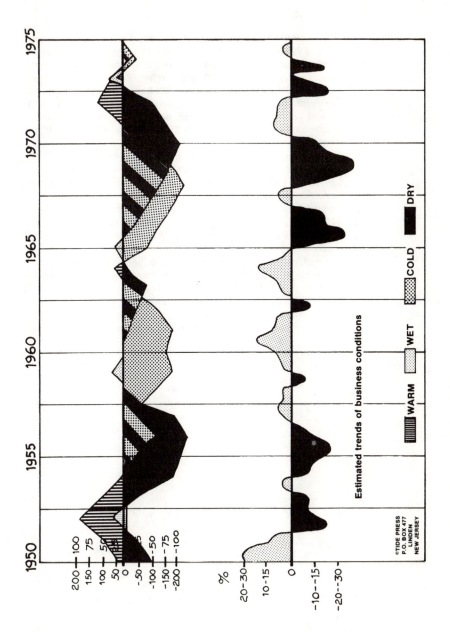

Estimated trends of business conditions

WARM WET COLD DRY

©TIDE PRESS
P.O. BOX 477
LINDEN
NEW JERSEY

Chart 18. Wheeler's Forecast of Weather and Business Trends, 1975-2000

Note that the forecast on this chart is for the period from 1975 to 2000 to be warmer and wetter than the previous 25 years. The number of warm and cold years is expected to be about equally distributed although it will on balance continue to average cold until the warm-wet phase of the next 100-year cycle around the year 2000. The number of wet and dry years are forecast to be equally divided from 1975 to the early 1990s after which almost continuous wet conditions are forecast through the end of the century.

Perhaps the most striking feature of this forecast is the vigorous period of prosperity lasting approximately four years in the early 1980s interrupting the last period of major depression ending around 1985. Thereafter, in parallel with the increasing amount of rainfall, prosperity will increase or, perhaps more correctly, conditions of extreme depression will moderate. However, the next era of vigorous prosperity is not expected until around 1995.

The main point to this forecast is that those people involved in long-term planning should not expect the present era of prosperity (in 1950) to last beyond 1952 unless there is a war. It is believed that although real, the chances of a war are slight.

The right side of the chart, beginning in the early 1990s represents what we have termed nation-building time.

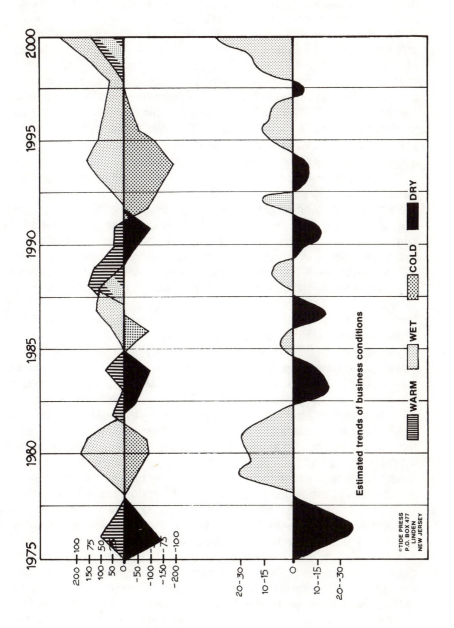

Estimated trends of business conditions

WARM   WET   COLD   DRY

©TIDE PRESS
P.O. BOX 477
LINDEN
NEW JERSEY

1975   1980   1985   1990   1995   2000

200 — 100
150 — 75
100 — 50
50 — 25
0
-50 — -25
-100 — -50
-150 — -75
-200 — -100

20 — 30
10 — 15
0
10 — 15
20 — 30

intense wet periods near 1980 and 1987. The late 1982, early 1983 floods throughout much of the central United States and the Northeast, the heavy snows in early 1983 in this same area, and the early 1983 coastal storms on the Pacific Coast confirm the validity of this forecast as it relates to intense wet periods. Wheeler's notes say conditions through 1997 would stay cold, although somewhat warmer than in the previous quarter century. Chart 18 seems to forecast a considerably warmer trend with indications of several warm periods centering on 1976, 1984, and 1988. Further, his comments in this book relative to the climaxing of both the 100- and 500-year cycles about the year 1975 suggests we are now in a lengthy transitional phase somewhat warmer than the preceding decade.

Wheeler anticipated serious droughts around 1955, throughout much of the 1960s, and into the 1970s, with two more near 1983 and 1991. The movement of people and businesses from the North to the Sun Belt throughout the 1960s and 1970s qualifies as typical cold-climate behavior, and his forecast of severe drought conditions during these decades was on target, as the rationing of water supplies in various parts of the country during these years will attest. His forecast of drought around 1983 is also correct although this drought appears to have come somewhat earlier and have been much milder than forecast especially if the heavy storms and flooding mentioned above signal the early demise of the 1980s drought period.

Just as the 1,000-year cycle's warm phase in this century is being punctuated by the current cold spell, it promises to be interrupted in the next century by a potentially strong, 10-year cold-wet period starting around 2015, according to Wheeler's weather forecast through 2050. This is to be followed by the hot drought climax of the 100-year cycle, about 2030. Shortly thereafter should come the hot climax of the 1,000-year cycle. Wheeler says evidence of this warming trend has been accumulating for years as glaciers and frost lines have steadily receded, interrupted from time to time only by the cold phases of the 100-year cycle. The interaction of the warm phases of both the 100- and 1,000-year cycles is expected to produce an abnormally hot sequence of years during the 2030s and 2040s as first the hot climax of the 100-year cycle and then the hot climax of the 1,000-year cycle occur. During these years, temperatures may soar higher than they did in the 1930s, to the accompanyment of droughts and depressed business conditions as bad or worse than those of the 1930s. Then, perhaps in the 2040s, the pattern of glaciers and frost lines should reverse, gradually receding again in line with a pattern that has repeatedly occurred in the past.

Comments and Observations on the Forecast of World Climate

To better understand the 100-year cycle, it might be well to compare it to a calendar year. The parallels between the seasons and the cyclical phases would be: spring — warm-wet; summer — warm-dry; autumn — cold-wet; winter — cold-dry. According to calendar time, each season is theoretically the same length, but we know from observation that some seasons are considerably longer or shorter than others, especially the transitional seasons, spring and autumn. The progression of seasons is further complicated by what Wheeler calls "saddles," or interruptions in the anticipated pattern; that is, spells of unseasonably warm weather when it should be cold, or vice versa. As a result, regardless of where one lives in the temperate zones, the variations are so numerous that no two seasons are alike in all respects.

For example, in parts of the Northeast, the last killing frost of the year may occur some years in early March, as late as June in others. As for moisture, the spring rainy season in drought years may consist of a few days of heavy scattered rains over a 4- to 6-week period, while in other years the rain begins early in February and continues well into the summer. One year this writer's locality received more snow on one April day than during the entire winter. Then it turned so warm that most of the snow melted the next day.

The point of this discussion is to show that just as the annual cycle of weather differs from one year to the next, so does the 100-year cycle of climate differ from one cycle to the next, evolving as a general pattern with an endless series of variations. The concept to grasp and understand is the outline and nature of the general pattern.

For approximately the first half of each 100-year cycle, average annual temperatures tend to be warmer than the average annual temperature of the entire 100-year period. Then, during the second half, they are cooler than the 100-year average. Furthermore, from the beginning of the warm phase of the cycle until some point more or less in the middle, temperatures get progressively warmer until they reach a climax and start to drop. This descent continues until average temperatures fall below the 100-year average to another climax on the cold side, from which they then begin a slow ascent.

This does not mean that temperatures move consistently in one direction, either up or down, year after year until the cycle changes. Instead, they fluctuate back and forth. Some years, during warm phases in the cycle, they may drop well below average, while during cold phases certain years will be much warmer than average. But over a span of years, most years during the first half of the cycle will have above average temperatures, while most years during the last half will be below average.

Within this 100-year temperature cycle are two rainfall cycles, each approximating 50 years long — one during the warm phase of the cycle and one during the cold. The rainfall cycle, however, is much more intricate than the temperature cycle because rainfall is greatest when temperatures are moderate and least when temperatures are either extremely hot or cold. Therefore, at some point in the hot cycle as temperatures move toward a climax, rainfall begins to taper off and a period of hot drought develops. On the cold side it first becomes too cold to rain, then it actually becomes too cold to snow. As a result, each warm phase is subdivided into warm-wet and warm-dry, while each cold phase is subdivided into cold-wet and cold-dry. The warm-wet years contain the last years of the previous cold phase, when temperatures are warming, as well as the early years of the current warm phase while the cold-wet years contain the closing years of the previous wet phase coupled with the opening years of the current cold phase.

This neat scenario is further complicated by the interaction of both longer and shorter cycles. For example, when the 100-, 500-, and 1,000-year cycles are all in their cold-dry phases, we would experience a major ice age and if mankind did not perish at this time, a person could drive a heavy truck across many temperate zone lakes and rivers during much of the year. At the other extreme, when the hot-dry cycles are all locked together as above, it would be possible to live comfortably in Iceland, Greenland, and areas well north of the border cities of Canada. Because the cold phase in our century's cycle is occurring within the warming phase of the greater 1,000-year cycle, and a 500-year cycle that is coming off a hot-dry climax reached in the 1930s, temperatures have not dropped to levels as low as those recorded in 100-year cycles of previous centuries. But during the hot-dry phase of the present 100-year cycle, because of this same phenomenon, the droughts of the 1930s were worse than anticipated; for the same reason, those of the early twenty-first century promise to be as bad as, or even worse.

Other factors that create complications in the 100-year pattern include sunspots, the rotation of the earth around the sun and of the moon around the earth, and the interaction of people with their environment. Within any climatic phase, as sunspots increase, the weather tends to get colder, while as these solar storms diminish, weather gets warmer. The rotation of the sun affects the earth's annual patterns, producing the seasonal variations, while the rotation of the moon around the earth tempers the monthly and daily variations. Philosophically, the idea that man affects the health and well-being of the earth in much the same way that the earth affects man is a venerable one, yet it is a concept that many people tend to dismiss. Nevertheless, many scientists and conservationists are becoming increasingly concerned by how people are affecting the earth's ecology through the dumping of toxic wastes, polluting the atmosphere, clearing oxygen producing forests and jungles for highways, housing projects, strip mining and so forth. All these things and more also interact to produce the variety of climatic conditions that we observe.

On examining Charts 17 and 18, several exceptions to Wheeler's general pattern become immediately apparent. First, the cold-wet phase supposed to center around 1945 appeared more warm- than cold-wet, although it was bracketed between two cold-wet years, 1944 and 1948. These years were followed by warm-dry 1949 and 1950 which, after a brief warm-wet interruption, flowed into the major cold-dry phase beginning about 1953. Now, a cynic might say that with virtually no cold-wet phase evident at this point, Wheeler's entire theory becomes invalid. But as the data show, 6 of the 9 years of the 1940s, for which data were available to Wheeler, were wet as forecast, and by a considerable margin over the 3 dry years. The temperatures were warmer than normal for this phase of the cycle, but not excessively so. Except for 1946 and 1949, they hovered very close to average, suggesting that, were it not for the effect of the sunspot minimum, the period would definately have been cold and wet.

The other seeming aberration occurs in the forecast for the 1980s and 1990s, as the cold-dry phase of one 100-year cycle draws to a close and a new one begins. Here Wheeler seems to project more warm and more wet years than seems logical at the close of a cold-dry phase. However in Chapter 7 Wheeler explains that the greatest instability occurs during transitions. This was amptly illustrated in early 1983 when reports of excessive rainfall, snows, and flooding over large areas of the United States came simultaneously with the declaration of a drought alert in New York City. This alert in turn was closely followed by the wettest March in New York City's history. During the transition from cold to warm, temperatures rise causing rainfall to increase. As rainfall increases, temperatures fall temporarily, creating an intervening cold-wet period. These transitions appear erratic because, like stocks, which bottom out on a rotating basis in a bear market, there is a great amount of instability as different areas "bottom out" on the cold and shift to the warm side at different rates throughout the world.

In terms of accuracy, Wheeler thought his forecasts would be 95% accurate when evaluated by decades, with a 65% year-to-year rate of agreement. We will leave his climate forecast at this point, inviting more detailed evaluation by interested climatologists, and move on to his business and social forecasts.

Projection of Business Cycles through the Year 2000

Just as Wheeler combined weather data to produce a forecast that he projected into the future, he also combined the data from Ayres' Index of Industrial Production into a curve with which to project business conditions.

His forecast as shown on the bottom of Charts 17 and 18, called for periods of depression in the early 1950s and the late 1960s through the 1970s. After a strong but brief recovery in the early 1980s, he forecast a lethargic period during which progressively weaker recessions would alternate with progressively stronger recoveries, through the end of the century. The last of these recoveries, starting about 1994, may inaugurate the first boom period in the next 100-year cycle.

As can be readily seen by correlating Wheeler's business forecast to actual business conditions from 1950 to the present, his forecast has for the most part correlated to actual business conditions despite the appearance of several distorting factors. The first was Wheeler's miscalculation of the likelihood that the United States would become involved in a war. In fact, it became involved in not just one war but two.

The first was the Korean war in the 1950s, shortly after this forecast was prepared, which broke out during a cold-wet period. Wheeler was aware of its possibility but discounted it. Nevertheless, he did state that, if a war did occur, it would distort the forecast by extending prosperity. I graduated college in 1950, shortly before hostilities erupted. That a depression was underway was obvious since only a few of my classmates received job offers. With the onset of the war, job opportunities rose dramatically, except for males of draft age, so to remove the obstacle, I volunteered to be drafted and within a week was in the Army. Business activity continued high until about 1956, when a postwar transition set in. Thus, the depression Wheeler forecast for 1951 did not materialize, while the post war transition was rather mild. In any event, Wheeler did recognize this possibility and spelled it out when he made the forecast.

The second war, in Vietnam, occurred during what Wheeler would term a "nation-falling" time in the 100-year cycle, and this particular war certainly had a detrimental effect on the nation. Vietnam occurred in the "winter" of the cycle, the time when plants and animals in tune with Nature hibernate to conserve their energies in preparation for the next period of growth and activity, and by analogy the time when intelligently led nations should be conserving their valuable national resources rather than rushing pell-mell to dissipate them. Instead, both presidents John F. Kennedy and Lyndon Johnson not only expanded Vietnam into a full-scale war, but they enacted many costly new social programs best left for other phases of the cycle. The result was that, however well intentioned the military actions and social programs may have been, they overstressed the capacity of the nation at a time when it was most vulnerable to these stresses. They demanded an excessive sacrifice from the productive elements of the nation beyond their capacity to respond and remain economically and competitively healthy. These pressures forced the nation at all levels — governmental, corporate, and individual — increasingly to dip into their capital bases, thus accelerating the pressures and compounding the problems.

To conceal the adverse effects of these actions for as much and as long as possible, the government prescribed a medication of accelerating inflation — the second major factor Wheeler did not anticipate. In a series of detailed chronologies to be published later, Wheeler lists the major kinds of events that occurred during each of the four major climatic phases of the 100-year cycle since 600 B.C. In these chronologies he lists higher prices as primarily a warm-wet and secondarily a cold-wet phenomenon. In the 1960s and 1970s, however, the inflation spilled over well into the cold-dry phase, permitting the government to finance its follies on an accelerating scale and to increase taxes while maintaining the illusion of a rising prosperity. This frustrated and angered those who were forced to reduce their living standards to pay taxes financing government activities that were poorly conceived, and all too often ineptly or even criminally managed, while being told that things were better than ever. Responding to their frustrations, many people moved into exotic tax shelters they did not understand in an attempt to protect their assets. More often than not, these investments turned out poorly, causing a further evaporation of the nation's capital base — an evaporation typical of the cold-dry phase of the climatic cycle.

A third factor Wheeler may not have fully appreciated or anticipated was the nation's infatuation with the use of "OPM" — other people's money. Seminars and books by the hundreds were promoted to show how to leverage one's limited assets to create fortunes in stocks, commodities, precious metals, real estate, business, and a host of other areas. What these people did not understand was that invariably the examples used had occurred during wet phases of the 100-year cycle because leverage and OPM works best only during prosperity phases. During depressions the indiscriminate use of OPM for many is a sure way to bankruptcy. It can be mathematically demonstrated in portfolio management, for example, that because some losses are inevitable when investing, the use of margin beyond a certain point guarantees total loss of one's capital, the only uncertainty being when it will happen. Unfortunately, most people only learn about the benefits of leverage after it has been practiced successfully by others for years, that is, just about the time the cycle is changing from a phase where the techniques could be employed profitably to one where they are no longer valid.

The negative aspects of OPM can be especially brutal if people are margined to the hilt and in addition pyramid their winnings. A story was published years ago about a sugar speculator who started with about $10,000. For a while his luck was phenomenal and he pyramided his winnings to the point where he was long several thousand contracts. Although his broker tried to get him to take some profits, the man refused. When prices finally broke, they gapped down for several days during which time it was impossible to sell any positions. By the time his account was liquidated, the man had lost well over $1 million on a $10,000 investment!

Closer to home, a friend and I once owned the same stock. He kept urging me not to sell on the basis of some inside information he claimed to have. The deal never materialized, as most such things don't. Eventually the stock plummeted, and my friend, who was heavily margined, almost lost his house on a stock in which he at one point had had a handsome profit. The point here is that the intelligent use of OPM is a cyclical thing. At some times it may be used with relative safety, while at other times it is better to pursue liquidity and the preservation of capital.

A fourth factor Wheeler could not fully appreciate was the speed with which the technology that will dominate the coming 100- and 500-year cycles would be developed and set in place in the closing years of the twentieth century. At the same time the old institutions, businesses, and ways of doing things were being tested, and if structurally flawed, were being forced to change or dissolve, the new technologies were taking over. If the recessions Wheeler forecast for the remainder of this century materialize, this disintegration of the old, and no longer useful, is likely to continue, not as a grand, preordained cosmic pattern, but as the result of business decisions that, at the time they are made, seem perfectly rational, but that later prove to have been flawed. The greed of my friend and the sugar speculator are two examples of how this works on a personal level. Both thought they were doing the right thing at the time.

The vast changes in the securities business offer a striking example of this process at work on the institutional level. Prior to the 1960s most Wall Street brokerage firms were organized as partnerships. Since then, most of these partnerships have disappeared. They have either been merged or driven out of business in large measure because of one major change they militantly refused to address when the problem first surfaced. In their place are a smaller number of corporations selling not only the traditional stocks and bonds but a wide variety of new, so-called "investment vehicles" including options, futures, tax shelters, etc. As the evolution of Wall Street continues, these new brokerage corporations are being further absorbed into larger organizations including banks, and insurance companies, mutual funds, even retailers who were formerly their customers and who now provide a variety of financial services.

While some change to the business known as "Wall Street" was inevitable, it need not have been so dramatic except for a decision made in the 1960s which seemed perfectly natural at the time, but which when examined in hindsight can be seen to have been a key factor in the lessened importance of Wall Street in the new financial organizations now evolving. At the time brokerage commissions were fixed by the New York Stock Exchange and everyone not a member of the Exchange had to pay the same commission per 100 shares regardless of the size of the order. If the commission on 100 shares of IBM for example was $60, the commission on a 100,000 share block was 1,000 times $60 or $60,000! This was great for the broker, and it did help subsidize the small investor to a degree but it was patently unfair to the increasingly powerful group of institutional investors then coming into prominence because while it took a greater amount of expertise and added effort to successfully trade large blocks of stocks, it did not take 1,000 times the effort to buy or sell 100,000 shares that to buy or sell 100 shares and therefore the commission should have been much less. Obviously a change had to be made but the brokers who were benefiting so handsomely from the status quo refused to compromise. Their decision was not to make a decision.

When this pressure to change commissions first started to build, it would have been easy for the brokers to build into the existing commission structure a series of discounts along the lines of those prevailing in industry. They could have offered deep discounts to competitive non-member brokers, a medium level of discounts to institutional customers and a moderate level of discounts for active individual customers. Although this would have meant giving up a large portion of their gross revenues, it would have kept control for pricing the service within their fraternity where it had always been. More important, for the brokers, it would have deflected and / or neutralized the pressures for change while they were still in the formative stages. This is not to say that this course was desireable, merely that, from a selfish point of view, retaining control of the commission structure should have been more important than keeping commissions high until the last possible moment. But although a proposal along these lines was suggested, it was never seriously considered.

In the meantime a coalition of the Securities and Exchange Commission, Merrill Lynch and the larger institutions managed not only to modify the fixed commission structure but to eliminate it entirely. That not only caused the demise of many brokers but it wrested control of the securities business away from the New York Stock Exchange, notwithstanding that the bulk of stock trading still takes place there.

What happened to the securities industry occurred as a seemingly natural evolutionary process. This is true of all change as Wheeler understood it because change is an integrated holistic process. Events occurred and decisions were made that seemed proper and logical to those in charge at the time. In retrospect, however, the results are often the opposite of what was expected, generating the excuse that "no one" could have anticipated what occurred. This of course is not true. Wheeler and many other perceptive people in all lines of activity who immerse themselves in their work, constantly prove that, viewed from the correct perspective, the future holds few surprises.

In like manner, many other industries and institutions that dominated the cycle coming to a close were and are being severly tested, while at the same time the technology of the next cycle, is gradually falling into place. Beginning with the gigantic room-sized Univac and IBM machines of the 1950s, successive waves of progress have brought the transister, miniaturization, integrated circuits, bubble memories, small home computers, and much more of the gadgetry that will enable people to achieve the higher levels of individual freedom Wheeler envisioned for the next 100- and 500-year climatic cycles. This process has accelerated since about 1975, the year Wheeler estimated in this text that both old cycles might come to a close.

As a result, two phenomena are simultaneously taking place during this phase of the cycle. On the one hand the predominating institutions of the past cycle have found themselves under increasing pressure. The way in which they respond to this pressure will largely determine whether, and in what form, they will survive into the next cycle. With the onslaught of each successive depression in this cold-dry phase, more and more institutions too rigid to adapt, or too levereged to recover from the pressures imposed on them by the mistakes they themselves created will either disappear, or through reorganization will rise from the ashes changed greatly. On the other hand, each successive period of recovery will see the emergence of additional new-cycle industries and the expansion of those that came early. This has tended to modify the intensity of what might otherwise have been more severe depressions, thus providing pockets of unparalled prosperity. In addition to the greater vitality of people during cold times, even when climate is dry, this development of new-cycle technologies may be one of the reasons why cold-dry depressions are less severe than hot-dry ones.

In any event, if they have not already done so, at some time in the 1980s the poor business conditions that predominate in the cold-dry era should climax. If this forecast is correct, although depressed business conditions will be an important factor into the early 1990s, future depressions promise to be milder than those in 1970, 1974, and 1982. Nevertheless, extreme caution would be advisable, especially where one is heavily leveraged financially. The record to date suggests that by the time this era of depression is over, there will be more bankruptcies, more unemployment, and more budgets out of control at all levels — individual, corporate, and government — than at any time since the 1930s.

Correlation with the Dow Jones Industrial Index

It is interesting to compare Wheeler's business forecast with the Dow Jones Industrial Index as a representation of the nation's prosperity level. Wheeler said that beginning about 1964 or 1965 a serious depression era would start, spanning about 20 years. After rising for years, the Dow first moved above the 1,000 level late in 1965. Since then, it has either approached or briefly exceeded 1,000 again in 1968, 1973, 1976, 1981, and 1982, but except for 1976, when it flirted with the 1,000 level for a whole year, it never moved considerably above 1,000 or stayed there for any great length of time until October,1982 when the Dow moved above 1,000 to new all time highs on very heavy volume possibly marking the beginning of a new secular bull market. On the other hand, Professor James Lorie of the University of Chicago called the 1970s the decade of the "Second Great Crash," a decade when common stocks on the New York Stock Exchange performed more poorly than at any time in all the decades since 1870.

By comparing Charts 17 and 18 to the Dow, we find Wheeler's forecast is remarkably accurate. Since 1950, on four occasions, the Dow has topped in the same year that Wheeler forecast a business peak, twice Wheeler's projection was a year early, and twice it was late. The following table shows when major business peaks were forecast compared with the actual peaks in the Dow Jones Industrials.

Forecast Year	DJI Peak	Comment
1953	Jan 1953	On time
1957	Apr 1956	1 year early
1961	Nov 1961	On time
1964	Jan 1966	2 years late
1967	Dec 1968	1 year late
1971	Apr 1971	On time
1974	Jan 1973	1 year early
1981	Apr 1981	On time

The record at bottoms is equally good. Of ten forecasted troughs, four coincided with actual Dow bottoms; three times the forecast was one year early, twice it was one year late, and once it was two years early. If this level of accuracy continues into the future, the remainder of this forecast will prove extremely valuable.

Forecast Year	DJI Low	Comment
1951	Jul 1950	1 year early
1955	Sep 1953	2 years early
1958	Oct 1957	1 year early
1962	Jun 1962	On time
1966	Oct 1966	On time
1969	May 1970	1 year late
1972	Dec 1971	1 year early
1974	Dec 1974	On time
1982	Aug 1982	On time

Although his forecast was not compared to any index of production, since the stock market is a leading indicator of business activity, it may be assumed the forecast has been equally valid in forecasting business conditions.

The 100-Year Cycle and the Kondratieff Theory

Until now, many economists and others who are cyclically oriented have looked to the long cycle popularly called the Kondratieff wave for guidance in forecasting long term economic conditions. Although this long cycle was named after the Russian economist Nikolai D. Kondratieff, who in 1926 published a paper in German on *The Long Wave in Economic Life,* a 52 year cycle had been recognized by the Aztec Indians of Mexico centuries earlier. Aztec priests actually performed a religious ceremony in order to forecast the upcoming 52 years; a modified version of this ceremony can be seen today in Acapulco performed by a group known as the "Flying Indians."

As popularly interpreted, the Kondratieff wave is said to average 54 years, with the current cycle having begun around 1940. Depending on the analyst consulted, the up phase is either presumed to have already peaked, or will peak, sometime between 1951 and 1985. It seems that the later the date of the particular forecast, the later is projected the timing of the peak, perhaps because almost everyone who has published a study of the Kondratieff wave has expected a depression exceeding the severity of the 1930s. Since an event of that magnitude has not yet materialized subsequent writers keep placing the date of the top further and further into the future. From the peak, the expectations are for a sharp break followed by a weak recovery to a gradually declining plateau lasting about a decade and flowing into a long "secondary depression" lasting about 20 years.

Wheeler's work does not challenge the validity of the Kondratieff wave or the general structure of this implied scenario. Instead, he adds new insights and dimensions to the nature of the cycle, having researched it back to 600 B.C., whereas Kondratieff examined it back only through four cycles. Wheeler agrees with the existance of an approximate 50-year cycle, but considers it to be merely one half of the 100-year cycle. Therefore, to fully understand the Kondratieff wave's implications and characteristics, it must be studied not alone, but "twinned" with another 50-year cycle. Coupled in this way, it is possible to see more clearly the similarities and differences between successive 50-year waves.

As for the similarities, both contain a long period of prosperity and a long period of depression. The difference comes from the fact that the first "K-wave" is a warm weather phenomenon, while the second occurs during the cold half of the century. During the first wave, the period of prosperity occurs during the warm-wet part of the 100-year cycle, forming an era with characteristics similar to the springtime of a single year. The period of depression during the first wave occurs in the warm-dry phase of the 100-year cycle, and its characteristics are similar to those of the summertime of an annual seasonal cycle. The prosperity phase of the second wave corresponds to the 100-year cycle's cold-wet phase, the seasonal autumn or harvest. The second wave's period of depression occurs during a cold-dry phase, with characteristics analogous to winter. Of the two periods of prosperity, the one during the warm-wet time tends to be longer, more vigorous, and more prosperous. Of the two periods of depression, the warm-dry depression is usually shorter but more intense while the cold-dry depression lasts longer. There are other significant differences, all of which will be examined in detail in a later volume.

The implications of Wheeler's forecast as it relates to Kondratieff seems to be that the K-wave depression for the present cycle began in 1965 when the Dow Jones Industrial Average first touched 1,000. Depending on how optimistically one cares to interpret Chart 18, the end of the depression phase was either signalled tentatively late in 1982 when the Dow moved to all time highs, or depressed conditions will continue through the mid-1990s. If the latter interpretation is correct, conditions may still not be as severe as forecast by the more pessimistic students of Kondratieff. The existence of the long depression era was most clearly evidenced by the long,steady decline in both bond and utility stock prices beginning in 1965. Utility stock prices declined steadily, as measured by the Dow Jones Utility Index, from 164.4 in 1965 to 57.1 in 1974. Since then they have recovered to over 125. Bond prices also topped in 1965 at about the same time as utilities but their decline continued until 1982. Thus 1974 may have marked the point of maximum intensity of this cycle's cold-dry depression even though conditions did not materially improve thereafter. If 1974 marked the low of the depression era, the period since then has represented a transition or long basing period and, in stock market terms, the 1982 depression may represent a "testing of the 1974 lows" or a "double bottom" from which a long term sustainable recovery could begin. The existance of the depression was also evidenced by the inability of common stock prices to move well above 1,000 since 1965, by their overall poor performance in the 1970s, and by the low levels of industrial production. During the real estate mania of 1978 and 1979, for example, although more money changed hands than ever before, far fewer housing units were built than in the previous housing peak in 1972, but this fact was masked at the time by the inflated prices being asked for houses.

Although many typical cold-dry phase activities have been occurring since the 1960s, it was not until 1982 that typical depression phenomena began to concern the nation. In addition to the lowest housing starts since World War II, automobile production was the lowest since 1961, bankruptcies soared to the highest levels in history, interest rates rose beyond levels ordinarily reached once every century,and unemployment rose above 11%. Industry was aggressively consolidating by either selling unprofitable corporate divisions where possible or closing them altogether. Both courses of action had the effect of removing excess capacity from the marketplace, thus shrinking overextended industrial production down to levels of actual demand. The Social Security System inaugurated in the hot-dry depression of the 1930s was pushed to the brink of bankruptcy in this cold-dry depression. Instead of hobos riding the rails and living in shanty towns in the 1930s, entire families began moving their belongings in station wagons from one public park to another in California and elsewhere in the Sunbelt states.

The one item most resistant to downward adjustment had been the price level, but by 1982 it too began to decline somewhat, except in the area of taxes. Despite the taxpayer revolt in California and increasing resistance by taxpayers to higher taxes, politicians, like the Wall Street establishment in the 1960s, continued to resist the need to make responsible changes while continuing to look for ways to maintain and expand the old Great Society programs. This had the effect of preventing both prices and taxes from dropping as they had in previous depression eras. Where ancient Chinese governments regularly placed moratoriums on the payment of taxes during depressions, contemporary American politicians, inclined toward fiscal arrogance and irresponsibility, kept looking for ways to increase them. With all the pressures on their constituents, political leaders into 1983 continued to covertly raise their salaries and increase their perks of office. To buy votes for reelection, many continued to approve pay raises for government employees beyond what they knew were prevalent wage scales in their communities and beyond what they knew was the ability of their tax structures to absorb.

This political mentality was explained to me when I noticed that during a series of meetings with corporate executive officers, a top Amex officer routinely offered positions on an advisory panel to virtually every one he spoke to. After he did this about 30 times to people, many of whom were obviously not qualified for a variety of reasons, I brought the matter up to his assistant, whose response was: "Alex (as we shall call him) doesn't really intend to have all those people on the board. But he knows that what people want more than anything else is to be "stroked" and made to think you care. He knows this will flatter their egos and that over 95% of all people he promises things to will never call on him to deliver, and he's learned to handle those few who do." It is this kind of cynicism that continues to govern the actions of far too many political leaders, who continue to believe, with much justification, that so long as they "stroke" the electorate before each election, the voters will continue to accept their looting of the tax coffers. It will be interesting to observe whether or not, during the remainder of the current cold-dry phase, the electorate will become sufficiently aroused for long enough to make some truly substantive changes.

Another area where flexibility has been lost is wages, especially in the highly organized, mature industries. But here some progress is being made to achieve the flexibility of prior cycles while protecting employees as much as possible from adverse depressionary effects. Where there have been truly serious problems, both labor and management are slowly learning to come together to do whatever is necessary to restore the soundness of their operations.

The lesson Wheeler has for students of the 50-year cycle is not to compare it to similar periods in the previous cycle but to events approximately 100-years prior. In this way Kondratieff students should gain more valuable insights in their attempts to forecast the future. Thus the most useful scenarios from which to forecast the current juncture will be found in analysing events in the 1780s and 1880s rather than the events of the 1930s alone.

Some Thoughts for Commodity Traders

Wheeler's observation about commodity prices was that they tend to rise and fall primarily in line with fluctuations in rainfall, not necessarily in line with business conditions or temperatures. He concluded, however, that this correspondance is due to the direct effect of rainfall on the human constitution, and not (as traditionally hypothesized) through the more obvious relationship between fluctuations in the size of grain harvests. His analysis shows that for about 200 years commodity prices have almost continuously followed business fluctuations in the United States because both are caused by the waxing and waning of human vitality and initiative in relation to rainfall. This analysis, as well as the interaction among commodity prices, rainfall, and cycles shorter than 50 years, will be covered in a forthcoming volume.

We will not examine this relationship here except to note that Wheeler's forecast projected a rainfall maximum in 1980 and a minimum around 1983 or 1984. For the record, during the period from 1980 through the fourth quarter of 1982, soybean prices dropped from about $9.60 to $5.20, wheat from $5.50 to $3.00, corn from $4.00 to $2.20, and nonagricultural gold fell from about $800 to $320. The forecast of a 1984 rainfall low suggests the possibility of still lower prices ahead. However, in interpreting this forecast, some allowance must be made for the heavier than average rainfalls throughout much of the nation late in 1982 and into early 1983. If there is to be a rainfall low in 1984, and if commodity prices do follow rainfall, then perhaps prices will rise sufficiently during this period of heavy rainfall to preclude significantly lower prices in 1984 than in 1982. Based on his observations, it appears that important future tops for many commodities will occur at projected rainfall peaks near 1987 and 1994, while important lows may appear about 1984, 1991, and 1998.

Political and Social Prospects for the Waning Twentieth Century

Of equal importance with Wheeler's observations dealing with climate and business are his comments on political and social events.

Political Leadership

Compared to despots like Adolf Hitler, who gain and consolidate power during the hot-dry phases of history, many cold-dry rulers tend to be either incompetent or would-be tyrants. Another category might be the truly competent leaders who know how to proceed but, because of the unsettled times, are unable to have their instructions carried out. During the cold-dry phase of the cycle, it may not be just a problem of incompetent rulers but of external pressures that either force otherwise competent people to make unsound decisions or to make no decisions at all. Then too, a problem may be so bad that even when a leader does all the right things, nothing positive seems to have been accomplished. An example would be a president who takes office at the onset of a depression. He manages to stabilize the situation and govern superbly, given the circumstances, but because there is no growth as in the previous time of prosperity, he is judged to be incompetent whereas a truly incompetent would have made the situation much worse. In any event, there is typically a rapid succession of leaders during the cold-dry phase. Recent history has been no exception. Since the commencement of the cold-dry phase in the 1960s, we have had Kennedy (assassinated), Johnson (forced to retire), Nixon (forced to resign), Ford (considered incompetent), Carter (considered inept), and Reagan (considered insensitive to the needy).

In substance, if not in form, the continuing presidential primary election challenges by Edward Kennedy against Democratic frontrunners, and by Ronald Reagan against President Gerald Ford, are much like the "palace wars" of which Wheeler speaks in his historical commentaries. It is interesting that important themes in the successful first presidential campaigns of both Democrat Jimmy Carter and Republican Ronald Reagan were idealistic, cold-dry themes based on the integrity and worth of the individual as opposed to that of the central government.

Individualism

According to Wheeler, individualism is another cold-phase phenomenon. Coming into the 1980s, it is being manifested in a large variety of ways. From a negative point of view, it is characterized by chaos, anarchy, and piracy. Numerous negative manifestations include urban and suburban muggings and robberies, the senseless "Tylenol murders" of 1982, the casualness of employee theft in terms of money, goods, and time, the self-centered "me" generation, an epidemic of narcotics smuggling and usage, the "shadow" governments of organized crime (sometimes run by the same people who govern in the official government), and maritime insurance fraud on unprecented levels (literally old-style piracy on the high seas). These behaviors create a concern for individual safety and a growing frustration that the governing structure cannot provide the requisite safety. From a positive point of view, it is characterized by the willingness and confidence of individuals to increasingly draw on their own resources to solve their problems and those of their neighbors without relying on an increasingly impotent central governing authority to solve their problems for them.

Wheeler notes that in warm times and among warm-climate peoples, the negative kinds of behavior are accepted, but in cold times resistance eventually stiffens. When it does, it results either in people taking the law into their own hands, in withdrawing, or in forcing the established structure to change. In the United States, taking the law into one's hands is probably best characterized by the vigilante committes of the Old West during the cold-dry phase of the nineteenth century. More recently, something similar has sprung up as people have begun to patrol their neighborhoods, attempting to rid themselves of criminal elements. The most publicized and controversial of these groups may be the Guardian Angels who patrol New York City subways. Controversial though this may be, the success of such groups can encourage others to do for themselves what the official law enforcement bodies cannot do and thus it sets the stage for a reversal away from the wholesale lawlessness and the danger of physical violence to individuals that is often so rampant as a negative behavioral characteristic during cold times.

While the pressure grows to "change the system", others withdraw into the "underground economy," an informal system of barter, or they otherwise work at jobs that pay "off the books" in nonrecorded transactions to avoid the payment of oppressive taxes. Initially, the official response to this is an attempt to close the tax "loopholes" but the net result usually is merely that the honest taxpayer, not in a position to underreport his taxes is increasingly harassed while the evaders remain undisturbed. This encourages the trend toward tax evasion to spread, creating the possibility that it will grow to the proportions of France and Italy where the art of evading taxes has developed into a national sport. Should this happen, a point is reached where the revenue service, despite its computers and other sophisticated information gathering techniques will be unable to function effectively. At that point it either has to accept the reality of tax anarchy as the status quo, or Congress will have to legislate a simplified system of taxes perceived to be fair and equitable by the majority of the people.

Still others form organizations to wrest control of various institutions and place them into new hands. This is the substance of the changes that wracked Wall Street, discussed above, of the increasing use of referendums like Proposition 13, of the many revolutions in the smaller nations of the world, and of the growth of organizations like the People's Medical Society founded by Robert

Rodale, editor of Prevention Magazine, who is looking to organize a confrontation with the $300-billion a year medical-health establishment. He claims medicine has become too expensive at a time when everything else is being cut back. Furthermore, he asserts the present system is misdirected and inappropriate in that it primarily focuses on dealing with a disease after it becomes entrenched in the body instead of teaching people to live more healthfully in order not to become sick in the first place. He promises to provide positive alternatives that will lower the cost of health care while maintaining its quality. He also promises to promote a climate in which the techniques of preventing diseases from occurring in the first place will take precedence over those emphasizing the containment of disease once it surfaces.

The Economic Ascension of Asia

Two of Wheeler's forecasts deal with the increasing dominance of Asia in world affairs and the rapid industrialization of backward countries. These forecasts tie in with his contention that major shifts in political and cultural hegemony between East and West follow the recurrent 500-year cycle of world climate. China has yet to become a major industrial power, but the dominance of Japan and the growing importance of Hong Kong, Taiwan, Korea, Singapore, and other Asian nations is well known. China is presently rising in industrial importance, as attested by the rising volume of high quality products it is exporting and reports that it may be sitting on a field of oil that will dwarf the reserves of the Middle East. Even small nations like Sri Lanka have begun to export such diverse products as clothing and semiconductors, making the transition from the past to the threshhold of the twenty-first century in a single leap.

Population

Another dry-phase characteristic is a decline in the birth rate, which has become the concern of demographers like Carl Haub working for the Population Reference Bureau. Most readers are familiar with the Malthusian idea that population grows geometrically. Starting with a couple who have four children, each of which has four children, by the fifth generation the original couple will have produced 1,024 descendents. At present (early 1983), in this cold-dry phase the fertility rate in many developed nations is "below replacement," causing a negative geometry to come into play. In West Germany, for example, at the current rate of reproduction, the population will shrink by the end of the century from 62 million to 52 million; by the end of the twenty-first century, it will be down to about 9 million; and by the year 2500, it will be less than the current population of Anaheim, California.

At the same time, population in the less developed nations is rising. Should these trends continue, Haub estimates that by the end of the next century the population ratio in favor of the less developed countries against the industrial world will rise from the present 3:1 ratio to 18:1 unless the people in the industrial world begin to do some real parenting. These developments tend to confirm Wheeler's view that cold periods make life more comfortable for people in warmer (and consequently less developed nations), accounting for an increase in their birth rates even during droughts, while droughts in the normally more temperate regions consistently result in lower birth rates there. The intrinsic balance of Wheeler's theories, however, offers consolation to the Western world. As precipitation rises again, so will the birth rate in the industrial nations as it has so often in the past; and as temperatures start to rise again, soon it will become too uncomfortable in the less developed nations and their birth rates should start to drop.

Wars

Ordinarily there are few international wars during cold times. When they occur, they are likely to be costly, as was the Vietnam war for the United States. Instead, civil strife increases either in the form of civil wars, as in the case of many emerging nations, in the form of riots, as this nation experienced in the 1960s, or in the form of increased resistance to a nation's bureaucratic machinery, as the trends toward barter and the underground economy. The Russians are increasingly experiencing this phenomenon, as exemplified by problems with their Jewish and other ethnic populations and with Poland and Afghanistan. Such difficulties may continue to increase within the Soviet Union and its satellites until civil strife becomes so widespread that it cannot be contained. Another of Wheeler's forecasts calls for the possibility of a civil war in Russia among the various population groups. With this in mind, and the fact that there is little historical precedent for international wars during cold periods, one could conclude that the emphasis in this country on military hardware and personnel in this cold-dry phase has been a misdirected use of valuable national resources that could be used more fruitfully in other ways.

Other Projections

Although Wheeler's forecasts from 1950 to date have proved fantastically valid and his theory of climatic conditioning comes closer to rationally explaining how things change during a business cycle than anything I have ever read, this neither suggests that his own forecast will hold through the year 2000 nor that the interpretation of his projections presented in this Postscript is the last word on the subject.

Wheeler himself never claimed omnipotence, but he spent enough of his life on this project to be confident of the general structure, if not the precise details, of his forecasts from decade to decade. For the 30 years since 1950, both his climatic and business forecasts have been generally on target. True, he may have miscalculated the intensity of some movements, but not their direction.

In addition to these climate and business forecasts, he made other projections, many of which have already materialized. Some of these include the disappearance of all official forms of discrimination in the United States (or at least far reaching steps in that direction); the rapid industrialization of the backward nations of the world; and the awakening of warmer countries and areas of the world, including the southern United States. In business he sensed the working classes would come to share the ownership and management of business, not through socialism but as a natural evolution of the capitalist system, and that they would become an extension of the middle class. Of all his forecasts, only the one dealing with the disintegration of Russian communism seems furthest from reality. But students of the stock market know that when stock prices break out of certain patterns, enormous price changes in the direction of the break often follow. Likewise, reactions to Soviet Russia's oppression of its people cannot be contained forever, especially with everyone else in the world leapfrogging forward to pass into the next century as democratic and technological equals. The Russians cannot forever stay suppressed if for no other reason than than the changing technology of the world requires increasing numbers of Soviet middle management and bureaucrats to travel throughout the world. So far, except for a few defectors, they apparently have been content merely to live the good life while abroad, but at some point they are going to demand the same good life at home. It is on this level of the mind and the pocketbook, not on the military level, that the "war" with the Russians should be fought, especially since the Russians who once thought capitalism would destroy itself during the next Kondratieff depression now see that depression is a world-wide occurrance from which they themselves are not immune. The bottom line is this: The extension of freedom in Russia, when it comes, may neither come from a revolution of the Russian masses nor from military intervention by the West, but from the sophisticated technocrats who increasingly run the country.

A personal anecdote may be appropriate to illustrate the point. The most expensive luncheon I ever hosted while at the American Stock Exchange was for two Russians who dropped in on me one day at noon unannounced and invited themselves to lunch.. At the time, I was the Exchange's listed company liaison officer, and these two Russians tried unsuccessfully to get me to persuade officials of various companies to do business with them on credit. The leader of the group knew how to savor the good life fully. Ordering in Italian (the maitre 'd was Italian), he had scotch-on-the-rocks, oysters on the half shell, filet mignon, spanish melon, cognac, espresso, and two cigars from the thermidor, one to smoke with the espresso, one to "go." The woman with him was an economist interested in visiting the trading floor of the Amex. She had been raised by a governess and privately tutored so that she too spoke several languages, including French with which she communicated with the maitre 'd because she felt hesitant in English. She seemed genuinely excited to step on the trading floor of a "decadent" capitalistic stock exchange, and she spoke nostalgically of the fact that there was once a stock market in St. Petersburg before the Revolution. When I suggested that perhaps as things changed, Russia might again have a stock exchange, she quietly and rather wistfully said she didn't think so — at least not in her lifetime. There was nevertheless a tone of hopeful anticipation in her last remarks.

The persuasiveness with which Wheeler shows depressions to be worldwide cyclical events also makes ludicrous the statements of competing political and business leaders as they blame each other for hard times and attempt to mislead voters and their fellow businessmen (and perhaps even themselves) with claims of what they plan to do to avoid or resolve such depressions. To use another personal example, I saw at rather close range how one aggressive, driving, activist of a chief executive officer took a highly profitable retailing chain from record earnings under his predecessor into bankruptcy in less than 3 years by a series of very highly leveraged decisions, many of which turned out to have been wrong. With a less aggressive executive at the helm, the firm might still be alive today. Likewise, had President Johnson not been so successfully persuasive in getting his Great Society programs enacted into law, not only would the depression era that followed have been far less severe but the expectations and required cutbacks would have been far milder.. Moderation in those years may have prevented the Social Security crisis of 1983, would have resulted in a much smaller federal bureaucracy with fewer programs to fund, and therefore a much smaller federal budget deficit to contend with. This in turn may have moderated the astronomically high interest rates of 1982 by several percentage points, and in general may have modified the severity of, though not prevented, the occurence of the present cycle's cold-phase depressions.

An important point Wheeler makes is that events recur in general but not in specific patterns. Events never happen in the same way twice. Of the many interacting factors, perhaps the perspective of the individual is the most important. It is one thing to sit back and impartially analyze a series of data or events, quite another to be a part of that data. When a person is part of an event, it is difficult not to get caught up in the exhilaration or gloom of the times. As a participant,it becomes very simple to set aside a logically developed course of action because "things are different this time around."

Wheeler's Accomplishment

A word about Wheeler's methodology is in order here. It is highly probable that two people looking at the same facts will arrive at different answers, depending on the perspective from which they analyze the information. Optimists and pessimists invariably propose different solutions to the same problems, as do liberals and conservatives. Further, mood is a function of climate with optimism predominating in wet periods and pessimism during dry times. Someone holding a job might fail to recognize as a period of adversity a time future historians will label an epoch of great depression. Similarly, someone who may be amply blessed with wordly goods but is psychologically insecure might consider every minor inconvenience to be a great tragedy. How, then was Raymond H. Wheeler able to see so clearly these relationships that completely escaped the attention of almost everyone else? The answer comes readily to anyone who has studied Wheeler in depth. It was because he was not just a scientist but a philosopher as well, a holistic thinker, and one of the world's first and foremost human ecologists. He did not work on a 40-hour-a-week basis, with lots of time off for vacations and sabatticals. Rather, he wholeheartedly immersed himself in his work. He was not merely concerned with how things worked but with why they worked as they did. And when he found answers that took him in directions not acceptable to his academic peers, the truth of his quest took precedence over the impulse to conform. The fact that most of his work is only now beginning to be published shows how dearly he paid for his independence. Even before he undertook the massive studies leading to the conclusions in this present volume, he resolved for himself the question of "Why?" He prepared a philosophical theory of relativity linking together the empirical and the theoretical, the inductive and the deductive, into one "principle of unity." The logical process to follow to examine and make forecasts on any subject is outlined in a paper (to be published separately) which alone should qualify Dr. Wheeler for Nobel prize consideration (albeit posthumously), for without it he may never have grasped the fundamental holistic relationships so eloquently revealed in his climatic research.

Beginning with "The Principle of Unity," and an overwhelming fascination with climatic research and human psychology, he and almost 200 assistants worked for over two decades to produce a tremendous data base, only a small part of which has been summarized here. But Wheeler was not looking just to amass data. He strongly believed that if a person didn't know what he was looking for, he could never amass enough data to find answers; when he ultimately found these answers, they wouldn't mean anything, and the person would go on collecting data ad infinitum. Therefore Wheeler first developed a theory as the framework for his research efforts. The analysis of his initial data convinced him he was on the right track, so he expanded the project. As he progressed, his vision of its implications also expanded to a degree only hinted at in this volume.

What the reader has learned in this volume is just the tip of the iceberg, a summarization of what Wheeler discovered after more than 20 years of concerted and productive research. Actually, the text of this volume may be a summary of what Wheeler believed was true as he first started his labors. He spent the rest of his life documenting his beliefs for those of us without his clarity and insight.

Beyond the Theory of Climatic Conditioning

At this point the question may come to mind, "What is there 'beyond Wheeler'?" Is there a coherent, fluctuating, primary causative factor for which the regularity of climatic change and its effects on human affairs is only a visual manifestation? Are there electromagnetic or solar wind cycles, for example, that tie Wheeler's climatic flux to even more profound, all-encompassing cosmic cycles?

Perhaps so. But if there are, the chances are good that Wheeler himself would not be spending his time searching for this "ultimate cause" if he were alive today.

In "The Principle of Unity" Wheeler explains that, by definition, there can neither be an ultimate, all-encompassing whole nor an irreducible minimum. No matter how small a particle one is examining, there is always something smaller; no matter how large the whole, there is always something larger. Rather than searching for the "ultimate," therefore, Wheeler suggests looking at the problem in the same way scientists study electricity. No one knows exactly what electricity is, and perhaps no one ever will, but over the years science has learned how to harness it in literally thousands of ways. Had science insisted on knowing the cosmic answers relating to electricity before learning how to use it, the world would not be where it is now with respect to practical application. And given the enigmatic subtlety that prevades the universe, it is entirely conceivable that the cosmic answers do indeed come only to seekers like Wheeler who immerse themselves wholly in their quest. Perhaps this is why, of the billions of humans who traveled this earth over the centuries, it remained for Raymond H. Wheeler to piece together with such clarity and simplicity these facts relating to climate and social institutions that have always been in plain sight for all to see.

Of course, Wheeler could be wrong. That's possible, although at this point the burden of proof must fall on the doubters. Assuming he was correct in his general theory of climatic conditioning in history, he still could be wrong about his specific forecasts for the decades immediately ahead. But it was never his intention that these forecasts be set in concrete. He was not on that kind of "ego trip." (If he were, the accuracy of his forecasts to date certainly qualifies him for an honored place in the prognosticator's Hall of Fame, even if his forecasts through the rest of the century prove to be incorrect.) Instead, what Wheeler was trying to show was that by understanding the nature of climatic cycles and how changes in climate affect the vitality and abilities of people, it is possible to make reasonable, educated guesses about many seemingly unrelated social and cultural activities far into the future, not in a precise but in a broad, general, directional, or relative sense that Wheeler describes as "more than" or "less than." For example, during periods of prosperity, when people are economically secure and the challenges of the day are easy to solve, they tend to think of the welfare of others "more than" they do during depressed periods when economic conditions may force them to become more self centered and think of others "less than" they do during periods of prosperity.

Four Scenarios for the Future

In these terms it is possible to draw several scenarios about climate and business through the end of this century. First, throughout the text of this volume, Wheeler consistently makes the point that the 100-year cycle invariably ends in a cold-dry phase. In one forecast he projected the next (and last) severe depression of the current cold-dry phase to center on 1985. This correlates most closely to the current Kondratieff wave consensus. According to this scenario, although no single depression since 1965 will be as intense as that of the 1930s, because the present cold-dry depression period is so long (from 1965 to about 1995), the total economic and social effects will equal those of the Great Depression. During this time, although there have been and will continue to be years of relative prosperity, the number of years recognized as depression years will far exceed those recognized as prosperity years.

On the climatic front something similar would be happening. Although there have been and will continue to be individual years of adequate rainfall, the rainfall during these future years would not generally be sufficient to completely replenish the reservoirs. Therefore each period of drought, although in absolute terms not as severe as the great drought of the 1930s, will be cumulatively more severe, especially because the demands on the nation's water supply today is many times greater than it was in the 1930s. This would inhibit a true sustaining recovery in most areas of business until the mid-1990s, in line with the forecasts of the most pessimistic Kondratieff theorists.

However, while Wheeler continually states that the climatic cycle ends in a cold-dry phase, he also affirms that the cold-dry phase is the least consistent of the four phases. Sometimes during the final years of the cold-dry phase, both temperature and rainfall rise and fall erratically, making the final years neither as dry nor as cold as the broad projection suggests. This is precisely the forecast Wheeler has indicated on Chart 18, and while he suggests that prosperity will moderately increase, he does not expect the next period of rampant prosperity to develop until about 1995.

In line with this reasoning, a second scenario can be constructed suggesting that until 1995, although business conditions may never reach levels of roaring prosperity, neither would they sink much lower than the depression levels of 1982. Instead, there would be short, alternating periods of both weak attempts at prosperity and failures that generate further recessions. However, because climate is gradually becoming warmer and wetter, the failures would no longer feed on themselves as severly as they did prior to 1982. Rather, each succeeding depression bottoming in 1987, 1991, 1993, and 1997 would be less severe than its predecessor, while each attempt at prosperity would be increasingly stronger.

This middle scenario would seem to indicate the continuing disintegration of those industries and institutions not strong enough to survive in their present form into the new 100-year cycle. However, as painful as this process might be, it would approximately be offset by the introduction of new-age industries, institutions, and technologies, and the expansion of those already in existence. This tug of war between the "old" and the "new" would continue with the "new" gradually taking command until about 1995, when virtually everyone connected with the old age technologies would either have passed away, retired, or been trained in the new technologies, when new-age industries would have achieved a firm footing, and when the vestigal organs of the old institutions would have wasted away.

A third and more optimistic scenario suggests that the strong advance of the stock market in the fall of 1982 to price levels not significantly bested since 1965 means that Wheeler may have miscalculated the period of brief, strong business prosperity. Instead of centering on 1980, as shown on Chart 18, it should perhaps be transposed to center on 1985. The move of the Dow Jones Industrials to all time highs might be signalling that the long, cold-dry phase may end sooner than anticipated. If this scenario holds, a period of prosperity lasting until 1987 or even later may evolve. This being the case, virtually all the economic damage likely to occur in the cold-dry phase of the present 100-year cycle has already happened. From here on, until the next nation-building period starts, business conditions would be inhibited primarily because business, individuals, and the government will have to unwind from, and pay off, the enormous debts their financial indiscretions have created. That is, the government would primarily focus on winding down inflation, lowering interest rates to past historic norms, paying off the national debt, making the Social Security System viable, bringing expenditures and revenues more in line, and so forth. Individuals and businesses would concentrate on regaining their liquidity, while institutions would work to adapt their activities to the requirements of the new age. An increase in wet weather accompanied by cold, but nevertheless slightly warmer, temperatures then in the years immediately ahead could conceivably permit such a scenario to unfold.

A fourth and most optimistic scenario follows along the lines of the third but suggests that rather than ending in 1982, the climax of this century's 100-year cold-dry period came in 1974. Under this scenario,

1982, in stock market terminology represented either a "double bottom" or a "testing of the 1974 lows" from which a broad new economic advance could begin. If conditions were worse in 1982 than in 1974 for certain economic units, it was because, rather than seeking financial liquidity in the interim period, these units continued to accumulate debts. This scenario can be drawn from Wheeler's statements in Chapter 8 that both the 100- and 500-year cycles could end about 1975.

Like everything in life, all four scenarios lead to conclusions not at first readily apparent. The first scenario details continuing difficulties until 1985, during which time increasingly severe economic pressures on virtually everyone would continue. However, by the end of the century all the excesses currently in the system would have been so thoroughly washed out that only the truly strong and competent would be left to take advantage of the opportunities that would present themselves in the nation-building time of the next 100-year cycle. There would be no old problems left to inhibit the progress of the next cycle.

The second scenario is far less severe but still allows for further pressures on various economic and social systems. It allows for further deterioration and disintegration of old-age industries. Under this scenario, most of the necessary changes would have been made and only a few nagging problems would be carried over to be resolved in the next cycle.

The third and fourth scenarios suggest that the breakdown process was for all practical purposes completed early in 1983, but that economic progress between then and the end of the century will be limited in many sectors, primarily because of the need to pay for the egregious excesses of the past. The biggest danger here is that some of the most important problems have not been sufficiently addressed and the governments and institutions where these problems reside not have been stressed badly enough to force their satisfactory resolution. For example, the resolution to the potential insolvency of the Social Security system proposed as this book goes to press is a patchwork solution which pleases no one and which virtually assures that the problem will resurface shortly in a form more serious than at present. Consequently these potentially destructive problems will carry into the next century to compound the next cycle's drought phase problems. Because the hot-drought of the twenty-first century's 100-year cycle will coincide with the hot-drought maximum of the larger 500-year climate cycle, these last scenarios may seem most optimistic near-term, but ironically their long-term ramifications on future generations could be most disasterous.

Perhaps the most important lesson to be derived from this summary of Wheeler's work is to understand that the existance of long climatic cycles that affect all our social and economic activities does not mean that we are slaves to climatic conditioning. Instead, it provides the key and the opportunity to achieve new heights of freedom and prosperity when one learns to harness these forces constructively.

For example, a friend in the hotel business who was concerned with high construction costs was nevertheless able to expand rapidly throughout the depression era of the 1970s. As the demand for lodging increased in many parts of the country in the early 1960s, this man noted that high building costs did not prevent people with access to lines of credit (other people's money) from going ahead with plans to build extravagent hotels. As a result, to carry the costs, the rooms and services had to be priced high, and during a recession hotels, especially new ones, are often unable to develop a sufficient cash flow to cover their overhead and are forced into bankruptcy. Rather than build hotels himself, this person waited and then went into the market during the depressions of 1970 and 1974 to buy the best hotels in his area when they went up for sale on their second bankruptcy. By then, the exhorbitant price the original builder had paid for his dreams had been squeezed out of the price tag; so had the bank's hope to make a profit on the loan. On the third go-round, the property would sell at a reasonable price relative to the income it could generate. Using this technique, the man was able to price his rooms lower than comparable properties in the area, insuring a high occupancy rate and a healthy profit. He denies profiting at the expense of others because he claims to have done nothing to encourage anyone to build any of the costly properties that he subsequently purchased. Instead, he insists they had access to the same information he had, but they chose to interpret it from a different perspective.

The principle of looking ahead and adjusting one's operations to changing conditions as a matter of choice rather than as a matter of involuntary pressure may sound good to some people, but others claim it is inappropriate in their business. Again resorting to a personal anecdote, I once had a discussion on this subject with one of the American Stock Exchange presidents to whom I reported over the years. He said it would be foolish and unrealistic for him to plan his operations on the basis of cycles or even to consider them as part of his arsenal of planning tools. He said it didn't make any sense for him to run the Exchange by attempting to anticipate changes in the level of trading volume, or by any similar yardstick. "Look," he said, "when a specialist who is also on the Board of Governors tells me he needs a new clerk at his post, I'd better hire one or the next time my contract is up, it won't be renewed. I can't tell him the momentum of trading is turning down. If volume does drop and we don't need the clerk, we can get rid of him, but my main job is to put out the fires." I was unable to convince him that by intelligently and accurately anticipating broad future trends, there would be far fewer fires that needed to be put out. For example, personnel in many industries should be hired while business is still low but clearly building up, so the new employees can be properly trained to handle the higher volume when it occurs; then while business is still good but topping, the correct procedure is to first stop adding to the staff, then to stop hiring replacements as attrition occurrs naturally. This way one is seldom if ever faced with the need to terminate large numbers of people at inopportune times, when they are psychologically least prepared for their terminations, and often just months before new people have to be hired and trained to replace those so recently let go.

But just cyclical analysis to buy, build, or hire at bottoms and sell or cut back operations at tops isn't enough. One needs to be able to translate these principles into one's area of specialization. I haven't tested this hypothesis, but it seems to me that by translating what Wheeler says into stock market principles, the best way to invest during the wet phases of the climatic cycle might be to focus on emerging growth companies and technologies. In this way, one would stand the best chance of discovering the companies that will dominate the coming cycle (such as I.B.M., Xerox, Polaroid, National Semiconductor and others have done in the present cycle). Then, in dry phases, the emphasis might well be on investments stressing capital and income safety. The son of one of the largest real estate developers in Florida told me his father had done just that in the 1920s. A year or so before the Florida real estate crash in that decade, his father sold all his real estate holdings with the exception of the family home. He converted the proceeds into cash, which he placed in a large safe in the basement. Then, during the height of the crash, he bought all his land back and much more, often at five cents on the dollar. This was the base for many of the well known planned communities that sprang up in Florida during the 1940s under the auspices of the company he subsequently founded, which continues to prosper to this day. Here is a memorable example of what can be achieved by fine-tuning one's sense of cycles.

Optimum holding periods for stocks might well shift according to the cycle. For example, a buy and hold strategy with respect to investments in promising companies might be appropriate during the warm-wet, nation-building phase. In the warm-dry depression, the emphasis might shift to cash or treasury bills. In the cold-wet phase, the emphasis might be to invest in successful, established companies with high rates of growth, and to invest in harmony with the four-year market cycle. Finally, during the long cold-dry depression phase, a program of trading according to the intermediate cycles to take advantage of short-term recoveries might prove most profitable.

The reader should be aware that these are untested, "top of the head" suggestions based on long exposure to the investment business. They are offered primarily to start the stream of ideas flowing as to how the information in this book might be put to practical use by the reader. Wheeler emphasizes throughout his writings that both climate and human social activity are in a constant state of change, fluctuating in a pattern that becomes predictable when understood. The obvious way to deal with the certainty of this change is not to resist it but to gradually change one's own activities and patterns of behavior to harmonize with these external changes. To resist is to be destroyed, not by the process of change, but by the intransigence of one's own mind.

While it may be appropriate to wear a warm fur coat during a blistery January snowstorm, that same fur is out of place on the beach on a sweltering summer day. Just as one's concept of what is appropriate in the way of clothing logically shifts with the seasons, so too should one's concept of what is appropriate in investing, in business conduct, and in all social endeavors shift with Raymond H. Wheeler's profound discovery - the four phases of the all-pervasive 100-year climatic cycle.